African Arguments

Written by experts with an unrivalled knowledge of the continent, *African Arguments* is a series of concise, engaging books that address the key issues currently facing Africa. Topical and thought-provoking, accessible but in-depth, they provide essential reading for anyone interested in getting to the heart of both why contemporary Africa is the way it is and how it is changing.

African Arguments Online

African Arguments Online is a website managed by the Royal African Society, which hosts debates on the African Arguments series and other topical issues that affect Africa: http://africanarguments.org

Series editors

ALEX DE WAAL, executive director, World Peace Foundation
RICHARD DOWDEN, executive director, Royal African Society
ALCINDA HONWANA, Open University

Editorial board

EMMANUEL AKYEAMPONG, Harvard University
TIM ALLEN, London School of Economics and Political Science
AKWE AMOSU, Open Society Institute
BREYTEN BREYTENBACH, Gorée Institute
PETER DA COSTA, journalist and development specialist
WILLIAM GUMEDE, journalist and author
ABDUL MOHAMMED, InterAfrica Group
ROBERT MOLTENO, editor and publisher

T0321542

Titles already published

Alex de Waal, *AIDS and Power: Why There is No Political Crisis – Yet*

Tim Allen, *Trial Justice: The Lord's Resistance Army, Sudan and the International Criminal Court*

Raymond W. Copson, *The United States in Africa: Bush Policy and Beyond*

Chris Alden, *China in Africa*

Tom Porteous, *Britain in Africa*

Julie Flint and Alex de Waal, *Darfur: A New History of a Long War*, revised and updated edition

Jonathan Glennie, *The Trouble with Aid: Why Less Could Mean More for Africa*

Peter Uvin, *Life after Violence: A People's Story of Burundi*

Bronwen Manby, *Struggles for Citizenship in Africa*

Camilla Toulmin, *Climate Change in Africa*

Orla Ryan, *Chocolate Nations: Living and Dying for Cocoa in West Africa*

Theodore Trefon, *Congo Masquerade: The Political Culture of Aid Inefficiency and Reform Failure*

Léonce Ndikumana and James Boyce, *Africa's Odious Debts: How Foreign Loans and Capital Flight Bled a Continent*

Mary Harper, *Getting Somalia Wrong? Faith, War and Hope in a Shattered State*

Gernot Klantschnig and Neil Carrier, *Africa and the War on Drugs: Narcotics in Sub-Saharan Africa*

Lorenzo Cotula, *The Great African Land Grab? Agricultural Investments and the Global Food System*

Marc Epprecht, *Sexuality and Social Justice in Africa : Rethinking Homophobia and Forging Resistance*

Forthcoming

Michael Deibert, *The Democratic Republic of Congo: Between Hope and Despair*

Gerard McCann, *India and Africa – Old Friends, New Game*

Adam Branch and Zachariah Mampilly, *Popular Protest in Africa*

Published by Zed Books with the support of the following organizations:

International African Institute promotes scholarly understanding of Africa, notably its changing societies, cultures and languages. Founded in 1926 and based in London, it supports a range of seminars and publications including the journal *Africa*.

www.internationalafricaninstitute.org

Royal African Society is Britain's prime Africa organization. Now more than a hundred years old, its in-depth, long-term knowledge of the continent and its peoples makes the Society the first stop for anyone wishing to know more about the continent. RAS fosters a better understanding of Africa in the UK and throughout the world – its history, politics, culture, problems and potential. RAS disseminates this knowledge and insight and celebrates the diversity and depth of African culture.

www.royalafricansociety.org

World Peace Foundation, founded in 1910, is located at the Fletcher School, Tufts University. The Foundation's mission is to promote innovative research and teaching, believing that these are critical to the challenges of making peace around the world, and should go hand in hand with advocacy and practical engagement with the toughest issues. Its central theme is 'reinventing peace' for the twenty-first century.

www.worldpeacefoundation.org

About the author

Alcinda Honwana is visiting professor of anthropology and international development at the Open University (UK). She was chair in international development at the Open University and taught anthropology at the University Eduardo Mondlane in Maputo, the University of Cape Town and the New School in New York. She was also programme director at the Social Science Research Council in New York. Honwana has written extensively on the links between political conflict and culture and on the impact of violent conflict on children and youth, conducting research in Mozambique, the Democratic Republic of the Congo, Angola, Colombia and Sri Lanka. Her latest work has been on youth transitions and social change in Africa, focusing on Mozambique, Senegal, South Africa and Tunisia. Alcinda Honwana's latest publications include: *The Time of Youth: Work, social change, and politics in Africa*, 2012; *Child Soldiers in Africa*, 2006; and *Makers and Breakers: Children and youth in post-colonial Africa*, 2005 (co-edited). She was awarded the prestigious Prince Claus Chair in Development and Equity in the Netherlands in 2008.

ALCINDA HONWANA

Youth and revolution in Tunisia

Zed Books

LONDON | NEW YORK

in association with

International African Institute
Royal African Society
World Peace Foundation

Youth and revolution in Tunisia was first published in association with the International African Institute, the Royal African Society and the World Peace Foundation in 2013 by Zed Books Ltd, 7 Cynthia Street, London N1 9JF, UK and Room 400, 175 Fifth Avenue, New York, NY 10010, USA

www.zedbooks.co.uk
www.internationalafricaninstitute.org
www.royalafricansociety.org
www.worldpeacefoundation.org

Set in OurType Arnhem and Futura Bold by Ewan Smith, London
Index: <ed.emery@thefreeuniversity.net>
Cover design: www.roguefour.co.uk

A catalogue record for this book is available from the British Library
US CIP data are available from the Library of Congress

ISBN   978 1 78032 462 3 hb
ISBN   978 1 78032 461 6 pb
eISBN 978 1 78032 464 7
ePDF 978 1 78032 463 0

Contents

Acknowledgements | ix
Political parties and associations | xii
Map of Tunisia | xv

Introduction 1

1 Disconnections 21

2 Mobilisation 48

3 Revolution 71

4 Transition 92

5 Elections 122

6 New government, new constitution 144

7 Women's rights 167

Conclusion 192

Afterword 203

Notes | 207   References | 228
Index | 236

Acknowledgements

This book depended on the willingness of many young Tunisian women and men across the country to sit down with me to share their lives, experiences and perspectives on the revolution, as well as their aspirations for Tunisia's future. I am deeply indebted to all of them for taking the time to provide me with such rich and detailed information. This book could not have been written without them.

Tarek Rekik, Yassine Lechiheb, Najmeddine Najlaoui, Nourddine M'hamdi, Dora Chaouachi, Hedia Ajmi and Hajer Araissia all invested their time and energy in assisting me during this research project. They organised interviews, planned our trips, and some travelled with me across the country, translated the discussions we held in Arabic and also shared their personal experiences and insights about the revolution and their country, which were very instructive. I thank them all for their friendship, unflagging contributions, dedication and commitment to this project.

During my visits to Tunisia I enjoyed the gracious hospitality of old and new friends. I am immensely grateful to Hakim, Elsa, Lina and Selime Ben Hammouda in La Marsa; Hajer Araissia and Sami Essid in Tunis; the Rekik family in Menzel Bourguiba; the Najlaoui family in Kasserine; the M'hamdi family in Regueb; and the Ajmi family in El Mazdour. I am also grateful to the directors and programme coordinators at the various *maisons des jeunes* and cultural centres in Tinja, Grombelia, Metline, La Marsa, Nabeul, Sousse, El Jem, Sidi Bouzid, Kasserine, Regueb and Tunis. I also thank the leaders and members of the various women's associations that welcomed me and shared their views and ideas.

I greatly benefited from innumerable discussions with Tunisian colleagues. Abdeljelil Bédoui, Mahmoud Ben Romdhane, Nadia Hadaoui, Hakim Ben Hammouda, Samir Rabhi, Zeyneb Farhat, Hélé Béji, Farida Ayari, Monia Lachheb, Sleheddine Ben Fredj, Monia Abed, Sami Essid, Aida Robbana, Nabil Mahâlel, Zouair El Khadi and Rezgui Mondher generously shared their knowledge and views about the processes going on in their country. Our conversations taught me an enormous amount about Tunisia's political and socioeconomic past and present, and the challenges that lie ahead. I am also grateful to Faiçal Nacer from Ennahdha's Bureau of Communications for the discussions we had and for contributing useful materials and information to my project.

Teresa Smart, Joseph Hanlon, Stephanie Urdang, Alex de Waal, Stephanie Kitchen, Ken Barlow, Hélé Béji, Hakim Ben Hammouda, Elsa Despiney, Farida Ayari, Dubravka Zarkov, George Joffé and Montserrat Badimon read and commented on drafts of the entire manuscript or on selected chapters. I thank them for their valuable comments and useful insights.

I am grateful to the Social Science Research Council's Conflict Prevention and Peace Forum programme for funding two of my visits to Tunisia. I thank Tatiana Carayannis for her support. In June 2012 I participated in a conference organised by TrustAfrica in Hammamet, Tunisia, that brought together scholars and activists from various countries in the Maghreb and sub-Saharan Africa to discuss the Arab Spring and its impact on the continent as a whole. This was a wonderful opportunity to present some of my field materials and get feedback from colleagues working on similar issues. My appreciation goes to all those whose presentations and comments contributed to expanding my thinking and analysis of these matters.

Portions of the material in this book appeared in my 2012 book *The Time of Youth: Work, Social Change, and Politics in Africa*, published by Kumarian Press.

It has been a pleasure to work with Grey Osterud, my

editor, whose incisive understanding of the intentions of this book was invaluable. I also thank Judith Forshaw for her great copyediting work.

I am particularly grateful to João, Nyeleti and Nandhi for their encouragement and unwavering support for my projects, and especially for the love and affection I receive from them each and every day.

Political parties and associations

Afek Tounes – Tunisian Aspiration

Al-Aridha Chaabia – Popular Petition Party

Alliance Démocratique – Democratic Alliance

Al Massar – Path of Social Progress

Al-Moubadara – The Initiative

Al-Waten – The Nation

Ansar al-Shari'a in Tunisia (AST)

Arrhma: Association des Femmes Nahdaouis – Association of Ennahdha Women

Association des Femmes Tunisiennes pour la Recherche et le Développement – Association of Tunisian Women for Research and Development (AFTURD)

Association Tunisienne des Femmes Démocrates – Tunisian Association of Democratic Women (ATFD)

Centre de Recherches, d'Études de Documentation et d'Information sur la Femme – Centre for Research, Documentation and Information on Women (CREDIF)

Congrès pour la République – Congress for the Republic (CPR)

Conseil National pour la Protection de la Révolution – National Council for the Protection of the Revolution (CNPR)

Conseil National pour les Libertés en Tunisie – Tunisian National Freedom Council (CNLT)

Destour Party – Constitutional Party

Ennahdha – The Renaissance Party (also Hizb al-Nahda)

Ettajdid Movement – Movement for Renewal

Forum Démocratique pour le Travail et les Libertés – Democratic Forum for Labour and Liberties (FDTL or Ettakatol)

Front Islamique Tunisien – Tunisian Islamic Front (FIT)

Front Populaire – Popular Front

Groupe d'Études et d'Action Socialiste en Tunisie – Socialist Study and Action Group (GEAST)

Hizb Jabhat al-Islah al-Islamiyya al-Tunisiyya – Tunisian Islamic Reform Front (JI or Jabhat al-Islah)

Hizb ut-Tahrir – Liberation Party

Instance Nationale pour la Réforme de l'Information et de la Communication – National Authority for the Reform of Media and Communications (INRIC)

Instance Supérieure Indépendante pour les Elections – Independent High Electoral Commission (ISIE)

Jeunes Indépendants Démocrates – Young Independent Democrats (JID)

Ligue de la Gauche Ouvrière – Left Workers' League (LGO)

Ligue Tunisienne des Droits de l'Homme – Tunisian League for Human Rights (LTDH)

Mouvement Baath – Ba'ath Party

Mouvement de la Tendance Islamique – Islamic Tendency Movement (MTI)

Mouvement des Démocrates Socialistes – Socialist Democratic Movement (MDS)

Mouvement du Peuple – People's Movement

Nida Tounes – Call of Tunisia

Nissa Tounsyat – Association of Tunisian Women

Parti Communiste des Ouvriers de Tunisie – Tunisian Workers' Communist Party (PCOT)

Parti de l'Indépendance pour la Liberté – Independence for Liberty Party (PIL)

Parti de la Justice et de la Liberté – Justice and Liberty Party (PJL)

Parti de la Lutte Progressiste – Progressive Struggle Party (PLP)

Parti de l'Unité Populaire – Party of Popular Unity (PUP)

Parti Démocrate Progressiste – Progressive Democratic Party (PDP)

Parti des Conservateurs Progressistes – Conservative Progressive Party (PCP)

Parti des Verts pour le Progrès – Progressive Green Party (PVP)

Parti du Centre Social – Social Centre Party (PCS)

Parti du Néo-Destour – Neo-Destourian Party

Parti du Travail Patriotique et Démocratique – Patriotic and Democratic Labour Party (PTPD)

Parti du Travail Tunisien – Tunisian Workers' Party (PTT)

Parti National Démocratique du Travail – National Democratic Labour Party

Parti Pirate Tunisien – Tunisian Pirate Party (PPT)

Parti Républicain – Republican Party (or Al-Joumhouri)

Parti Socialiste Destourien – Destourian Socialist Party (PSD)

Parti Social-Libéral – Social Liberal Party (PSL)

Parti Tunisie Verte – Green Party (PTV)

Parti Tunisien du Travail – Tunisian Labour Party

Pôle Démocratique Moderniste – Democratic Modernist Pole (PDM)

Rassemblement Constitutionnel Démocratique – Constitutional Democratic Rally (RCD)

Syndicat National des Enseignements – Secondary School Teachers' Union (SNES)

Syndicat National des Journalistes Tunisiens – National Union of Tunisian Journalists (SNJT)

Union Démocratique Unioniste – Democratic Union (UDU)

Union des Tunisiens Indépendants pour la Liberté – Union of Independent Tunisians for Freedom (UTIL)

Union Générale Tunisienne du Travail – Tunisian General Workers' Union (UGTT)

Union National de la Femme Tunisienne – National Union of Tunisian Women (UNFT)

Union Patriotique Libre – Free Patriotic Union (UPL)

Union Tunisienne de l'Industrie, du Commerce et de l'Artisanat – Union of Industry, Commerce and Artisans in Tunisia (UTICA)

Unionistes Nassériens – Nasserist Union Movement

Watad – Democratic Patriots Party

Introduction

The youth uprisings that led to the Arab Spring started on 17 December 2010 in the small town of Sidi Bouzid, in central Tunisia, after Mohamed Bouazizi,[1] a 26-year-old fruit vendor, set himself on fire as a protest against unemployment, difficult economic conditions, and mistreatment by the police.

According to various sources in Sidi Bouzid, Fayda Hamdi, a 45-year-old female officer of the municipal police, confiscated Bouazizi's goods and scales because he did not have a vendor's permit. Bouazizi was furious and reportedly insulted her. Some people reported that he said something like: 'What can I do now? Should I weigh my fruit with your two breasts?' Reacting angrily, the officer slapped his face in front of everyone. Being slapped by a woman in public is a grave offence against a man's self-respect. As Tunisian journalist Mohamed Kilani pointed out, 'only those who understand the meaning of honour in certain regions in Tunisia ... may be able to imagine the depth of his humiliation' (Kilani 2011: 55). A couple of Tunisian analysts contested the veracity of this story, which they saw as an attempt to portray Bouazizi as disrespectful to the older woman, thereby diminishing or devaluing his act as worthy of national recognition. They saw Bouazizi's self-immolation as a politically motivated act of protest that stemmed directly from his outrage over massive youth unemployment and the regime's unsound socioeconomic policies.

Deeply upset about losing his goods and offended by the treatment he had received from the policewoman, Bouazizi tried to lodge a complaint with the municipal authorities. Apparently the governor refused to see him, even after Bouazizi threatened: 'If you don't see me, I'll burn myself.' True to his word, he acquired a can of paint thinner, doused his left arm, and held a lighter in

1

his right hand while standing in front of the main government building of Sidi Bouzid. After voicing his protests about the lack of jobs, the high cost of living and police abuses, attracting the attention of many onlookers and passers-by, Bouazizi set himself alight. He succumbed to his wounds at a military hospital in Ben Arous 18 days later, on 4 January 2011.

There have been self-immolations in the past, but Mohamed Bouazizi's self-immolation and subsequent death struck a chord and created enormous outrage, leading thousands of young men and women out onto the streets of Sidi Bouzid in solidarity with Bouazizi to protest about unemployment and poor living conditions. A number of factors, such as the soaring rate of youth unemployment and increasingly high levels of economic hardship, coupled with intense political repression and government corruption, might explain why at this particular juncture Bouazizi's self-immolation was the straw that broke the camel's back. After a couple of days, demonstrations spread across the central region as young people came out in force to confront the regime. In several instances, the national police used tear gas and fired on protesters, causing deaths and injuries. What began as an individual expression of outrage over a personal offence and loss of livelihood turned into a region-wide youth protest against police abuse and the lack of jobs.[2]

As the uprising grew, an alliance developed between urban middle-class youths and the young unemployed protesters from the interior regions of the country. Groups of young cyber activists from Tunis rapidly descended on Sidi Bouzid and Kasserine, the remote inland areas where the protests were taking place, and joined the demonstrations. They marched alongside other protesters, challenged the police, and skilfully used the internet to publicise, in real time, the confrontations between youth and the police, exposing the political repression and brutality of the Ben Ali regime. Their actions, along with those of local internet users, helped to transform an initially localised uprising into national and international news. In a matter of seconds, Tweets, Facebook messages and YouTube videos with images of young protesters being violently attacked by the police reached millions of viewers across the country and abroad. Major international media outlets, such as Al Jazeera, France 24 and CNN, accessed the information and broadcast it immediately. The worldwide exposure of the regime's bloody repression of unarmed demonstrators gave a new dimension to the protests. The dictatorship could no longer conceal what was happening inside its borders, nor describe these events as isolated disruptions by fringe groups. Moreover, the government had no effective means of attacking the insurgency's virtual networks: shutting down the internet did not work because young people quickly turned to proxy sites.

Revelations of government atrocities in Sidi Bouzid, Kasserine and other towns in the central region appear to have created tremendous popular outrage and stimulated young people to join in the uprisings. Street protests mushroomed all over the country. The alliance between middle-class and unemployed youths helped expand the revolt's demands, as urbanites sought to end internet censorship and to defend civil liberties. The regime's violent response to the protesters helped forge the connection between socioeconomic and political demands and contributed to the transformation of what was a largely spontaneous and localised youth protest against poor living conditions, police abuse and a lack of jobs into a determined national revolt (ICG 2011).

The insurgency by unemployed and disaffected young people in the interior of the country provided new momentum to the ongoing cyber war against the regime, mainly led by urban middle-class young people in Tunis and the other major cities. The cyber war reached a new level with the involvement of Anonymous, an international group of activist hackers, and the subsequent hacking of important government sites. These two fronts – fighting in the streets and fighting in the cyber world – fed into each other and strongly contributed to the advance of the protest movement.

The escalation of the conflict between young people and the government attracted the attention of some civil society groups, which played a significant role in expanding the protest. At the end of December 2010, the Bar Association joined in and called

3

upon its members to stage national demonstrations. Hundreds of lawyers came out onto the streets of Tunis, Sfax, Djerba and other cities to denounce human rights violations and demand respect for civil liberties. The lawyers did not escape police brutality; they were beaten severely.[3] Other civil society groups that supported the youth revolt as it developed included the Union Générale Tunisienne du Travail (UGTT), the association of journalists and teachers' associations. The legal opposition parties, which until then had been watching the protests from a distance, decided to become involved around 10 January 2011.

Although the national leadership of some civil society groups, for example the UGTT, initially adopted a 'wait and see' attitude, they joined the movement when they realised that it had grown beyond anyone's expectations and appeared to be unstoppable. Neither sticks nor carrots were effective in preventing protests. The escalation of police repression and the shutting down of the internet, along with offers of amnesty for a few insurgents, did not deter demonstrators, and grandiose but vague promises of more job programmes for youth did not dissuade others from joining. As young people continued to stand up against the regime, they continued to attract supporters from other groups. The social movement initiated by young Tunisians rapidly grew into a national coalition of forces from all sectors of Tunisian society, spanning age, gender and ethnicity, and socioeconomic, political and religious ideologies. Indeed, there was a general malaise and widespread discontent with the regime, which the youth movement was able to galvanise. At this juncture, the revolt shifted its immediate focus from socioeconomic reform, freedom of expression and civil liberties to regime change. The slogan of the social movement became 'Ben Ali Dégage!' ('Ben Ali Go!'). Following just 29 days of intense street protests, on 14 January 2011 Ben Ali fled the country, opening a new chapter in Tunisia's history. This radical change came at a cost. According to a United Nations human rights investigation, at least 219 Tunisians were killed during the uprisings and another 510 were injured.[4]

The spark lit by Mohamed Bouazizi in Sidi Bouzid ignited a

regional youth protest against police abuse and unemployment that spread into a youth movement fighting for better living conditions and freedom of expression, which was then transformed into a nationwide coalition that managed to overthrow one of the most entrenched dictatorial regimes in North Africa. How was this evolution of the social movement possible? What conditions permitted the establishment of an alliance between the elites and the masses, the young and the old, the rich and the poor, and the Islamists and the secularists to oust the regime? This book begins with an analysis that tries to tackle some of these questions.

The Tunisian revolution had enormous national, regional and international implications. The determination and tenacity of young Tunisians inspired many youths across the globe, particularly in the Arab world. A few weeks later, young Egyptians occupied Tahrir Square in Cairo and staged protests that led to the removal of Hosni Mubarak. In Libya, insurgent youths joined other groups to defeat the well-armed security forces of Muammar Gaddafi, who was killed in October 2011. These events signalled the beginning of what I prefer to call the 'African Awakening'.[5] On the African continent, and in many other parts of the world, young people are protesting against unemployment and socio-economic inequalities, and are demanding social justice and civil liberties. Young people's demonstrations across the globe gained new momentum after the events in North Africa. Youth also led protests in Yemen, and after almost a year of unrest they voted President Saleh out of power in February 2012. Protests also took place in Bahrain and in Syria, where they have turned into a drawn-out war against the Assad regime.

In Senegal in January 2011, a group of young activists established the Y'en a Marre (Enough is Enough) movement to fight government corruption, massive unemployment and the lack of future prospects. Rallied by Y'en a Marre in June 2011, young people clashed with police as they denounced attempts to change the constitution to favour the sitting president. Amidst clouds of tear gas, young protesters managed to stop the approval of the constitutional amendments (Honwana 2012). Galvanised by

5

this victory, the Y'en a Marre youth movement embarked on a national campaign to encourage young people to vote freely. Under the slogan '*Ma carte d'électeur, mon arme*' ('My voting card, my weapon'), they managed to vote President Abdoulaye Wade out of office (ibid.). A number of other youth protests took place during the course of 2011–12 in countries such as Sudan, Angola, Uganda, Kenya, Burkina Faso and South Africa. While they have not led to regime change, these demonstrations are already signalling the power of a politically motivated younger generation ready to stand up for itself.

In Europe, too, young people came out onto the streets to express grievances over economic hardship and massive unemployment. In March 2011, there were riots in Greece and in Portugal more than 30,000 young people filled the streets to protest about unemployment and the absence of career prospects for what is known as the *geração à rasca* (the struggling generation). In May 2011, the Indignados (indignant) movement (also known as 15M)[6] in Spain protested against soaring unemployment rates and the failures of governance and democracy. In the UK in August 2011, riots and looting by youths occurred, sparked by the shooting of a young man of colour by the police. These violent events exposed inequalities and existing disconnects within British society, as well as the failure of government to respond to the needs of a disaffected younger population (ibid.).

North and South America also experienced a wave of youth uprisings. In Chile, an estimated 100,000 young people took to the streets of Santiago, in August 2011, to protest about bad governance and to demand free, quality public education. And in the United States, many young Americans struggling to find work and pay for their college education joined the Occupy Wall Street movement in protest at socioeconomic inequalities, corporate greed and corporations' undue influence over government (ibid.).

Despite their diverse socioeconomic and political situations, young people, in rich and poor countries alike, appear to be affected by the same problems of unemployment, political disempowerment and restricted futures. Using the streets as the place of action, and social media and electronic messaging to organise itself, this generation has begun to assert its rights as citizens, and to claim a space for itself in the world. While the outcomes of these youth social movements are impossible to predict and will vary from one country to another, it is clear that the world will never be the same after the Tunisian revolution.

For young Tunisians, overthrowing the dictatorship was only the first step. Major challenges arose during the immediate post-revolution transition period. Political parties, old and new, quickly moved to fill the political vacuum and exercised control over the transition process. The heterogeneous group of young activists had no clear leadership and was not organised to enter or play a role in the political arena. Watching from the outside, young people became increasingly disgruntled with the slow pace of change; not only did their situation remain the same, but their hopes for significant socioeconomic and political transformations began to fade. The transitional authorities, still strongly attached to the former regime, moved away from the logic of revolutionary rupture and towards what many perceived to be a pseudo-democratic order based on the maintenance of existing institutions. The progressive left-wing parties that decided to stay out of the transitional government pressed for the complete dismantling of the previous regime's institutional apparatus. Left-wing opposition challenged the interim government by creating alternative bodies, such as the 14 January Front and the National Council for the Protection of the Revolution. Once again, young people took to the streets to force radical political reforms. This combined approach succeeded; changes were made in the composition of the government, the institutions of the old regime were dismantled, and elections were set up for a National Constituent Assembly that would have the task of writing a new Tunisian constitution.

Nevertheless, the struggle was far from over. During the run-up to the elections, competing political parties did not engage sufficiently with the pragmatic concerns of the youth, which centred on employment opportunities, freedom of expression, equal opportunities and social justice. The electoral debates led

7

by the political parties focused on identity politics and polarised secularists and Islamists. The secular perspective, defended predominantly by the liberal, left-wing, largely Francophone upper middle class, was based on a modernising agenda for the protection of individual freedoms and women's rights. The Islamist outlook, espoused essentially by conservative, mostly Arabic-speaking groups with strong ties to organised religion, called for the restoration or installation of Islamic law and the rejection of Western influences. While both perspectives have moderate and radical tendencies within them, this characterisation has broader nuances; for example, some Islamists are also upper-middle-class Francophone speakers who had been in exile. Many young Tunisians I spoke to were at odds with this shift in the political discourse, which disregarded the issues that mattered most to them. Younger voters' low turnout in the October 2011 elections reflected their disaffection from the transitional process.

Ennahdha, the Islamist party, won a plurality but not a majority, obtaining 89 seats in the National Constituent Assembly (41 per cent of the total number of seats), and was compelled to form a coalition with the Congrès pour la République and the Forum Démocratique pour le Travail et les Libertés (also known as Ettakatol), both secular centre-left parties. This troika was in charge of managing the country during the post-election transition period, with the aim of producing a new constitution and preparing for presidential and legislative elections in 2013. Major challenges confronted both the National Constituent Assembly and the troika government; in such a deeply divided political environment, coming up with a constitution that would achieve national consensus was a difficult undertaking. The troika government was expected to provide physical and economic security as well as public services to Tunisians at a moment of tremendous political and social turmoil.

Meanwhile, tensions between Islamists and secularists have intensified. Members of extremist groups such as the Salafist[7] movement have called for strict observance of religious law in the new Tunisian state, and the issue of women's rights has moved to the centre of public debate as women's bodies have become the terrain upon which battles over identity are being fought. The Tunisian women's movement has been fighting against the imposition of Sharia law and the reversal of existing women's rights; it has been trying to reframe the debate, beyond secularist versus Islamist divides, to focus on the issues that matter most to the majority of Tunisian women. At the same time, the secularist movement has been actively reorganising and rethinking its own strategy against religious extremism.

How can Tunisians negotiate a new place for Islam in a political culture that, since independence, has defined secularism as the touchstone of national identity? The immediate struggle has centred on which political forces have the greatest sway in the drafting of the new Tunisian constitution, and thereby in determining the future of the country. To what extent will Tunisians be able to reconcile the positions of the secularists with those of the more conservative Islamists? These critical questions continue to preoccupy Tunisians today.

The various youth groups that led the revolution remain politically unorganised and appear to be less united than they were during the fight against the dictatorial regime. The poor and the unemployed seem more concerned about jobs and improving economic opportunities in their regions, and some have taken a pro-Ennahdha position if not a pro-Salafist one. Urban youth, mostly secularist, appear to be primarily worried about individual liberties and ending political repression, especially police violence and government censorship of the internet. Both groups refrain from playing formal political roles and engage mostly in civil society associations, although they tend to do so in isolation from each other. Indeed, Tunisian youth are questioning the relevance of 'politics as usual' and have been struggling to find new responses to the challenges they face in the post-revolutionary period. Their expressed desire for radical socioeconomic and political change appears to include the rejection of all traditional forms of politics, as they continue to refuse to be co-opted by political parties (Nigam 2012).

There is no doubt that young people were the trailblazers of the revolution and contributed to opening up space for political dialogue and contestation in Tunisia. However, while they struggle to articulate what the 'new political' will look like, 'traditional' political forces have been occupying the existing political space. Many young Tunisians fear that the country may risk becoming merely a slightly reworked version of its past or, in a more radical shift, be transformed into a conservative Muslim society. In these circumstances, and without entering the formal political arena, how can young people actively play a political role that will push for fundamental socioeconomic changes in Tunisia? While young Tunisians believe that there are platforms for political activism outside formal party politics, will their work in civil society associations be enough to steer the country in the right direction? Or will street protests continue to be their main mechanism for exerting pressure on those in power?

This analysis of young people's involvement in the Tunisian revolution is based on interviews I conducted with activists just six months after the overthrow of the government and during two other visits in April and June 2012.[8] The book's main concerns are:

- to understand how the youth movement evolved into a revolution that overthrew the regime;
- to investigate the roles played by the various groups that constituted the revolutionary coalition;
- to examine the process of 'democracy in the making' in Tunisia, especially the tensions between various political forces and the position of youth in politics;
- to interrogate the future of a society divided between a conservative Islamic majority and a modern secular elite, as well as between a younger generation yearning for radical change and an older generation playing 'politics as usual'; and
- to examine the promise, achievements and challenges of a youth social movement with no clear leadership for claiming political power.

In Tunisia, young people no longer appear to be bound by

hegemonic political discourses and party ideologies, and are creating their own spaces of intervention to engage the state and society. They understand that the revolution is a long process and it will take time to achieve profound socioeconomic changes and a new political culture. The Tunisian revolution, led mainly by disenfranchised youths, was a powerful example of 'citizenship from below' that has emerged outside traditional political structures and has opened up a space for major transformations. The success of the first stage of the revolution depended on young people's ability to draw people from different sectors of society into the fight against the dictatorship. The success of the post-revolutionary transition, however, will depend greatly on the capacity of Tunisians, in all their diversity, to find common ground to rebuild the country.

First encounters

I arrived in Tunisia for the first time in June 2011. At the time, I was writing *The Time of Youth: Work, social change, and politics in Africa*,[9] a book on youth transitions and participation in social change, and I was struck by the magnitude of the events that occurred in Tunisia and Egypt and by young people's pivotal role in both revolutions. That was when I decided that the book had to include material about the events in North Africa, and I travelled to Tunisia. I was able to access diverse networks of young people, activists, scholars, journalists and politicians, whose contributions, insights and perspectives were invaluable to my research.

I define youth not on the basis of chronological age (for example 15–24 or 15–34)[10] but rather as a socially constructed category characterised by particular cultural views about roles, rights and obligations. Indeed, and as Pierre Bourdieu pointed out, 'youth and age are not self-evident data but are socially constructed, in the struggle between the young and the old' (Bourdieu 1993: 95). In this sense, youth is defined here primarily on the basis of societal expectations and responsibilities. The vast majority of Tunisians I encountered have been struggling to make a smooth transition into adult life. Many have university degrees but are jobless and survive through insecure, temporary and low-paid jobs, mostly in the informal economy. In my 2012 book *The Time of Youth*, I discussed the notion of 'waithood', a portmanteau term combining 'wait' and 'hood', meaning to wait for adulthood (Singerman 2007; Dhillon and Yousef 2009). Waithood describes a period of suspension in which young people are unable to attain the social markers of adulthood – find stable employment, marry and provide for their families, and contribute to society as fully fledged citizens (Honwana 2012). In this period of limbo, young people are no longer considered to be children in need of care, but are not yet social adults, capable of taking on the social responsibilities of adulthood. Like many young people across the continent, many young Tunisians are living in waithood. And, indeed, the revolution in Tunisia was carried out mainly by those aged between 18 and 40 years of age, many still unemployed and dependent on their parents and others, trying to make ends meet through odd jobs and very precarious livelihood strategies. Therefore, the term 'youth' in this context should be understood in this broad sense, and must include all those who have yet to attain social adulthood despite their chronological age (ibid.; El Difraoui 2012).

During my three visits to Tunisia in 2011–12, I travelled to many towns and villages throughout the country, where I felt welcomed by everybody I came across. People were very warm and hospitable, and many showed appreciation of my interest in them and in what was happening during the revolution. In fact, many in Sidi Bouzid, where the revolution started, complained that foreigners and international media groups had literally swamped the region during the beginning of the upheaval, to then leave abruptly to focus on the Egyptian revolution that took place just a couple of weeks later. Tunisians felt that the world had lost interest in them, their struggles and achievements; that they did not have a chance to rejoice in their victory against the dictatorship with the rest of the world; and that the world's attention had turned to Egypt. In this context, my interest and my visits to the interior were well regarded and welcomed. There was tremendous enthusiasm, particularly on the part of the youth, to talk to me, share stories about the revolution, and show me the places where important events had occurred.

I met young men and women from diverse social and economic backgrounds and I conducted individual interviews and focus group discussions with students, young professionals and entrepreneurs, cyber activists and many unemployed graduates. Graduate unemployment is a major problem in Tunisia and one of the factors that fuelled the revolution against Ben Ali. Reforms in the education system greatly widened access to higher education, but young graduates' expectations of a job, a career and possibilities for upward mobility have been shattered by the challenging economic situation and the lack of employment. In long individual interviews I listened to their narratives about life, family, education and future prospects. I listened to their struggles to become independent adults and fully fledged citizens in the context of unequal regional development, lack of civil liberties and widespread government corruption.

I also conducted several focus group discussions with young people in both single-sex and mixed groups. Most focus groups concentrated on particular themes, and the participants were encouraged to debate and exchange views among themselves. I visited several *maisons des jeunes* (youth clubs) across the country and interacted with young people as they carried out their cultural and civic activities. I went to universities, professional training centres and enterprises. I also talked to young unemployed men sitting in street cafés, where they spend most of the day chatting or playing table games, and I met with several young women in youth associations, university foyers and their homes.

I was fortunate to be invited several times to visit their homes and share a meal with the family. On these occasions I had the opportunity to meet parents, grandparents and siblings, and to savour delicious Tunisian food. It became apparent that many of my hosts were genuinely surprised that the foreign researcher their children had brought home was a black woman from sub-Saharan Africa. And these encounters became truly two-way interactions as I found myself answering my fair share of questions; my hosts wanted to know more about me, my own family and the traditions of my country, Mozambique. In the towns and cities of the Tunisian interior especially, people were hugely curious about sub-Saharan Africa. Several Tunisians reminded me that they see themselves as primarily Africans, and shared that in the old days their region was called *Ifriqiyah*, and they felt closer to Africa than to the people from the Persian Gulf.

The fact that my local research assistants were themselves young and well plugged into local youth networks – the universities, the cyber activists and the *maisons de jeunes* – greatly facilitated my access to these networks. I met their friends and then the friends of those friends, creating a snowball effect. My research assistants mediated between my young informants and me, advising on how to broach sensitive subjects and providing useful insights about local culture. They even taught me some key words in Arabic that were very helpful to show respect and break the ice during interviews.

The research also included discussions with politicians, academics, journalists, trade unionists, religious leaders, intellectuals and activists. These interviews provided me with the broader picture and relevant information about Tunisian society's views of young people and the role they played in the ousting of the old regime. They also offered insights into the availability or otherwise of specific policies for the young and their place within the economy, society and culture.

Methodologically, this book tries to bring young people's voices to the centre of the narrative and then construct a wider sociopolitical analysis from their personal histories and experiences. Young Tunisians I met described their political mobilisation, recounted their participation in crucial events, and reflected on the problems they and their country face in the transition to democracy. The significance of allowing them to speak for themselves and narrate their experiences and views directly in the text is tied to young people's appreciation of their role in the revolution, which provided them with a sense of personal autonomy and ownership of the process. In some ways, the book tries to capture that spirit of the revolution by placing them at the forefront of the narrative.

Encounters of occupation, resistance and liberation

In this section I examine the recent revolution and the political tensions of the transition period against the broader historical context. In the past, young Tunisians were actively engaged in processes of social transformation as they resisted and confronted colonial domination. Also, previous tensions and debates surrounding post-independence vision, policies and alliances can arguably be connected to, and shed new light on, some of the political processes happening in Tunisia today.

Tunisia has a long history of repression and resistance. Numerous monuments across the country bear silent witness to the country's history of foreign invasions, occupations and resistance. Home to the ancient Phoenician city of Carthage, Tunisia's location at the centre of North Africa made it attractive to the rulers of the Roman, Arab and Ottoman empires, who all recognised the geostrategic importance of the country. Under the pretext of Tunisia's debt owed to its European creditors, and the fact that some Tunisians strayed into the neighbouring French colony of Algeria, French forces invaded and occupied the country. Despite resistance by the locals, the treaty of Bardo (also known as Al Qasr as Sa'id) established Tunisia as a French protectorate in 1881.

As with all forms of colonial rule, under the French, Tunisia's land and native population were exploited for the benefit of the colonisers. Young Tunisians at the time were instrumental in the resistance against French colonial rule. In 1920, Tunisian nationalists formed a political party – the Destour (Constitutional) Party – to claim and fight for Tunisian autonomy. Through a judicious blend of repression and concessions, however, the French managed to ensure that the young party made little progress. By 1934, a group of young nationalists, namely Habib Bourguiba, Salah Ben Youssef and Farhat Hached, decided to break away from the Destour Party, creating an offshoot that they called Neo-Destourian Party. It was in this period that Habib Bourguiba, the secretary-general of the new party, gained national prominence as a politician and went on to play a central role in Tunisia's political life. Bourguiba was just 31 years old at the time.[11] Despite banning the party and having its secretary-general imprisoned for several years in France, the French authorities were unable to suppress the Neo-Destourian Party.

The Second World War brought brief German rule in the country, with the French regaining control towards the end of the war. As the movement for independence intensified, in 1946 Farhat Hached abandoned the communist-led Confédération Générale du Travail (the French General Confederation of Workers) to establish the UGTT. This was the first indigenous attempt to organise Tunisia's workers, and the new union worked closely with the nationalist movement.[12]

Hached was assassinated in 1952 by the French para-military hit squad La Main Rouge (the Red Hand).

In 1954, Pierre Mendès-France, a socialist, became prime minister of France and introduced a policy for partial French withdrawal from two colonies, Tunisia and Indochina. Mendès-France promised internal autonomy to the pro-independence bey – the provincial governor under the suzerainty of the Ottoman empire. After long negotiations, a French–Tunisian convention was signed in 1955 granting Tunisia's internal autonomy.[13] Bourguiba, who had been exiled, returned to Tunisia and a Neo-Destourian government was formed. Tunisia became fully independent from France in March 1956 and Bourguiba became head of state. However, Salah Ben Youssef, one of Bourguiba's contemporaries and fellow Neo-Destourian, denounced the French strategy as being too restrictive and refused to join the government. He turned against Bourguiba, who accepted the French proposal, left the party and organised a brief armed resistance in the south, which was soon suppressed. Ben Youssef fled the country to escape imprisonment and was assassinated in 1961.[14]

The new Tunisian state managed to maintain good relations with France as Bourguiba was able to crush the radical Youssefist movement. Larbi Sadiki, a Tunisian political scientist, stressed that the Bourguiba regime replaced colonial hegemony with an indigenous hegemony, crushing rival centres of power and leaving no space for competing visions (Sadiki 2002). Bourguiba pursued a nationalist model of non-doctrinaire socialism.[15] In the 1960s, however, he adopted drastic socialist policies of state control and agricultural cooperatives, but the failure of these policies led to his return to a more moderate approach. The regime embarked on an economically liberal model of development that led to the flourishing of private businesses and consolidation of the private sector. On the social front, his regime undertook a number of reforms with regard to public education and literacy campaigns, women's rights, family planning and a state-run healthcare system. In the international arena, Bourguiba sided with the West during the Cold War, and challenged the leadership of the Arab League by Egyptian President Nasser, a pro-Arabist and supporter of Salah Ben Youssef's ideals.

Despite having been unanimously voted president for life by the Tunisian National Assembly in 1975, Bourguiba was deposed by his prime minister, Zine El Abidine Ben Ali, in 1987. Ben Ali became president of Tunisia and renamed the Neo-Destourian Party the Rassemblement Constitutionnel Démocratique (RCD). Ben Ali continued Bourguiba's liberal economic development model and instituted economic reforms that increased Tunisia's growth rate and foreign investment. While maintaining Bourguiba's pro-Western foreign policy, Ben Ali also worked to improve ties to the Arab Muslim world. Internally, his presidency was repressive and suppressed political dissent; the regime arrested and forced into exile several leaders and militants from the opposition parties, as well as outlawing Ennahdha (also known as Al-Nahda), which became one of the main targets of government hostility.

The scope of the book

Following on from this introduction, Chapter 1 focuses on the antecedents of the revolution and addresses four critical areas of disconnect between the Ben Ali regime and the Tunisian population: unequal regional development and massive youth

17

unemployment; corruption and nepotism; political repression and lack of civil liberties; the shortcomings of women's rights reforms and the repression of Islamic identity. The chapter argues that these disconnects, which cut across a wide range of sectors and social strata in Tunisian society – from the disenfranchised poor through the middle class to the business elite – were crucial to the emergence of the broad national coalition that led to the demise of the dictatorship.

Chapter 2 discusses four groups that played critical roles in various stages of the protest movement: young cyber activists; unemployed university graduates; civil society organisations; and opposition political parties. It examines the specific struggles faced by each of these groups and the strategies they adopted to fight the regime. The chapter argues that youth mobilisation for this uprising grew steadily from the frustrations expressed on internet social networks and through cyber activism; in interactions at street cafés and bars; during breaks in telemarketing call centres, on construction sites and at other workplaces and educational institutions; as well as from the lack of economic opportunities and a sense of social injustice and repression that permeated Tunisians' everyday life. When the right opportunity arose – Bouazizi's self-immolation – young Tunisians were ready for action.

Chapter 3 describes the series of events that occurred during the 29 days of protest all over the country. This chronology is compiled from the recollections of young people who took part in the specific events they describe. The chapter enquires whether what happened in Tunisia was indeed a social and political revolution or, rather, an uprising that did not substantially change dominant patterns and power relations. The analysis also considers the Tunisian youth protests in light of existing theories on social movements. The chapter argues that the analysis of the revolutions of the early twenty-first century calls for a reformulation of the notion of 'the political' and the rethinking of old models in order to devise new ones more adequate to the realities of our times.

Chapter 4 explores the tensions and negotiations between the various political forces that occurred immediately after 14 January

2011. It analyses the formation and actions of the interim government and discusses young people's views of the key political and social developments that marked the post-revolutionary transition. Understanding the process of building a multiparty democracy in Tunisia involves surveying the new political landscape, the development of various political discourses, and the common and divergent visions for a new Tunisia. Young people are largely disconnected from the debate surrounding identity politics that has been adopted by political parties. They are consciously rejecting 'politics as usual' and are choosing to remain outside formal, traditional political structures. Instead, they engage in civil society associations and use street protest to continue pressing for meaningful political and socioeconomic change.

Chapter 5 looks at youth participation in the elections and the significance of the low youth turnout. It discusses the challenges young people faced in navigating the maze of political parties, and describes their engagement in voter education during the electoral campaign. Finally, it considers the election results and the constitution of the coalition government. The main argument of this chapter is that young Tunisians' absence from the polls was due to their conviction that neither the established nor the emerging political forces would steer the country towards positive change. Campaign discourses focused on issues of identity, revolving around debates between secularism and Islamism, rather than addressing the key concerns of the revolution – unemployment, social justice and civil liberties.

Chapter 6 examines the challenges faced by the newly elected National Constituent Assembly as it has set out to establish its role and mandates during the transitional period leading to the presidential and legislative elections planned for late 2013. It also explores the tensions within the coalition government and its ability to deliver on the promises of the revolution. The chapter also analyses the role of the opposition parties in the post-electoral period and ends with a discussion of young Tunisians' views of the government, the opposition, the new constitution and the future of the country.

Chapter 7 explores the context of women's civil society movements in Tunisia and young women's perspectives on current debates about women's rights and position in society. It begins with an examination of the contested issue of women's rights in Islamic law and of the political and legal reforms relating to women and the family undertaken by the Bourguiba regime in the 1950s. The chapter then analyses the evolution of the feminist movement in Tunisia from independence to the post-revolution period, highlighting its diversity and women's activism during the political transition. It shows that, although women's rights reforms began as part of a top-down, state-centred modernisation project, women have become increasingly engaged in public debates and are now speaking for themselves.

The concluding chapter considers the challenges that lie ahead for the Tunisians and the role of youth in effecting meaningful social change. It also examines some of the achievements of the youth revolution so far and the lessons that can be taken from it. However, there is no doubt that the revolution is still ongoing and events unfolding. Only time will tell how far Tunisians have progressed in improving their socioeconomic conditions and in consolidating civil liberties and other gains of the revolution.

1 | Disconnections

Tunisia was a fertile ground for the spread of this massive youth-led uprising. Social and economic malaise in the country had been deepening over the previous two decades. The self-immolation of Mohamed Bouazizi ignited protests that expressed longstanding discontent with structural problems and governmental policies that underpinned Ben Ali's dictatorship. Frustrations among Tunisians from various groups and walks of life stemmed not only from economic hardship and high levels of unemployment but also from suffocating repression, the absence of political freedoms, and a ruling family that was increasingly condemned as a kleptocracy.[1]

This chapter addresses five critical areas of disconnect between the Tunisian authorities and the population: unequal regional development and massive youth unemployment; corruption and nepotism; political repression and lack of civil liberties; the short-comings of women's rights reforms; and the repression of Islam and the quest for religious identity. The chapter argues that these disconnects, which cut across wide sectors and social strata, from the disenfranchised poor through the middle class to the business elite, were crucial to the emergence of the broad national coalition that led to the demise of the dictatorial regime in Tunisia.

Unequal regional development and massive unemployment

Regional imbalances in the Tunisian economy appeared during the regime of Habib Bourguiba, the first president of post-independence Tunisia who led the country between 1956 and 1987. Initially, Bourguiba's economic development strategy was marked by socialist redistributive policies. His prime minister, Ahmed Ben Salah, launched state-led programmes for agricultural cooperatives and public sector industrialisation, but the socialist experiment was short-lived because of opposition within Bourguiba's ruling coalition (Murphy 1999). The economic hardship and malaise that ensued in the 1970s, with weak agricultural performance and high urban unemployment, led to increased migration to Europe. In January 1978, the Union Générale Tunisienne du Travail (UGTT) organised a nationwide general strike to protest against the government's economic policies. Over 50 demonstrators were killed and 200 trade union officials, including UGTT secretary-general Habib Achour, were arrested.

In the 1980s, the economy continued to perform poorly, and in 1984 the International Monetary Fund (IMF) forced the government to raise the price of bread and semolina (wheat flour), causing severe hardship and a wave of food riots. In 1987, following a bloodless coup, Bourguiba was overthrown and replaced by his prime minister, Zine El Abidine Ben Ali.[2] The new president and his government embarked on a series of economic reforms aimed at generating economic growth and accelerating development. According to Tunisian economist Hakim Ben Hammouda, reforms were undertaken in three main directions. First, the government sought to reduce its deficits and curb inflation. Second, it privatised public enterprises; between 1987 and 2008, the sale of over 200 enterprises netted the state almost 6.1 billion Tunisian dinars (about US$3.8 billion). The corruption and nepotism that marked this process created many problems, however. The third reform was the liberalisation of the economy through free trade agreements aimed at helping local enterprises cope with increased competition from foreign companies. In July 1995, the government signed a free trade agreement with the European Union that not only covered economic issues but also included political, social and cultural aspects of the relationship between Tunisia and its neighbours across the Mediterranean (Ben Hammouda 2012).

As various Tunisian economists have pointed out, this programme of reforms lifted the country out of the economic crisis of the late 1980s and stimulated economic growth. Yet the dynamics of market-led growth generated serious regional economic imbalances. The structural adjustment policies required a further opening of the Tunisian economy to foreign goods, investment and finance, leaving Tunisian society with greater levels of economic stratification and a proliferation of low-skilled jobs. An increased number of Tunisians were living in poverty and unable to meet their economic needs or achieve their life aspirations.

The neoliberal economic policies of Ben Ali's regime led to a pattern of uneven economic development that has marginalised the central, western and southern desert regions and has con-centrated wealth – i.e. investment in tourism and infrastructure – in the northern and eastern coastal regions of the country. For example, the road network centres on Tunis and serves the coast, while the interior remains more isolated.

The decline in farming and mining in the inland regions has contributed to widening regional inequalities. By 1999, about 25 per cent of the country's labour force was engaged in agriculture, which accounted for 12 per cent of gross domestic product (GDP), but fertile land was limited to the north, where cereals, olives, fruit, grapes and vegetables are produced. In the central-west and southern regions, desert farming was and continues to be precarious; with neither irrigation nor soil conservation systems, yields are very low. Endemic poverty gives rise to despair. Although nationally the poverty rate is estimated at just 10 per cent, in the central and western regions close to 30 per cent of the population live in poverty (Hibou et al. 2011). Entrepreneurial activity is also highly unequal. Rather than making public investments in the inland regions, the government offered tax breaks and incentives to private businesses in the vain hope that this would encourage local development.[3]

Tunisians in the central, western and southern desert regions were angered by the government's neglect. They lacked such basic social infrastructure as schools, hospitals and roads. With little public and no private investment there, few jobs were created. 'There are no industries that provide jobs for people in this region. There is only the paper factory, where my father and my uncles worked. But the government did not build new factories; that's why there are no jobs for our generation,' said Amin, a 28-year-old man in Kasserine. The Société Nationale de Cellulose et de Papier Alfa, established in Kasserine in 1963, is the sole industry and the main employer in the region. For half a century, however, the paper mill has been poisoning the adjacent communities with the chlorine it releases. The government has never addressed the problem, leaving Kasserinians to suffer from illnesses caused by the factory's pollution.[4]

Explaining some of the reasons for his discontent, 27-year-old Khaled stressed that:

Ben Ali's government has not invested in Kasserine at all. We are one of the poorest regions in the country. More than 80 per cent of what we consume here comes from Algeria, not from Tunisia. You see those jerry cans of fuel that are being sold in the streets? That is fuel from Algeria, which is much cheaper than Tunisian fuel. Here everything comes from Algeria: food, clothes, furniture, everything ... We survive because of Algeria, not because of the Tunisian government.

Samir Rabhi, a college teacher in Kasserine, contended that this underdevelopment was deliberate:

Kasserine is an agricultural region but it has been neglected by the Tunisian government. No investments have been made in this region and, even worse, government policies were designed to impoverish the inland regions. The regional imbalances did not happen by default, but rather by design.[5]

To deal with steady declines in state revenue, the government implemented unpopular programmes aimed at reducing subsidies on commodities including food. Popular dissatisfaction in the inland regions was widespread. Major revolts began in Gafsa, Sidi Bouzid and other economically marginalised regions. The January 2008 protests in Redeyef, Gafsa, constituted one of the first open demonstrations against Ben Ali's regime. Protests were led by unemployed non-union workers and students who were unable to get jobs in the phosphate mines. The miners' union and the ruling political party (Rassemblement Constitutionnel Démocratique or RCD) cooperated with the Gafsa Phosphate Company, the major employer, in limiting and controlling access to jobs in the mines. Protesters called for an end to unfair and fraudulent recruitment practices (Allal 2010). Supported by miners' widows and families, they also demanded better living conditions. The unrest in Redeyef quickly expanded to other mining areas and paralysed the industry for several months (Amnesty International 2009). That same year, unemployed youths staged protests in Skhira in the south-east and in Ben Gardane.[6]

The government's neoliberal economic approach resulted in lower wages and job insecurity and failed to generate enough jobs to employ young people entering the workforce. Unemployment skyrocketed among university graduates during the 1990s. The global economic downturn had especially serious effects on the Tunisian economy between 2007 and 2009: rates of unemployment and underemployment, which were already high, soared, particularly in the tourism industry. Each year about 140,000 people are ready to enter the labour market while only 60,000 to 65,000 jobs are created, mainly in Greater Tunis and the coastal regions. Among these 140,000 new jobseekers, 70,000 are university graduates, 40,000 have completed professional training, and 30,000 have no training (Hibou et al. 2011). In 2009, the unemployment rate among people aged 18 to 29 rose to nearly 30 per cent, while it reached 45 per cent among university graduates (World Bank 2008). Yet even these figures underestimate the extent of youth unemployment, as they do not include many of those who, after failing to find work, enter the informal economy or migrate to Europe. Young women, who comprise almost half of new jobseekers, have more trouble finding jobs than young men.

Reforms in the education system have made higher education more accessible to Tunisians. The state guarantees free higher education to anyone passing the baccalaureate or high school diploma.[7] Largely as a result of this policy, the number of Tunisians graduating from college has tripled in a single decade, producing many more graduates than the labour market is able to absorb. According to a World Bank study, in 2008 unemployment affected graduates in all fields. Among those with technical and master's degrees, the unemployment rate was about 50 per cent. Graduates with professional degrees were the most vulnerable, while those from higher institutes of technology had a slight advantage. University graduates in management, finance and law had higher rates of unemployment, reaching 68 per cent for those with master's degrees in legal studies. Among the technical fields, graduates in specialties linked to agriculture and agribusiness also had much higher unemployment rates, around 70 per cent for technicians and over 31 per cent for engineers (ibid.). The World Bank's study stressed the fact that graduates lacked the skills required for lower-level jobs.

The upward trend in the unemployment rate of university graduates in Tunisia was viewed by the African Development Bank as resulting from a mismatch between the demand for and supply of skilled workers, as well as from the relatively low quality of training received by many graduates (African Development Bank 2011). Tunisian economists have criticised the education policies of the last two decades for focusing on quantity rather than quality. Nabil Mâalel, from the ESSEC[8] at the University of Tunis, and Zouhair El Kadhi, from the Institute of Qualitative Studies at the Ministry of Development, have stated that Tunisia has always complied with the advice of the IMF. El Kadhi explained:

> The government was often more preoccupied with pleasing the international institutions rather than looking at what was good and effective for the country, and the education policy was one such instance. We suddenly started producing an excess of graduates, there were graduate schools everywhere, some of the fields of study were quite atypical, and there were no links between the educational system's outputs and labour market needs.

Mâalel added that there was no foreign investment in the private sector to help absorb this trained labour force, despite the attractive financial incentives offered by the government. In

Tunisia, the state has been the main employer and the public sector has been the only avenue for secure work.

Entrepreneurial schemes to support unemployed graduates to develop their own businesses were tentative and badly managed. The government established the Banque Tunisienne de Solidarité (BTS) in the mid-1990s to provide business loans to young graduates, facilitate the development of small enterprises and expand employment. The National Employment Fund, set up in 2000 to deal specifically with graduate unemployment (Kallander 2011), encouraged graduates to apply for microcredit at very competitive interest rates (Hibou 2006).

According to French sociologist Béatrice Hibou, however, the BTS quickly became an instrument of political control, with credit lines being offered to members of the ruling party, the RCD, often without any expectation of a good return. Many of the young people I interviewed found the BTS scheme corrupt. Nassir, a 31-year-old man from Tozeur, pointed out that the BTS 'could have been a good thing, but these BTS funds had strings attached ... because you had to be from the RCD, or be willing to sign up to the RCD, in order to benefit from it'. Hibou's analysis concurred with the young man's views, emphasising that 'young people are reluctant to join the party ... which suggests that, more than disaffection, there is a real rejection of that framework, which they feel is heavy, outdated and ineffective for obtaining full employment' (ibid.: 233). The National Employment Fund, too, became an instrument of the state used for political control and clientelism. Access to public and private sector jobs became tightly controlled by those connected to the regime (Goldstone 2011; Kallander 2011; Paciello 2011).

International migration was one route out of this situation, especially in the most impoverished regions. In the past decades, Tunisia has witnessed a steady exodus driven by the limited opportunities and constraints people face at home.[9] The Tunisian National Institute for Statistics reported that in 2009 there were about 1 million Tunisian migrants living abroad (around 10 per cent of the total population), the vast majority in Europe. Young

Tunisians constitute the largest proportion of these migrants. However, the tightening of border controls in Europe due to the weakening economic situation has made migration more difficult in the last decade.

Tunisian economists Nabil Mâalel and Zouhair El Kadhi have attested that Tunisia's development model was quite popular with the World Bank and the IMF. These institutions praised Tunisia's development model because it encouraged foreign investment, created a flexible workforce and lowered taxes on businesses. Indeed, the World Bank, IMF and European Union propagated the image of the Tunisian 'economic miracle' (Hibou et al. 2011). Mâalel has emphasised that, while in the past few decades the Tunisian economy has grown substantially enough to generate considerable wealth and produce a positive macroeconomic performance (see also Ben Romdhane 2011), the fruits of that growth have not been distributed evenly across the regions.

Although young people saw the expansion of the higher education system as a positive development that created tremendous opportunities, massive unemployment and underemployment have foreclosed those opportunities. The achievement of a higher degree raised expectations among a generation that is more closely connected to the global world through television, cellular telephony and the internet. Earning degrees that led nowhere shattered this generation's dreams of getting better jobs than those held by their parents and of enjoying the advances and commodities of the modern world. In reality, many have ended up financially worse off than their parents despite their academic and professional training. These socioeconomic disconnects, especially unequal regional development, massive unemployment and difficulties in labour migration and entrepreneurship, have been at the heart of young people's discontent and were central issues in the youth uprisings of December 2010 and January 2011.

Corruption and nepotism

The notorious excesses of the authoritarian regime in Tunisia played a major role in exacerbating popular dissatisfaction and, in particular, alienating the middle class. Tunisians have long been aware of state repression, but in the last few years they have become more conscious of the disproportionate power and influence wielded by a tiny elite concentrated on Tunisia's first family. The publication of *La Régente de Carthage: Main Basse sur la Tunisie* (*The Regent of Carthage: A stranglehold on Tunisia*) by investigative journalists Nicolas Beau and Catherine Graciet in France in 2009 and the release of the WikiLeaks memos in 2010 exposed the magnitude of the ruling family's plundering of the country's resources. Despite government bans, both the book and the memos were widely circulated among Tunisians.

The book depicted the president's wife, Leila Trabelsi, as a cunning businesswoman building a mafia-like network involving her brothers and other relatives that amassed amazing wealth. Ben Ali's and Leila's families controlled all major businesses in the country and were known among Tunisians as 'the family'. This closed group's interests extended to virtually every corner of the economy, from information and communication technology through banking to manufacturing, retail, transportation, agriculture and food processing.[10] The family gained control of several key industries through privatisation of state assets and benefited from the government's efforts to encourage competition.

According to cables written by Robert Godec, the US ambassador to Tunisia, in July 2009 and made public by WikiLeaks, the Ben Ali/Trabelsi family was increasingly flaunting its opulence in public, arousing outrage among the poor and unemployed. The cables identified Imed Trabelsi, the favourite nephew of Leila Trabelsi, who controlled the construction industry and had a franchise of the French company Bricorama, and Ben Ali's son-in-law, 28-year-old Mohamed Sakher El Materi, who owned a shipping cruise line, concessions for Audi, Volkswagen, Porsche and Renault, a pharmaceutical manufacturing firm, and several real estate companies. Leila's brother, Belhassen Trabelsi, was able to launch a new airline, Karthago, in part because of government privatisation incentives. Corruption was so extensive that this private airline took over lucrative charter flights previously operated by Tunisair, the state-owned airline, and borrowed Tunisair planes whenever it wanted (ibid.).

The pervasive and high-level corruption in Tunisia had negative consequences for foreign investment, which in turn hurt job creation. As Tunisian sociologist Slaheddine Ben Fredj pointed out, the Ben Ali/Trabelsi clan controlled the economy so tightly that it discouraged direct foreign investment and economic growth. Everything had to go through the family, which would force potential investors into partnerships and joint ventures and would threaten those who would not play by their rules (Hibou 2004; 2006). In early 2006, L'Institut Arabe des Chefs d'Entreprises (Arab Institute of Business Managers) in Tunisia released an investment climate survey that pointed to the decline in business confidence, suggesting that 'good connections required for business success', 'cumbersome administration' and difficulty accessing capital were notable obstacles for investments in the country.[11]

Many Tunisians were familiar with what happened to McDonald's. A WikiLeaks memo describes the situation:

> McDonald's undertook lengthy market research, obtained necessary licenses and real estate leases, entered commercial agreements, secured a local partner, and established necessary product supply chains. Their investment, however, was scuttled by a last minute intervention by First Family personalities who reportedly told McDonald's representatives that 'they had chosen the wrong partner.' The implication was clear: either get the 'right' partner or face the consequences. McDonald's chose to pull out completely at great cost.[12]

The family also stifled the development of successful companies outside its control by intimidating legitimate businessmen and deterring any promising local entrepreneurial activity. The Tunisian middle class was gradually excluded, in favour of a small, close-knit clique of relatives that included siblings and in-laws as well as more distant kin of Ben Ali and Leila Trabelsi (Hibou 2004; 2006).[13] Elite Tunisians boldly, but not publicly, denounced Ben Ali and the Trabelsi family as uneducated and uncultured nouveaux riches whose conspicuous consumption was an affront to all Tunisians. Some feared that this new phenomenon would suck the lifeblood out of the country, leading to a spiralling educational, moral, social and economic decline. Many civil society activists considered the state to be a fundamental impediment to meaningful political liberalisation.[14]

The family threatened small entrepreneurs and the lower classes as well as big businesses. During my 2011 visit to the country I heard several stories of potential young entrepreneurs being stifled by the president's family. Nassir, a 31-year-old man from Tozeur I met in Tunis, shared this story with me:

> I know of a young man who had a brilliant business idea. After he deposited the project for approval at the ministry in order to be granted the necessary permits, a representative of the Ben Ali/Trabelsi family contacted him to offer a partnership. Stressing the connections and the power held by the family (to open doors within the state bureaucracy and business community), the representative guaranteed business success and proposed a 75/25 per cent split, with the young man taking the lower figure. The young man thought the deal was not fair, but he had no option but to accept it, otherwise he risked being completely ostracised.

After telling me this story, Nassir raised the question: 'How did this person get hold of the young man's project?' And he went on to answer it: 'Only senior people at the ministry could have passed it on. This shows how corruption works; the family controls the state apparatus.' He concluded: 'The state and the law are there to work just for them.'

Corruption in Tunisia extended beyond the predatory activities of the president's family and the large businesses that supported or accommodated the family in order to preserve their own positions and status. In a broader sense, corruption in Tunisia also operated at a lower level, for example in the form of appeals to acquaintances, friends, colleagues or relatives to obtain favours or to get around rules, or the payment of sums of money to avoid a fine, get a job, obtain a bursary, get the right papers at the right time, open a shop, and even be able to sell in the street. Corruption among policemen as well as among lower- and mid-level civil servants directly affected the everyday lives of the majority of Tunisians.

Young men and women I spoke with during my investigations told numerous stories of corrupt officials within the government administration, private companies, educational institutions and law enforcement agencies. This was affirmed by 31-year-old Ali from Kasserine:

> The lower officials see what is happening at the top and they copy it at their own level ... They know nobody will punish them because the bosses are also doing it. It is a vicious cycle and a set of practices that are hard to change.

Both the lower-level officials who demand bribes to facilitate access to services and goods and those who empty their pockets to pay them are struggling to survive in an economic environment infested with corruption, nepotism and favouritism. They all understand that this is the way society operates and they are trapped within the system.

State nepotism and high-level corruption coupled with these everyday experiences created particular resentment among the youth, especially unemployed graduates, who were seeking some form of employment or livelihood – applying for jobs or subsidies to start small businesses – in order to try and carve out a relatively decent future. The prevalence of these practices alienated young people from a state that was supposed to uphold the social contract with its citizenry but instead allowed the plundering of the country's riches by a small clique.

Political repression and lack of civil liberties

Political repression and a lack of civil liberties were equally important sources of popular resentment against the regime. Ben Ali had pledged to respect human rights and to allow greater openness in the political arena when he took office in November

1987. His promises soon rang hollow, as his regime became more repressive than that of his predecessor. Civil liberties were severely restricted. Torture, arbitrary arrest and restrictions on freedom of speech and assembly were prevalent.

In a desperate attempt to depoliticise the Tunisian people, the regime closed the political space. No form of political dissent was tolerated. Freedom of association was almost non-existent. With few exceptions, civil society organisations that worked on political issues were denied legal registration (Kausch 2009; Ben Hammouda 2012). Opposition parties and civil society organisations suffered from periodic crackdowns and had a very limited margin for manoeuvre. Freedom of assembly was severely restricted, particularly for political parties and human rights organisations; they were not allowed to hold public meetings or engage in any sort of public criticism of the regime (Kausch 2009; Paciello 2011). In early 2005, Tunisian authorities banned demonstrations by student groups, opposition parties and human rights organisations protesting against the government's invitation to Israel's prime minister, Ariel Sharon.[15] The police forcibly dispersed protesters and injured a number of men and women. Radhia Nasraoui, a human rights lawyer, was beaten up in the street by police officers and sustained a broken nose, cuts and bruising. No action was taken against those who attacked her.[16]

The number of detentions and political trials and the level of harassment of dissidents rose considerably during Ben Ali's regime. Human rights activists, journalists and members of the opposition were subjected to constant surveillance, harassment and imprisonment (Kausch 2009). Ben Ali's main foes were Islamists, who were summarily detained or imprisoned after sham trials in the early 1990s. International human rights organisations, as well as a small group of local activists, ceaselessly criticised Tunisia's human rights record. According to an Amnesty International report, in 2007 at least 12 people were sentenced to lengthy prison terms following unfair trials on terrorism-related charges, while around 50 others were still on trial at the end of the year. Torture and ill treatment continued to be reported. Hundreds

33

of political prisoners sentenced after unfair trials in previous years, including prisoners of conscience, remained in prison. Many had been held for more than a decade and were reported to be in poor health.[17]

International political issues figured prominently in the revolution. Because of the regime's position as a collaborator in the 'war on terror', the United States and European governments disregarded any criticism of its human rights abuses. Outraged Tunisians sought an end to the subservience of the Ben Ali regime to Western powers. They saw the government's pursuit of repressive policies in response to Western demands and military aid incentives as a loss of independence and sovereignty.

Moreover, the government tightly controlled all forms of public expression and severely punished those who did not toe the government line. Journalists and dissidents who crossed the regime have been imprisoned, beaten, harassed, threatened or removed from their jobs. In February 2000, the United Nations (UN) Special Rapporteur for freedom of expression characterised the Tunisian media as showing 'uniformity of tone' and lacking criticism of government policies. Indeed, no critical press, radio or television was allowed. Legislation used to exert pressure on journalists and editors was amended to tighten restrictions on freedom of expression.

Another form of repression arose after the introduction of new technologies of communication and information. In the late 1990s, the country entered the world of the internet, which offered Tunisians new forms of communication, including the instantaneous transmission of videos and photographs. The rapid spread of new technologies created a new community and a cyber society, made up mainly of young people, that escaped the control mechanisms of the state. In response, the Tunisian government developed a sophisticated approach to online censorship and blocked access to a number of internet sites. The authorities engaged in large-scale phishing operations of its citizens' websites and private accounts.

In addition to suppressing the media and the internet, the regime repressed any popular criticism of the government and its leaders. As Nassir from Tozeur put it, 'in my 31 years of existence, the first time I heard someone criticise the president and say things against the government was during this revolution ... Nobody dared to voice any criticisms before.' In Bizerte, the 24-year-old Ayoub told me: 'If Ben Ali was still in power you wouldn't be able to speak freely with us about our views regarding our country and our future ... You could only do that in the presence of an agent of the regime.' Soufien, a 25-year-old man from Menzel Bourguiba, said that:

> Ben Ali's regime was very harsh; he was a dictator in the true sense of the word. We were forbidden from expressing our opinions about the government or anything political ... Everyone avoided talking about politics because you never knew who was part of the RCD or who was an informer for the regime. Our parents discouraged us from talking about politics for our own protection.

Modernisation and women's rights

Tunisia's struggle for modernisation and to extend women's rights dates back to the nineteenth century when Tunisian thinkers and reformists began to call for women's emancipation and to lay the basis for a more modern Tunisia. Early reformers included Ahmed Bin Dhiaf, an intellectual and government official who raised the issue of women's emancipation and the need for women's education in the 1860s. In 1877, Kheireddine Pacha also emphasised the need for girls' education and for a new status for women in Tunisian society (Zlitni and Touati 2012).

In the early twentieth century, Tahar Haddad,[18] a scholar and modernising Islamic reformer, called for women's emancipation from traditional social norms. An advocate for women's rights, he linked the progress of Tunisian society to the emancipation of women. In 1930, his controversial book *Our Women in the Sharia and Society* utilised Islamic texts to call for women's rights to formal education, work and self-determination as well as for ending polygamy and other practices that subjugated women. For example, Haddad compared the veil to a muzzle and considered the negative effects the veil had on women, namely a sense of submission, confinement and, for married women, a dependence on their husbands. He also stressed the need to abolish forced marriages of underage girls to much older men and parental intervention in the choice of a husband (Zlitni and Touati 2012). Contesting assertions that such practices were inscribed in the *Quran* and were permissible to Muslims, Haddad declared:

> Islam is innocent of the oft-made accusations that it is an obstacle in the way of progress. Rather it is the religion of progress par excellence, an endless source of progress. Our decadence is the consequence of the chimera with which we have filled our minds and the scandalous, paralysing customs within which we have locked ourselves. (Curtiss 1996: 34)

Haddad further argued that the question of veiling was a social problem, rather than a religious one, and considered the debate surrounding the veil to be secondary. Instead, he pronounced education to be the key to women's emancipation and proposed reforms in marriage and divorce laws (Mamelouk 2007; Charrad 2008; Jones 2010). The book sent shock waves across the Islamic world. Conservative Islamic scholars vehemently rejected Haddad's reformist ideas as a gross misreading of religious texts; they also accused him of agnosticism. He was also charged with blasphemy and forced to resign from his positions as a professor and a notary (Zlitni and Touati 2012). The controversy surrounding Haddad's book, which was banned, did not subside until after his death in 1935 (Jones 2010).

Building on Haddad's ideas, Muhammad Zarrouk founded in December 1936 a women's periodical called *Leïla: Revue illustrée de la femme*. The magazine was published monthly until November 1940, and then as a weekly newspaper until it was discontinued in July 1941. *Leïla* stood out from other periodicals because it carried articles on the social and cultural debates about the changing role of women in Tunisian society (Mamelouk 2007). In 1955, Bashir Ben Ahmed took up the name and started the new magazine *Leïla Speaks to You* with Dorra Bouzid, a Tunisian journalist studying in Paris at the time, who was its only woman editor, and later became the first female Tunisian journalist. After a few years with *Leïla Speaks to You*, Dorra Bouzid joined forces with Safia Farhat and in 1959 they co-founded the magazine *Faiza*, the first feminist Arab-African women's periodical. *Faiza* played an instrumental role in the Bourguiba post-independence reform but was discontinued in December 1969.

According to Sami Zlitni and Zeineb Touati, Muslim women from the Tunis elite used the momentum created by the intellectual debates to start claiming the right to be educated, to work and to be fully emancipated, as in the cases of Manoubia Ouertani, a woman who took off her veil during a public event in January 1924, and Habiba Menchari, who also took off her veil during a conference she was giving in January 1929 entitled 'Tomorrow's Arab women, for or against the veil'. Their actions received strong condemnation from theologians, the colonial authorities and other conservative groups (Zlitni and Touati 2012).

It is clear, therefore, that a long and meaningful debate, which had been initiated in the nineteenth century, paved the way to the process of reforms regarding women's rights that took place under Bourguiba's rule after Tunisia's independence.

Bourguiba's state feminism Haddad's and other intellectuals' thinking and writings about women and Islam became the basis for the post-independence reforms of women's rights undertaken by Tunisia's first president. Habib Bourguiba understood that his modernising and secular project would be compromised if women had no social or economic rights. A few months after independence, on 13 August 1956, Bourguiba gave a famous speech in which he formally enacted an unprecedented piece of legislation, known as the Code du Statut Personnel (CSP), or *majalat* in Arabic, that radically reformed Islamic family law in Tunisia. When it came into force in January 1957, it offered Tunisian women a set of rights and a degree of access to the public sphere that were unparalleled in the Arab world.

Heavily influenced by Tahar Haddad's vision, the CSP's provisions dealt directly with issues relating to the position of women in the family and society. It abolished polygamy, with Article 18 stating that 'Polygamy is forbidden ... [and] is punishable by imprisonment of 1 year or a fine of 240,000 francs or both' (République Tunisienne 2001: 7). Bourguiba equated polygamy with slavery and argued that the Quranic requirement of equal treatment of four wives was nearly impossible to achieve. The CSP established the equality of men and women with regard to divorce. *Talaq*, or extra-judicial divorce, was prohibited, and Article 32 stipulates that both men and women can initiate divorce procedures after reconciliation efforts fail. The CSP declared that marriage could not take place without the consent of both spouses, and set the minimum age at 20 for men and 17 for women[19] (ibid.). Following the provisions of the CSP, the Tunisian Constitution promulgated 'the principle of equality' of men and women in relation to citizenship.

As a consequence of Bourguiba's reforms, from the late 1950s Tunisian women enjoyed the right to vote, change their place of residence, seek public office, work outside the home, open bank accounts and establish businesses without the permission of their husbands. In a speech delivered on 26 December 1962, Bourguiba stated: 'Work contributes to the emancipation of women. By her work a woman or a girl assures her existence and becomes conscious of her dignity.'[20] That same year, Tunisian women gained access to birth control, and contraceptives were made freely available. Abortion was legalised in 1965, and women were entitled to obtain abortions for personal as well as medical reasons without permission from their husbands. Bourguiba initiated a family planning campaign through clinics and educational programmes. A law limiting to four the number of children per family that were allowed to benefit from state subsidies helped reinforce the state's family planning policies.

Bourguiba denounced women's veiling and confinement to the home as hindrances to the new nation's modernising and development goals. He stated that to achieve progress Tunisians had to fight against 'anachronistic traditions and backward mentalities' (quoted in Charrad 2001: 220). The government subsequently led a campaign against the veiling of women (Jones 2010).

Bourguiba's efforts were also supported by *Faiza*, the feminist women's magazine founded by Dorra Bouzid and Safia Farhat. Reflecting on that period, Dorra Bouzid wrote in 2011 that Bourguiba was an attentive reader of the magazine, pointing out that he commented on articles that passionately supported feminist struggles and that he even tried to address the injustices raised by the magazine. As she recounts:

> I was honoured to be invited to his wedding to Wassila Ben Ammar and *Faiza* ran a special issue on the wedding, but he [Bourguiba] had only one condition: that he read the text before publication ... I still have the manuscript with the annotations he made with his famous green pen.[21]

Bourguiba's regime developed an official discourse of women's rights that broke fundamentally with some existing cultural and religious traditions. Of course, his reforms of women's and family rights were not well received by conservatives. Although he was careful to ground his reforms on a modern reading of Islamic texts, his critics saw them as an affront to Islam. Some called for amendments to certain provisions in the CSP, such as the prohibition of polygamy and the equality of men and women in divorce matters; others requested the revocation of the entire CSP. Critics regarded Bourguiba's modernising projects as imports from the West that contradicted Islamic norms and values.[22] In January 1968, the Association for the Preservation of the *Quran* was founded to protect Islamic values and safeguard the provisions contained in Sharia.

Although modernist in its foundations, as inscribed in legislation, Bourguiba's CSP contained several contradictions. While it reformed aspects of Islamic family law, it did not fundamentally undermine traditional family relations. The CSP failed to reform inheritance laws, and women continued to be adversely affected by the preference for male heirs. Indeed, scholars have shown that the CSP preserves and promotes masculine privileges. Running for public office, for example, remained in practice a male prerogative, and women were largely confined to jobs as nurses, teachers and seamstresses. In Bourguiba's nationalist project, women's social roles were still mainly determined by their positions as mothers and wives (Bessis 1999; Zayzafoon 2005). Thus, from their inception, Bourguiba's reforms appeared to be both revolutionary and restricted.

Equally significant is the fact that the legal reforms to women's rights undertaken by Habib Bourguiba were imposed from above and within a context of restrictive political systems dominated by urban elites. In fact, Bourguiba's policies have been called *féminisme d'état* (state feminism)[23] and the CSP has been deemed a mechanism for replacing the traditional, patriarchal model of the extended family with the nuclear family and an individual rights model. Feminist scholars have pointed out that while governmental reforms have certainly improved the lives of many women, these top-down reforms did not address the underlying problems of a social and family structure in which women are positioned as unequal or dependent (Brand 1998; Hatem 1992). They argue that state feminism was primarily motivated by political calculations and manoeuvrings rather than by the desire to promote gender equality (Brand 1998; Charrad 2008; Jones 2010). These reforms, critics stress, were instruments to serve the interests of the state's modernising secular project against the Islamists.

The 'Ben Aliste' reforms of the Personal Status Code During the 1990s, feminist groups lobbied to reform some critical issues concerning women's rights that the CSP failed to address: the view that women have a duty to obey their husbands, and the inequality between the sexes in relation to inheritance. They were successful with the first provision, which was modified by Ben Ali in 1993, but they did not manage to change inheritance laws. Although Ben Ali continued Bourguiba's state feminism when he took over, the country experienced the rise of Islamic fundamentalism, with Islamist groups launching attacks on the CSP. Indeed, Bourguiba's departure revived the debate on Arab Muslim identity. As quoted in Zlitni and Touati's article, a member of parliament at the time said: 'The Personal Status Code is not part of the sacred texts'; and the Mufti[24] of the Republic concurred with him by saying that: 'It [the CSP] infringes on Islamic texts' (Zlitni and Touati 2012: 50).

The Mouvement de la Tendance Islamique (MTI), established in 1981 by Rached Ghannouchi, soon after Bourguiba legalised multiparty politics, was the precursor to Ennahdha. The MTI had been fostering cells of militant women to promote the use of the veil and respect for Islamic values. Veiled militant women were tasked to Islamise their sisters, and gradually the number of women wearing veils grew significantly (ibid.). In October 2006, Ben Ali's government launched a very strong campaign to enforce more rigorously the 1981 ban on the wearing of the veil in public places such as schools and government offices, and embarked on a strategy to crack down on Islamic fundamentalism.

According to Tunisian historian Sophie Bessis, three dominant ideas marked the Ben Aliste phase of state feminism:

1 the claim that Tunisia's progress towards modernity was irreversible;
2 the recognition of the deep changes at work in Tunisian society, particularly the shift from an extended to a nuclear family model; and
3 the need for women to participate in the construction of modernity by joining the struggle against Islamic fundamentalism.

In 1992, Ben Ali created the Office of the Secretary of State for Women and Family and appointed several women to high political positions. He also established the Centre de Recherches, d'Études de Documentation et d'Information sur la Femme (CREDIF) to develop a database and analysis of the situation of women in the country (Bessis 1999). However, Ben Ali did not modify the discriminatory inheritance law or remove from the CSP the provision stating that women must relate to their husbands 'in accordance with custom and tradition', an ambiguous clause prone to conservative interpretations.

As the result of these reforms, Tunisia today has a fairly solid

41

set of legal provisions regarding women's rights that is unparalleled in the Arab world. Many Tunisian women have pointed out, however, that in practice women are not always able to exercise those rights. Tunisian sociologist Monia Lachheb asserts: 'The CSP is a beautiful piece of legislation but its implementation leaves a lot to be desired ... The text per se has been insufficient to change practice; we need to establish clear mechanisms for women to benefit from these rights.' Because of the regional imbalances in contemporary Tunisian society, most women in the impoverished areas of the country are not aware of their rights and do not know about the specific provisions of the CSP that might benefit them. There are serious discrepancies in women's positions between the developed eastern coastal towns and the economically struggling interior. Rural women are considerably more attached to Muslim traditions and do not have as much access to education, employment or social and legal services as urban women.

Monia Abed, president of the Tunisian Association of Women Lawyers, contends that the legal system still has several lacunae in relation to provisions to implement women's rights. For example, the CSP has not been effectively translated into other types of legislation such as the penal code. A number of legal procedures create difficulties for women seeking to file complaints and hinder their access to the courts. Feminist groups recognise the disconnects between state policies and the situation of most Tunisian women. As Abed affirms: 'Women's rights have been used as a political tool ... There is a lot that needs to be done by feminist organisations in order to guarantee social, economic and political rights for all Tunisian women.'

The issue of women's rights was not raised during the December 2010–January 2011 uprisings because women's demands were the same as those of other Tunisians: employment, better living conditions and civil liberties. In the political transition that followed the revolution, however, women's rights issues rapidly became the central question as secular and Islamist parties began to debate the place of Islam in the new Tunisian state.

Anti-Islamism and the quest for religious identity

When Ben Ali took over power from Bourguiba, he promised to liberalise the regime and allow greater pluralism and dialogue with opposition parties. He was initially tolerant of the activities of Ennahdha (the former MTI), allowing its members to run in the 1989 parliamentary elections as independents. They performed well in the elections, garnering an estimated 13 per cent of the national vote, and accused the regime of manipulating election results; the RCD claimed victory with 90 per cent of the votes.

Clashes between the regime and the Islamists escalated, which led to the banning of Ennahdha in 1991. Following claims of an Islamist plot against the government and a plan to assassinate the president, an open 'war' was declared and the regime initiated a crackdown on the Islamists. From 1992 onwards, thousands of Islamic militants were detained and convicted in military courts without due process (Arieff 2012). Many received steep sentences and remained in prison until 2006 (Alexander 2010). Those who managed to leave the country were sentenced in absentia, while others went into exile after serving long prison sentences. As part of the strategy to repress Islam in Tunisia, more than 5,000 mosques were placed under government surveillance and submitted to rigid controls by government officials, who appointed prayer leaders and censored the topics for Friday sermons.[25]

Following the 11 September 2001 attacks in the United States, the Tunisian regime became a strategic ally of the West in the fight against Islamic extremism – the so-called 'war on terror'. In 2003, Ben Ali's government promulgated far-reaching anti-terrorism legislation and many Islamists were on the radar of the security services because of their physical appearance and attire or because of their regular visits to mosques. Many were continuously brought to police stations for questioning, were always under pressure from the security services, and felt marginalised socially.[26]

Human rights activists criticised this legislation for preventing the exercise of fundamental freedoms. They also accused the Tunisian government anti-terror trials of relying on 'excessive pre-trial detention, denial of due process, and weak evidence' (Arieff 2012: 9). According to Amnesty International, the trials did not meet international fair trial standards.[27] The UN Special Rapporteur on the promotion and protection of human rights was also critical of the anti-terrorism law of 2003, stating that its definition of what constituted terrorism was extremely vague, 'hence deviating from the principle of legality and allowing for wide usage of counter-terrorism measures in practice' (cited in ibid.). The UN Special Rapporteur urged the government to amend the law and restrict its application so as to exclude those who had been convicted improperly of 'terrorism'.[28]

It is estimated that about 2,000 Tunisians were detained, charged or convicted on terrorism-related offences between 2003 and the fall of Ben Ali.[29] Some were tried and sentenced in absentia. Confessions under duress and torture were accepted as evidence in court without proper investigation. The International Association in Support of Political Prisoners published a report that analysed a sample of about 1,200 Tunisian political prisoners jailed on the basis of the anti-terrorism laws. As pointed out in the report, half (48 per cent) of the prisoners were aged between 25 and 30 years, while another 30 per cent comprised a group aged between 19 and 24. Almost 39 per cent were from the working class and 34 per cent were university or secondary school students, with 15 per cent being traders or shopkeepers.[30]

Among the most significant consequences of the repressive campaigns against Islamism, in both the 1990s and the 2000s, was the absence of religious freedoms and open forms of religious socialisation for Tunisian Muslims. Some analysts believe that 'the marginalization of public religious displays together with an increasing culture of soulless materialism had deeply affected a number of young people during the 2000s, giving rise to what can be termed "spiritual needs"'.[31] The worsening socioeconomic conditions in the country compounded the high rates of youth unemployment, while the younger generation's sense of alienation and disempowerment fostered a quest for religious identity and spirituality. In this regard, a prominent Ennahdha leader stated:

Young people did not have much of a choice. Some of them retreated into personal activities with no political significance, others replicated the consumerist behaviour of their western counterparts, and some found a refuge in extremist views of Islam that led them on the wrong path. The blame for this has to be squarely on the regime.[32]

Although political Islam did not have a prominent role in the revolution, the unprecedented openness of the transition in the post-Ben Ali period favoured the emergence of new and diverse political actors and Islamist movements have been able to take advantage of the democratic process (Hamid 2011). It is within this context that Ennahdha was able to become a key actor and perform well in the October 2011 elections. And it is also within this atmosphere that we have witnessed in Tunisia the emergence of Salafism, a form of Islamic extremism. Political scientist George Joffé describes extremism as involving an ideology and praxis aimed at delegitimising and rejecting the state and its elites, often through the use of violence. He contrasts it with radicalism, a form of political dissent over normative and hegemonic assumptions, which does not necessarily presuppose the elimination of the state (Joffé 2012; 2013).

The Salafists propose a conservative interpretation of Islam in politics and social life, and call for Sharia to become the law of the state. However, rather than being a recent foreign import, some scholars have stressed that:

> Tunisian salafism, in both its scientific and Jihadi versions, has its roots in the dissatisfaction of some Islamists with the political thinking and strategies of its 1980s predecessor, Ennahda or the Mouvement de la Tendance Islamique (MTI), which had accepted the principle of democratic procedures to govern society. (Torelli et al. 2012: 142; Amghar 2011)

In 1986, a group of Islamic militants, among them Mohammad al-Khoujah and Mongi al-Hachmi, broke away from the MTI and formed the Front Islamique Tunisien (FIT), a more conservative

45

and purist Islamic organisation. The FIT was also banned and most of its members were jailed, fled into exile or were completely marginalised by the regime. Thus, radical Islamic tendencies were already present but dormant in Tunisia. They seem to have found fertile ground in which to re-emerge after the fall of the dictatorship and with the onset of democracy (Amghar 2011; Hamid 2011; Torelli et al. 2012).[33]

The term Salafism, according to Islamic scholars, derives from the Arabic word *salafiyyun*, which means 'the ancestors' and refers to the 'first three generations of Muslims, deemed to be the most pious believers' (Torelli et al. 2012: 144). *Salafiyya* thus entails a return to original or 'true' Islam and the suppression of all external elements that over the course of history have tarnished the essence of the religion (Amghar 2011; Hamid 2011; Torelli et al. 2012).

Analysts point to the presence of two different strands of Salafism in Tunisian society: the scientific Salafism and the jihadi[34] Salafism. The crucial difference between the two is the use of armed struggle to attain political objectives. Scientific Salafism is fundamentally based on non-violent religious ideologies, and most Tunisian Salafists fit into this category as they advocate political engagement and acceptance of democracy within the confines of Sharia law (the Jabhat al-Islah). However, some Salafist groups are involved in preaching a more purist version of Islam (groups influenced by the *dawa* and Wahhabism), which may include an armed struggle.[35]

Although this has not happened so far, reports of Tunisian jihadi fighters in Iraq and a call for jihad on the Ennahdha government by a Salafist imam on national television in November 2012 have renewed debates among Salafists about the validity of jihad as a form of political expression. The resurgence of jihadism in the national political discourse has also raised serious concerns among other political forces and ordinary Tunisians, because it may compound the already volatile political situation in the country.[36]

The current political transition has indeed been marred by tensions between secularist and Islamist groups, as well as between

Salafists and more moderate Islamist forces. As many observers have pointed out, these tensions are not new but result from unresolved disconnects in Tunisian society during previous regimes. These disconnects are now being experienced by a younger generation of Tunisians still grappling with issues of religious identity and politics in a modern and democratic context.

Conclusions

Economic grievances have caused widespread discontent among Tunisians, especially in the impoverished areas of the country and among unemployed graduates. The rise of a mafia-like group around the president and the corruption that surrounded it affected entrepreneurs and created disaffection among the middle class. Islamists and secular opposition groups alike were banned or marginalised; civil society activists were censored and controlled. The stifling of the media and the aggressive repression of the cyber community were unprecedented and generated antipathy towards the regime. The top-down political and legal reforms to women's rights and the absence of solid mechanisms for implementing those reforms would come back to haunt Tunisians. It can be argued that the heavy-handed repression of Islamism and the lack of religious freedoms may have forged radical forms of religious extremism, and may have created a quest for identity and spirituality among the younger generation. The toxic combination of widespread political and religious repression, economic stagnation and social exclusion deprived the regime of popular legitimacy and provided a fertile ground for a series of uprisings that culminated in the December 2010–January 2011 revolution.

2 | Mobilisation

The Tunisian revolution originated in the economic hardship experienced by residents of impoverished regions, the discontent of marginalised urban elites, and resentment at the suppression of political and civil freedoms among the majority of citizens. The mobilisation of a range of different groups from across Tunisian society transformed the popular protests led by the youth into a nationwide movement. As some observers declared, if the uprising had remained confined to the poor and marginalised, it would have been possible for the regime to contain and repress it. But the national character that the movement assumed and the involvement of Tunisians from different social classes, political and religious tendencies, age and gender groups, and urban and rural areas enabled it to overthrow the government.

This chapter discusses four groups that played crucial roles in various stages of the protest movement: young cyber activists; unemployed university graduates; civil society organisations; and opposition political parties. It examines the specific struggles of each group and the strategies they adopted in the fight against the regime. The chapter argues that mobilisation for this uprising grew steadily from frustrations expressed through internet social networks, via interactions in cafés, at breaks in telemarketing call centres and on construction sites, and from a sense of social injustice and repression that permeated everyday life. When the moment came, Tunisians, especially the youth, were ready for action.

Cyber activists

The Tunisian revolution was fought not only on the streets but also on internet forums, blogs, Facebook pages and Twitter feeds. Young bloggers used online social networks to expose government abuses and atrocities and distributed information about the situation in Sidi Bouzid and other regions through web-based social networks, while the government-controlled print and broadcast media completely ignored the popular uprising for as long as possible.

The internet has developed rapidly in Tunisia, and the country's level of internet usage is among the highest on the continent. There are internet cafés everywhere, and growing numbers of young people access cyberspace. In 2007, there were 188,844 internet subscribers in Tunisia, while the number of users was much higher (Ben Hammouda 2012). By 2009, the number of internet users had risen to about 2.8 million, and the ADSL networking rate stood at 11.1 gigabytes per second.[1] By March 2011, one-third of the population, 3.6 million people, used the internet. In March 2011, Facebook had 2.4 million users, more than one-fifth of the population. It is estimated that, in 2012, 84 per cent of internet users accessed the internet at home, 76 per cent did so at work, and 24 per cent used public internet cafés.[2] In Tunisia, as elsewhere, young people are the most comfortable with new information and communication technologies.

The Tunisian regime censored the internet for many years. In 1996, the government created the Agence Tunisienne d'Internet (ATI) under the Ministry of Communications to promote, regulate and exercise control over internet usage in the country. Internet censorship was widespread; the government blocked popular video-sharing websites, such as YouTube and Dailymotion, while social networking sites, especially Facebook, were shut down periodically. In February 2003, the regime arrested nine young internet users in the southern Tunisian town of Zarzis on accusations of terrorism. According to their lawyers, their only crime was visiting banned websites. Following the case of the 'Zarzis internauts', and faced with heavily censored cyberspace, young Tunisians developed political and informational websites in the form of individual or collective blogs (ICG 2011). Tunisian cyberspace became gradually politicised, leading to the emergence of a

49

new form of political and generational contestation. A cyber war between the government and young cyber activists was declared.

Young internet users rose to the challenge and fought to keep internet access free from government interference. Ben Ali's regime selectively targeted and blocked websites and intimidated bloggers who disseminated information against the regime. With cyberspace under siege, Twitter became the activists' bastion. Because people could access Twitter via clients rather than going through the website, many Tunisians could still communicate online. The web-savvy used proxies to browse censored sites, but many users were unable to access blogs.[3] In April 2010, the government carried out heavy censorship of web pages, blocking more than 100 blogs as well as many other sites. The government's approach was invasive and paranoid. Cyber activist Aziz Amami pointed out that 'in this country we didn't really have the internet; what we had was a sort of national intranet'.

In May 2010, cyber activists Slim Amamou and Aziz Amami planned a demonstration in Tunis to protest about internet censorship. Tunisia's constitution included the right to protest, and they decided to formally apply for an authorisation to hold the demonstration. They attempted to deliver the necessary documents to the Ministry of the Interior, but officials refused to accept them. They then mailed the documents with a request for proof of delivery, but proof never came. Slim and Aziz documented their efforts online. The day before the planned demonstration, both were arrested and interrogated by the police. They were threatened with torture, although they were not physically harmed. Slim was forced to record and post online a video calling off the demonstration. Despite that, on 10 May 2010, young Tunisians gathered in 'flash mobs' in Tunisia and in France, Canada, New York and Ghana, wearing white T-shirts with slogans against internet censorship.[4]

During their war against internet censorship and for freedom of expression, young Tunisian cyber activists connected with Anonymous,[5] a loosely knit group of cyber activists acting secretly in a decentralised but coordinated manner. Anonymous strongly opposes internet censorship and provides support to cyber communities under siege worldwide. The group drew world attention for supporting the whistle-blowing website WikiLeaks. Anonymous became a sort of internet vigilante group and led a campaign against companies that stopped providing services for WikiLeaks, which they called 'operation payback'. The US government received the most serious blow when this 'anti-secrecy' organisation released sensitive diplomatic cables and Pentagon information about the wars in Afghanistan and Iraq (Stryker 2011; Olson 2012).

Tunisia became a target of Anonymous's wrath by censoring a Tunisia-based website set up to host the WikiLeaks memos.[6] According to an Anonymous member, the group's concerns changed over time: 'We did initially take an interest in Tunisia because of WikiLeaks, but as more Tunisians have joined [us] they cared more about the general internet censorship there, so that's what it [our intervention] has become.'[7]

Tunisian cyber activists were instrumental in letting Anonymous know the kind of outside help they required as well as the focus and targets of the group's interventions in the country. They had full control of the situation and knew exactly what they could do themselves and how external support could contribute to their struggle. Bullet Skan, a 17-year-old cyber activist from Tunis, recounted: 'We told Anonymous that their initial interventions in Tunisia to retaliate for the censorship of WikiLeaks were not effective enough. We asked them for help with specific targets.' Attacking government websites was a lot more dangerous for those living within the country because of the risks of being identified and arrested by the authorities. Tunisian web activists found a valuable ally in Anonymous.[8]

In conjunction with Tunisian activists, Anonymous launched a series of 'distributed denial-of-service' attacks that succeeded in disrupting at least eight government websites, including those of the president, the prime minister, the Ministry of Industry, the Ministry of Foreign Affairs, the ATI and the stock exchange. A week after the attacks began, the government appeared to have taken steps to protect its websites from attack by making them inaccessible from overseas.

Mobilisation

Nevertheless, Anonymous found ways of continuing the attacks with internal support. The arrest of several young Tunisian bloggers on 6 January, following the attacks on official websites, was a desperate attempt by Ben Ali's regime to silence online activism. The wave of arrests came as the regime felt it was losing the bitter cyber war it had helped to ignite. Among those arrested were four young cyber activists whom I interviewed during my visits to Tunisia: Slim Amamou, Aziz Amami, Sofiane Bel Hadj and Bullet Skan. Who are these young internet activists?

Slim Amamou is the best-known Tunisian cyber activist, not just because of his active role in the revolution but also because he became a member of the transitional government after the fall of Ben Ali. He was 33 years old when I met him in Tunis in 2011. Born in Tunis, Amamou comes from a middle-class family. His father was born in Moknine and is a professor of medicine, and his mother, originally from the island of Djerba, is a gynae-cologist. Slim obtained his high school degree (baccalaureate) from a *lycée* in Tunis and went on to study computer science at the University of Sousse, located on the eastern coast. After finishing his *licence* (degree), Amamou decided to start work and joined a large computer company before establishing his own. His company, created in 1999, develops web applications and software for businesses. Combining his computer skills and his political activism, Amamou soon became a cyber activist, fighting against internet censorship and advocating for the protection of intellectual property, civil liberties and freedom of expression.

Aziz Amami worked closely with Slim Amamou on cyber activism for many years. Now 29, he holds a degree in computer science from the University of Tunis but told me that his real passion is anthropology and cultural studies. Since he came from a family of modest means, he did not have the luxury of pursuing studies in these fields. 'My family encouraged me to choose a course that would help me make a living,' and computer science was more promising than anthropology or cultural studies. Aziz confessed that when he had to set aside his intellectual inclina-tions to do something more practical, 'I clearly understood the meaning of our socioeconomic condition'. His parents were born in Sidi Bouzid (where the revolution started); his father worked for the postal service and his mother was a housewife. His two sisters earned university degrees in law and agronomy, but neither was able to find employment after graduation. Aziz, too, had no regular employment and spent his time on cyber activism. He acknowledges that his father, a Marxist who read a lot, served as a model of independent thinking. Marxist literature was a major influence on his life; he recalled reading Mao Zedong at home as a teenager. When he was arrested on 6 January, one of the books the police took from his desk when they raided his room was Hegel's *The Phenomenology of Spirit*.

> Since high school I have always challenged the status quo. I have been involved in organising strikes and protest marches while at high school, one of them during the period of the [second Palestinian] intifada. In 2008, I was expelled from university because I was the main organiser of a protest in solidarity with the revolts in Redeyef in Gafsa.

Amami's class background contrasts with that of Amamou, but they share a commitment to freedom of expression as well as valuable computer skills.

Sofiane Bel Hadj was 29 years old when I met him in Tunis in 2012. Like Amamou, he comes from a middle-class family, but his experience is international. Born of a Tunisian father and a Belgian mother, Sofiane grew up in the textile town of Ksar Hellal near the city of Monastir. He enrolled in a local *lycée* in Nabeul but did not finish his secondary education as he was expelled from school for rebelling against the teaching of religion. Two years later his mother sent him to the French *lycée* in Tunis, where he finished his baccalaureate in 2003. Sofiane then moved to Europe to study political science at Brussels Free University. In his second year at university, Sofiane attended a public conference on campus presented by the renowned Tunisian human rights activist Radhia Nasraoui and Hamma Hammami, the leader of the then illegal Parti Communiste des Ouvriers de Tunisie (PCOT).

It was after meeting Nasraoui and Hammami that he decided to do something for his country.

Through Facebook, Sofiane came into contact with a number of websites of Tunisian dissidents, such as Nawaat, El Sabil and Takriz, and established his own Facebook group called 'I have a dream: for a democratic Tunisia'. The Facebook group engaged in a critical examination of the policies of the dictatorial regime and mobilised members to criticise the abuses perpetrated by Ben Ali's government. It became very popular, catching the attention of the regime's cyber agents who then attacked it. So he created a new Facebook group where he appeared under the pseudonym of Hamadi Kaloutcha. When the Tunisian government closed Facebook, Sofiane and other cyber activists mounted a strong campaign against the government, collecting thousands of letters of cancellation of service that they intended to send to internet access providers, which they knew were controlled by the Ben Ali/Trabelsi family. 'Such a massive termination of subscriptions would have a negative impact not only on the family's business but also on the country's human development indexes, and they would not take the risk,' stressed Sofiane. The next morning, *Le Temps*, a local newspaper, broke the news that thousands of Facebook users were threatening to cancel their subscriptions, and in response the government reinstated Facebook. Through these new forms of communication, a Tunisian student in Brussels was able to play a key role in his homeland.

Sofiane returned to Tunisia in March 2010 and connected with other cyber activists operating in the country. Among his many actions, Sofiane established a website where he posted the WikiLeaks memos translated into French and Arabic. Following the government crackdown on cyber activists, on 6 January 2011 he was arrested by Ben Ali's secret police and jailed for four days.

A very young cyber activist and computer whizz-kid who went by the pseudonym of Bullet Skan was also involved in the protests. He was just 17 when I met him in Tunis in 2011, but his life story was already richer than that of many adults. Bullet Skan was only three when he started playing games on his parents' computer at home. By the age of five he had completely dismantled and reassembled his parents' old computer in an effort to understand how it worked. At seven, when he was spending entire afternoons at his cousin's house navigating the web, he asked his parents for access to the internet at home. After his wish was granted three years later, he spent most of his free time on the internet.

Bullet Skan comes from a middle-class family and grew up in Tunis. His father is the chief executive officer of a food distribution company, and his mother teaches French in a primary school. His two brothers are much older and both have careers. As the youngest child in the family, Bullet Skan was often left on his own playing with the computer. But he quickly moved from computer games into hacking.

> I had no idea hacking was a crime and I had fun entering people's email accounts and taking control of them. In my internet adventures I came across a group of Algerian hackers and befriended them, and they taught me a number of hacking tricks ... During my summer vacation in 2007 I hacked a major Tunisian company and I disrupted their work during the three months of my summer vacation; then I wrote to them and I said I was the one who did it. Of course, they took me to the police, but because I was only 13 years old and the police did not have a good understanding of what hacking was they let me go after I signed a document saying that I would never do it again.

When Bullet Skan realised that certain internet sites were blocked, he took it upon himself to discover proxy ways of accessing them. He soon came across the internet sites of Tunisian dissidents and the Takriz network. Takriz[9] is an anonymous network of Tunisian dissidents founded in 1998 and was one of the most critical cyber voices against the dictatorship of Ben Ali. Through Takriz, Bullet Skan became a cyber activist at the age of 15, moving away from hacking towards helping expose the abuses of Ben Ali's regime. He became involved with other cyber activists in the fight against internet censorship and freedom of expression, connecting with Slim Amamou, Aziz Amami and Sofiane Bel Hadj. He ended up behind bars with them on 6 January 2011, when he was just 16.

Lina Ben Mhenni, a 27-year-old female cyber activist, was not imprisoned in January 2011, although the police raided her home several times. Lina was born in Tunis, earned a master's degree in English language from the University of Tunis, and worked as a teaching assistant in linguistics at her university. She comes from a middle-class family. Her father, Sadok Ben Mhenni, was a leftist and former government minister who was imprisoned because of his opposition to Habib Bourguiba. Lina began her blog 'A Tunisian Girl' in 2007, the year her mother donated a kidney to her to replace her failing organs. Six months after that surgery, she competed in the World Transplant Games; competing again in 2009, she won two silver medals in race walking.[10] On 'A Tunisian Girl', Lina Ben Mhenni advocated freedom of speech and human rights and fought against internet censorship. She soon found herself at odds with the government, which blocked her site inside Tunisia, and she had to use proxy sites to access her pages. In 2008, Lina spent a year abroad as a Fulbright scholar teaching Arabic at Tufts University in Massachusetts, USA. That same year, she was invited to be Tunisia's contributor to Global Voices Online. In April 2010 the secret police raided her family home. 'They took my computer, my cameras, my everything,' she said. 'It was clear it was them because of the way only I was targeted and the way they went after my equipment.'[11]

A few days after Mohamed Bouazizi's self-immolation, Slim Amamou, Aziz Amami and Lina Ben Mhenni, as well as other activists, descended on Sidi Bouzid and Kasserine to join the protesters. Amamou recounts how they got involved:

> On 18 December 2010 I learned about the uprisings in Sidi Bouzid through the internet postings made by Ali Bouazizi, the cousin of Mohamed Bouazizi. I saw videos of people demanding jobs, better life conditions and freedom. Because I am an activist for freedom of expression on the internet but also in

life in general, I became interested in the events in Sidi Bouzid. I was already working with a group of activists on freedom of expression and I decided to engage our group in publicising the events in Sidi Bouzid. I went down to Sidi Bouzid with a few colleagues and we made our own videos of the events in Sidi Bouzid, Kasserine and other areas. We placed our information on the web, which was immediately picked up by people all over the country and by the international media.

Defying police repression and brutal attacks against participants, the cyber activists from Tunis joined in the street protests alongside unemployed youths from the area. On 25 and 27 December, Aziz Amami and Slim Amamou, along with other colleagues, organised two large demonstrations in Tunis in solidarity with protests in Sidi Bouzid. During these demonstrations, which brought hundreds of youths from the capital onto the streets, Slim Amamou was able to capture the event on his mobile phone; Al Jazeera picked it up and transmitted it in real time to the entire world.

Other bloggers and cyber activists in Kasserine and Sidi Bouzid were also instrumental in sending out information denouncing police brutality during the demonstrations in their towns. Houssem Hlali is a 27-year-old blogger from Kasserine. He completed a degree in culture, cinema and theatre at the Higher Institute of Applied Studies in Humanities in Le Kef in 2008. He has not been able to find employment, so he sometimes takes temporary jobs and works as a volunteer in various youth associations. When the protests started in Kasserine there was no media coverage at all, so Houssem took pictures and videos with his mobile phone and posted them on his Facebook page. After a few days he started posting them on Al Jazeera's site as well. As the volume of information increased, Houssem enlisted the help of his 30-year-old friend, Ahmed, to upload the images and videos online.

I was so happy and proud to see my postings about the events in Kasserine on Al Jazeera. I never posted any information on France 24, but they too used my videos. I also saw that some of my pictures were published and used under other people's names. That's when I decided to add a strip to all my images that read 'L'Artistou-Gass', which is my Facebook name ... I also started another Facebook page in Arabic and French which I named 'Chabeb Tounes' [Tunisian Youth].

As the protests intensified in Kasserine, reporters from Al Jazeera, France 24 and other foreign media descended on the city and invited Houssem Hlali to assist them locally. Upon their departure, these international groups invited him to continue providing them with regular updates about the events in Kasserine and Sidi Bouzid. He declined the invitations because he felt that:

the foreign media abandoned Tunisia to focus on Egypt. As soon as the demonstrations started in Egypt they all left and lost interest in our revolution ... But I am sure that our revolution will feature in history as the one that opened the door to other revolutions in the Arab world.

Widespread internet availability in the country raised expectations which were then stymied as the government blocked popular sites and censored internet activity. Young Tunisians were frustrated by their inability to access the cyber world freely, and many tried to bypass government restrictions by using proxy sites. The internet, and especially Facebook and Twitter, connected young Tunisians from urban and rural settings and undermined the regime's strategy of building a consumerist and apolitical middle-class youth culture (ICG 2011). Those who used Facebook and Twitter appear to have developed a sense of solidarity and activism that they then expressed through direct action. A young cyber activist explained to the ICG: 'Facebook allowed us to overcome our fear of the regime. With Facebook I knew before going to a protest that I would not be alone. We felt like we belonged to a group which, even though it was virtual, would protect us' (ibid.: 8).

With nearly 2.5 million Facebook users in Tunisia, 42 per cent of whom were between 18 and 24, and a core group of about 2,000 active bloggers and cyber activists, social networks were critical in shaping the youth movement. The internet provided national and international visibility to youth protests in ways that print and broadcast media did not, in part because of the prohibitive expense involved in having professional reporters and editors. The fact that young activists and commentators had direct access to the internet and could post their own content was crucial in sustaining and propagating the democratic, participatory character of the movement. New media contributed to the radicalisation of youth against the regime through the images of the crackdown posted on the web. Social networks made mobilisation easier as the communication and circulation of information among youths was almost instantaneous, which facilitated the coordination of the uprising. However, the biggest contribution of the internet was, without a doubt, the emergence of new social actors, who brought with them their own political culture.

Unemployed university graduates

During my 2011 visit to Tunisia I spoke with dozens of unemployed graduates who were looking for jobs. Aïcha is a vibrant and outspoken 24-year-old woman whom I met in Nabeul, a tourist-oriented coastal town in north-eastern Tunisia. She has been living there for almost a year since she got a job as an administrator at a local cultural centre. Aïcha obtained a first degree in cultural animation – that is, in planning recreational and cultural programmes for children and youth – from the Bir El Bay Institute in Tunis in June 2009. Her father was an accountant and her mother a nurse, but, after her father's death following a long illness, the family struggled to make ends meet. Aïcha went to Tunis to pursue her university studies in 2005, receiving a government loan of 1,500 Tunisian dinars (TND) a year (about US$960) to cover her living expenses (university fees were covered by the government). She has been paying back her student loan since getting her job in August 2010.

Aïcha was very active at university in protests against the steady increase in graduate unemployment and political repression. In her own words:

It was at university that I became aware of the situation in the country. I remember taking part in a student strike at my institute in 2006, which was organised to protest against the lack of employment for graduates ... The output of the institute was 400 graduates a year and the government was only absorbing 30 graduates a year. We were demanding the creation of more posts or alternatively that the government should stop producing more graduates without jobs. I was still a student when I realised that my prospects for the future were very bleak. Our strike was met by heavy police repression and various students were arrested. Some of us who escaped prison were considered a risk to national security and placed under police surveillance. From then on I became very involved in political activism, fighting for student causes.

After finishing university, Aïcha was unable to find full-time employment in her field.

Like many unemployed graduates, she took a couple of temporary jobs for foreign call centres based in Tunisia. She spent three months at a call centre in Tunis for a French telephone company calling clients in France to persuade them to buy new products. This job paid a monthly salary of 400 TND (about US$250). After deciding to go back home, she worked for a month at a call centre in Korba. She soon realised that the sales scheme involved defrauding customers.

We had to call older people, senior citizens in Europe, and tell them that they had won special gifts and ask them to give credit card details and home addresses in order for the gifts to be sent to them ... I did not stay long there as I soon realised it was a centre for fraud ... There are call centres of foreign companies operating here that are very shady.

Working in call centres has enabled young graduates who are fluent in French to make some money by selling products over the phone to customers overseas. Foreign call centres have proliferated, especially in the northern part of the country. These companies prefer to hire young women because managers believe that women are more patient, more polite and more persuasive than men. Many young people claimed that call centres exploit young labour because they are aware that these are often the only jobs available to graduates with a good command of foreign languages. Workers have no proper contracts and are employed for short periods; monthly renewals are dependent on the supervisor. Employees generally work ten- to twelve-hour shifts with only a one-hour break for lunch and one or two 15-minute breaks to use the restroom. They are under constant surveillance to ensure that they do not take unauthorised breaks and that they make calls continuously and interact with customers in a polite and persuasive manner. They are supposed to be persistent and encourage clients to purchase whatever they are selling, and they cannot let the customers know that they are operating from outside the clients' own countries.

Zeinab, a 24-year-old from Tunis, shared her experience:

> I worked in a call centre in Tunis. I would start my day at 8.00 a.m. and end at 6.00 p.m. with only one hour for lunch and one occasional 10-minute break. Even during Ramadan they did not give us more time to rest. We were given a script and a supervisor was always controlling us so we did not deviate from the script. I was paid 350 TND [about US$225] each month but they did not pay me the first month as the supervisor said it was a month for training … I was furious; they took advantage of me because they know we need jobs.

Not only are some firms involved in shady transactions with customers, but also they exploit workers by avoiding state regulation. Meriam, a 25-year-old from Metline, said: 'Most call centres are not well organised and the conditions of work are not good … Many do not offer contracts and they do not declare their revenue to the state.'

Aïcha, Zeinab and Meriam, like many other young university graduates who could find work only in these exploitative call centres, grew frustrated with their situation. They could not put the skills they had acquired at university to good use and had to sit for long hours answering phones and selling products to European customers. Aïcha commented:

> We were really revolted by the lack of opportunities for the youth; we felt the government was not doing enough to resolve the situation, which became more dire every day ... Meanwhile, we were all aware of the wealth being accumulated by the president, his family and his friends. There was a lot of injustice.

Sami, a 27-year-old university graduate, has also suffered from unemployment. Both his parents were born in Metline, a town on the north-east coast, and he and his two sisters and younger brother grew up there. Sami finished his baccalaureate in Metline and then went to the coastal city of Mahdia, near Sousse, to study information technology and management. Since finishing his degree, Sami has been unable to secure full-time employment despite having sent his CV to various companies. While waiting to get a job, he earns a bit of money as a day labourer in construction and agriculture. He continues to live at his parents' home with his younger siblings and depends almost entirely on his parents' financial support. Sami had a girlfriend for four years, but last year she left him because he lacked the resources necessary for them to marry. He was visibly frustrated and desperate about his situation because he could not see a way out. He had considered emigrating to Europe like some of his friends had done, but 'you need money to do that ... You must pay the people who take you across ... and it is a lot of money. I can't afford it.'

Migration to Europe has long been an alternative for young unemployed men. For many years Tunisians found work overseas, but in the last two decades it has become more difficult as Europe has restricted immigration. Nevertheless, many youths have tried to cross illegally to the Italian island of Lampedusa, located just 200 miles away from Metline. They have risked their lives in small fishing boats, hiding from the maritime patrols and trying to cross rough and even treacherous seas. In Italy, they applied for asylum or obtained papers through dubious networks, and many ended up being sent back to Tunisia. Illegal emigration of youths to Europe, known among Tunisians as *haraga* (*brûlé*, meaning to burn your papers so that they cannot know where you come from), was a response to high rates of youth unemployment.

In the central and southern parts of the country, many young men also tried to escape unemployment by migrating to Libya, an oil-rich country where the standard of living was quite high. It was estimated that in 2004 10 per cent of Tunisian emigrants went to Libya (Boubakri 2004). Khalifi, a 21-year-old I met in the town of Regueb in Sidi Bouzid, comes from an impoverished working-class family. His father abandoned the family when Khalifi and his twin brother were only ten years old. Khalifi did not finish his high school studies and decided to work to help his mother and siblings, but was unable to find a job in his home town. At the age of 19, Khalifi made the three-hour road trip to the border and crossed illegally to Libya to find a job in construction in Sirte, where he worked for about two years. With the outbreak of war in Libya, Khalifi and other Tunisians were forced to flee the country and return home. He plans to go back eventually, but he worries that the long war and ensuing political instability in Libya will have negative consequences for young Tunisians who depend on working there in order to support their families. Many Tunisians were also involved in smuggling goods, such as clothing, electronics, foodstuffs and even cars, from Libya into Tunisia. 'Some customs officers belong to these smuggling networks,' attested Khalifi.

During the revolution, unemployed youths quickly rallied on the streets, and Khalifi was one of the first to go out in support of the events in Sidi Bouzid a few days after Bouazizi's self-immolation. In the course of the demonstrations, Khalifi was shot in the right leg by a sniper from the state police who was trying to disperse the protesters.

Nourdinne, a 28-year-old man from Sidi Bouzid, affirmed:

> We didn't have jobs and we sat in the cafés chatting for long hours and everyone expressed frustration although we could

not openly criticise the government [because] we were afraid of the RCD [Rassemblement Constitutionnel Démocratique] ... When the opportunity came we all knew what we had to do ... We were already tired of this situation, we just needed something to push us into action.

Cross-border trading and smuggling were common activities for unemployed youths in the area of Kasserine, located a few miles from the Algerian border. Khaled, a 27-year-old graduate student in Tunis, was expecting to finish his degree in 2012, but he had no hope of finding work that would utilise his education. I was invited to lunch at Khaled's parents' home in Kasserine and had the opportunity to meet his parents and sister. Their mother raised Khaled and his siblings alone while their father spent 14 years in France working in the car manufacturing industry. He sent remittances home and visited the family every year. Khaled's mother began her cross-border trade business to help support the children. Three or four times a month, she crossed the border to the nearest town in Algeria to buy carpets, textiles and women's fashions, which she sold to small retailers and in the local market. Merchandise 'is much cheaper in Algeria' because, according to Khaled, the Algerian government subsidises the cost of foodstuffs, clothing and other products. 'Everything is much cheaper in Algeria ... We survive thanks to our proximity to this country.'

After completing his secondary education in Kasserine, Khaled enrolled on a programme in cultural studies and youth programming in Tunis. He receives a small grant from the Ministry of Education, but it does not cover all his costs. During his summer vacations, Khaled travels to Algeria to buy goods to resell in Kasserine. With his mother's assistance he has found his niche buying and selling young men's clothing. An investment of 300 TND (about US$200) yields a net profit of about 150 TND (about US$100), which he uses to subsidise his living expenses in Tunis. He finds travelling across the border difficult and risky: 'Customs officers can confiscate your merchandise, or people can rob you before you have a chance to sell your products.' Aware of the high rates of graduate unemployment in the country and the difficulties faced by his friends and relatives who have graduated, Khaled thinks:

> It doesn't look like I will have a full-time job when I finish my course next year ... That's why I have to continue doing this trade business during my vacations, so that I will have something going in case I am unable to get a job.

Hafsia is a 34-year-old woman who lives in Kasserine. She is still single because her Tunisian boyfriend did not have the means to marry her. Hafsia enrolled in a law faculty at the University of Sfax but soon realised that that was not her calling. At the end of her first academic year she left and went to Tunis, where she graduated with two professional certificates, one in accountancy and banking techniques and the other in audio-visual animation. Five years after finishing her studies, Hafsia has been unable to find stable employment. The longest she has worked in the same job was as a substitute teacher at a primary school in Kasserine. She was never paid for that job because the ministry misplaced her files; after pursuing the matter for a year with no success she gave up. She has held a number of short-term jobs, but mainly she volunteers in the community. She lives with her parents and helps with the household chores.

Without any serious support from the state, unemployed young graduates have resorted to temporary work and informal ways of earning a living. They work in foreign call centres, migrate to Europe, and take up cross-border trading. But these are temporary strategies and do not offer any job security. The sense of hopelessness and despair experienced by unemployed graduates fuelled massive resentment towards a government that raised their expectations but failed to generate jobs that would enable them to realise their aspirations. Their disaffection was shared by students who faced a similar future, and so the General Union of Tunisian Students was quick to join the movement. These disillusioned young men and women became the main actors in the Tunisian revolution. They are knowledgeable and full of energy, but they had no real prospects for the future. They had nothing to lose, so they came out in force onto the streets to protest and skilfully used the internet and other networks to accomplish their goals.

Civil society

Civil society groups played significant roles in widening the movement once it had begun among the youth. Lawyers staged large demonstrations in front of courthouses in Tunis and other cities to protest against government abuses and to defend human rights. On 31 December 2011, the Bar Association called upon its members to stage national demonstrations. In Tunis, Sfax and Djerba hundreds of lawyers came out onto the streets, dressed in their robes, and demanded respect for human rights and civil liberties. The lawyers did not escape police brutality and were beaten violently.[12]

The Bar Association's activism was not entirely unprecedented. For many years lawyers and judges had engaged in the defence of prisoners of conscience, denouncing a justice system that functioned at the beck and call of the regime. For example, in April 2005, lawyer Mohammed Abbu was sentenced to two years in prison for publicly expressing his political views; his conviction mobilised many members of the Bar Association against the regime (ICG 2011).

Other civil society groups that attached themselves to the youth movement included the Tunisian Human Rights League, the Tunisian Association of Democratic Women and the National Syndicate of Tunisian Journalists. Particularly important was the role played by the Union Générale Tunisienne du Travail (UGTT). The UGTT, with about 520,000 members, is Tunisia's largest civil society organisation, and was the cornerstone of the nationalist movement during the colonial era. The UGTT has always played a key part in Tunisian politics and has been able to link social needs with political demands by acting independently from the state apparatus.[13]

Although initially during the 2010–11 youth uprisings the leadership of the UGTT decided to stay out of the conflict and play a mediating role between the government and the protesters, it soon changed its approach. Local and regional UGTT unions decided to join the youth and forced the national leadership to come on board (Ben Hammouda 2012). The Syndicat National des Enseignements (SNES, the Secondary School Teachers' Union) also immediately joined in to support the youth. Members of the SNES in Sidi Bouzid are reported to have taken Mohamed Bouazizi to a local hospital for treatment. The SNES, which was dominated by the left, had always adopted a strategy of political confrontation towards the regime (ICG 2011). Similarly, other groups within the UGTT, including the Primary School Teachers' Union, the Health Workers' Union and the Postal Workers' Union, immediately aligned themselves with the young protesters (ibid.).

On 11 January 2012, the national leadership of the UGTT called for peaceful marches all over the country. In the city of Sfax, the unions declared a strike on 12 January; they counted on the support of local businessmen who were bitter about the city's economic marginalisation relative to Sousse and Monastir, where the ruling families were well established (Ben Ali was born in Hammam near Sousse, and Bourguiba in Monastir). With about 30,000 people in the streets (ibid.), the city of Sfax hosted the largest demonstration in the country before the fall of Ben Ali. The grand finale came on 14 January, when the UGTT organised a national strike that brought hundreds of thousands of Tunisians out onto the streets and led to the departure of the president.[14]

The participation of the UGTT helped form a broader national coalition against the regime. As Hakim Ben Hammouda pointed out, it was at this point that the youth revolt was transformed into a revolutionary movement as the demands shifted from socioeconomic grievances to regime change (Ben Hammouda 2012). The dissident network Takriz, which operated through a virtual community, has also been credited with infusing political demands into their protests. But some young people, especially cyber activists and unemployed university graduates, have stated that the youth were well aware that regime change would be necessary in order to bring about radical change. As 37-year-old Hichem emphasised: 'Jobs and food without freedom would not be enough ... If we went for a minimalist approach we would soon be disappointed and want more ... Freedom is paramount.'

Political parties

When Ben Ali's regime was toppled, only seven opposition parties were legally recognised.[15] Most had no significant weight, as the RCD completely dominated the political and state apparatus. The opposition parties were systematically repressed; their members and activists were often arrested, their newspapers were banned, and their candidates at the elections, when not invalidated, had merely a symbolic presence. Only the three principal legal opposition parties – the Parti Démocrate Progressiste (PDP), the Ettajdid Movement, and the Forum Démocratique pour le Travail et les Libertés (FDTL), also known as Ettakatol – were able to have even a limited political presence. The Ettajdid Movement enjoyed parliamentary representation, having won two seats in the October 2009 legislative elections. The Islamist movement Ennahdha was banned and its leaders exiled in Great Britain.

Political opposition parties were severely weakened by the regime and had no social base. As Mahmoud Ben Romdhane asserted: 'We were elite clubs of 200–300 members at most, with extremely limited political activity.' When the revolution came they were caught unprepared and took time to react. At first the political parties participated indirectly, rallying their grassroots activists to support the movement, and issuing press releases and calls for action on the internet. Some members of the PDP, Ettajdid and Ettakatol took part in the protests, but only in the final days before the fall of Ben Ali. Having joined the movement very late in the process, the opposition parties had little effect on the revolution itself.

The illegal leftist parties, such as the PCOT and Watad (the Democratic Patriots Party), immediately supported the youth protests in Sidi Bouzid. On 12 January, the leader of the PCOT, Hamma Hammami, was arrested in Tunis following a statement issued two days earlier in which his organisation called for the end of the Ben Ali dictatorship. Ennahdha was also absent as a political party; its militants had been repressed by the regime and its leadership had left the country. However, some Ennahdha activists joined the protests and called for jobs, freedom and regime change. Religion was not an issue, and the Ennahdha party did not issue any statements during the uprisings.

The vast majority of young protesters had no political affiliations. As the ICG report put it: 'The youth movement was neither apolitical nor partisan. It was deeply politicised but did not have a political leadership' (ICG 2011: 8). The actions of opposition parties became central during the transition when they moved into the political vacuum left by the hasty departure of Ben Ali. The young activists who had led the revolution were not prepared to take on formal political roles and assume power, as they struggled to engage with the existing political system and preferred to locate their actions in the realm of civil society associations.

Conclusions

Mohamed Bouazizi's desperate act was the catalyst of the revolution, and the protests that immediately followed his self-immolation in Sidi Bouzid began the process of political mobilisation that spread through the country. The community of cyber activists and unemployed university graduates emerged as the most significant actors in this bottom-up protest movement. Their efforts were supported by various civil society organisations, particularly the UGTT and the Tunisian Bar Association, which mobilised their members across the country to come out and join the youth. The UGTT's strong nationwide network of labour union activists played an important role in the geographical extension of the protest movement. The Bar Association, the Human Rights League, the Association of Democratic Women and the National Syndicate of Tunisian Journalists helped expand support for the protests and consolidate their focus in the capital by involving public intellectuals and middle-class social and political activists. The existing political forces on the left, centre and right, including the Islamists, had difficulty carving out a role for themselves and joined the youth movement only in the last few days (Ben Hammouda 2012).

The younger generation of Tunisians became unstoppable in their protests against unemployment and lack of civil liberties. Their demands grew with the movement itself as they sought to create a new political culture based on equity, social justice and freedom of expression that was completely distinct from the empty ideological appeals of the past.

3 | Revolution

The self-immolation of Mohamed Bouazizi on 17 December 2011 in Sidi Bouzid brought hundreds of thousands of young Tunisians onto the streets to express their solidarity with Bouazizi and to protest against the difficult conditions they shared, especially economic hardship, unemployment and police abuse. Clashes between demonstrators and the police erupted as more people joined in the rallies. Protesters set up a coordinating committee that began relaying information to demonstrators within and beyond Sidi Bouzid.

Crucially, internet-based social networks both facilitated internal communications and generated international visibility. Photographs and videos of police brutality against courageous, unarmed young demonstrators surfaced through Facebook, YouTube and other sites, while Twitter conveyed eyewitness reports and propagated protesters' evolving demands, all in real time. The uprising spread very rapidly as more and more Tunisians outraged about the situation in the country supported the young people's demands joined the protests. What began as an isolated event in Sidi Bouzid developed into a broader social movement that led to the fall of the dictatorship in Tunisia and spilled over to Egypt and Libya, in what soon became known as the Arab Spring.

During my first visit to Tunisia a few months after the demise of Ben Ali's regime, young people who had participated directly in the revolution were eager to talk and tell their stories about what they did, how they did it, why they did it, and what they saw during those historic days. Tunisians were feeling a sense of abandonment as world attention quickly turned to the events in Egypt, a much larger country with greater geopolitical and strategic importance. Tunisians missed the opportunity to celebrate and take stock of their achievement with the rest of the world.

This chapter describes the series of events that occurred during the 29 days of protests all over the country. This chronology was compiled from the recollections of young people who took part in the specific events they describe. It asks whether what happened in Tunisia was indeed a social and political revolution or, rather, an uprising that did not substantially change dominant patterns and relations of power. The chapter ends by considering the Tunisian youth protests in light of existing theories on social movements. It argues that the new revolutions of the early twenty-first century require the reformulation of the notion of 'the political', with the rethinking of old models and new ones devised that are more adequate to realities in the global South at the present time.

Twenty-nine days of protests

On 17 December 2011, Mohamed Bouazizi's self-immolation took place in front of the governor's office in Sidi Bouzid at around three o'clock in the afternoon. A couple of hours later a few hundred people assembled in the same place to express their solidarity with Bouazizi. On 18 December, even more young people demonstrated in front of the governor's office, protesting about economic hardship and unemployment. Protesters were met with tear gas and police brutality. Some demonstrators were arrested, and many others were injured.

On 19 December, clashes between the police and the demonstrators continued in Sidi Bouzid as more people joined the rallies. Protesters began organising to protect themselves from the police and set up a coordinating committee to relay information to participants. Although still and moving images of these events were posted on the internet, the Tunisian national media were silent about the uprising.

On 20 December, young people in the neighbouring towns of Kasserine, Gafsa and Sfax staged protests in solidarity with Sidi

Bouzid. Over the next few days these protests spread to Regueb, Meknassi and Menzel Bouzaiene. Protesters responded to police violence by throwing stones, burning tyres in the middle of the street, and torching official government buildings and cars. The police in Menzel Bouzaiene fired on the demonstrators, killing two 18-year-olds, Mohamed Ammari and Chawki Hidri. Many more were injured, but the protesters did not retreat. During that week, particularly on 22 December, young bloggers and cyber activists from Tunis and other regions flocked to Sidi Bouzid, Menzel Bouzaiene and other towns to join in the demonstrations and to record and report the events to the country and the world. Images and videos they posted on the internet were picked up by international media, particularly Al Jazeera and France 24.

On 23 December, Hassen Ben Salah Néji, a 24-year-old unemployed man from Sidi Bouzid, electrocuted himself by touching a high-voltage electrical pole after shouting 'No to misery! No to unemployment!' A government official commented: 'As much as we regret this painful incident, we are outraged by attempts to use this isolated incident, to take it out of its true context, and to exploit it for unhealthy political ends' (quoted by the Tunisian News Agency). Aside from police repression, that was the first public notice that the government took of the demonstrations.

On 25 December, the regime's development ministers announced urgent measures to deal with youth unemployment in the regions where young people were demonstrating against the government. The demonstrators were not placated; protests continued to grow, and participants defied curfews and police repression. A group of cyber activists organised demonstrations in the capital, Tunis, in solidarity with those in Sidi Bouzid. Anonymous, an international group of cyber activists, started focusing its 'operation payback' in support of WikiLeaks on Tunisia and launched several cyber attacks against the government.

The next day, demonstrations spread across the country as Sousse, Ben Gardane, Mahdia and Bizerte joined in. That night, young people in Regueb fought the police. Abidi, a 30-year-old unemployed man, recounted how the protests in the town began.

We learned of the events in Sidi Bouzid through Facebook. We started contacting our friends, and friends of friends, and the word got out through Facebook, and so in the afternoon of the 22nd we were out in the streets to support Sidi Bouzid and to demand jobs ... We were out on the 23rd, 24th and 25th, but things turned sour on the 26th of December. At that point the demonstrations become more intense, as did police brutality. They beat us, used tear gas, and fired on us ... and we had to fight back to defend ourselves. We used stones, we burned government cars and buildings ... It was a war!

On 27 December, thousands of people gathered in Tunis in front of the headquarters of the Union Générale Tunisienne du Travail (UGTT) in solidarity with the youth protests in Sidi Bouzid. The UGTT leadership remained lukewarm about the protests, although UGTT members in Sidi Bouzid and other regions had already joined the youth movement. The protests became national, as young people and trade unionists took to the streets in unprecedented numbers.

A day later, President Ben Ali, who was on holiday in the Persian Gulf, returned home to restore order. To appease the demonstrators, he immediately visited Mohamed Bouazizi at the burn and trauma centre of the Ben Arous hospital. He then made an impromptu television address to the nation criticising the protesters as:

a minority of extremists and agitators in the pay of others, and against the country's interests, [who] resort to violence and street disturbances ... This is negative and anti-civil behaviour ... and impedes the flow of investors and tourists which impacts negatively on job creation ... The law will be enforced rigorously against these people.

He argued that 'these events were triggered by one social case, of which we understand the circumstances and psychological factors and whose consequences are regrettable', and declared that:

the exaggerated turn that these events have taken [is] a result of their political manipulation by some ... who resort to some foreign television channels, which broadcast false and unchecked allegations and rely on dramatisation, fabrication and defamation hostile to Tunisia.

Ben Ali's speech was not well received, and protests continued. On 29 December, the police crackdown on demonstrators intensified. The next day, in an act of desperation, the government made scapegoats of some officials and appointed new governors for Sidi Bouzid, Jendouba and Zaghouan.

On 31 December, the Bar Association called for national demonstrations, and lawyers staged large protests in Tunis, Sfax and Djerba. Hundreds of jurists dressed in their robes came out onto the streets and demanded respect for human rights and civil liberties. Cyber activist Lina Ben Mhenni reported to Global Voices Online that:

> Tunisian lawyers have been protesting regularly to denounce what happened in Sidi Bouzid and the social situation in Tunisia ... The government has decided to 'punish' them. Every day, news of the kidnapping, arrest or assault of lawyers is surfacing on social networking sites ... December 31, 2010, was the most horrible day for the lawyers ... [as] police officers did not hesitate to beat them violently when they were gathering in the Bar House located in front of the courthouse in Tunis. Security forces used their truncheons, causing many injuries to the lawyers.[1]

On 1 January 2011, as criticism of Ben Ali's regime mounted, the Rassemblement Constitutionnel Démocratique (RCD) held a meeting and unanimously reaffirmed its support for the president. Two days later the cyber war intensified as Anonymous, in coordination with Tunisian cyber activists, launched attacks on the government's internet sites. The president's website and those of the ministries of foreign affairs, industry and commerce, as well as that of the Tunisian stock exchange, were severely disrupted. In retaliation, the government hacked numerous Facebook pages and email accounts, with Yahoo users apparently being the most vulnerable. To help users protect their accounts, nawaat.org, an independent group blog run by Tunisians, offered technical guidance. The Tunisian Pirate Party[2] was also reported to be distributing USB sticks containing free software for an open network that helps to defend against surveillance.

On 4 January, Mohamed Bouazizi died of his burns. After the announcement of his death, protesters gathered in the streets of towns and villages across the country. His funeral took place on 5 January at Garât Benour, a village located 16 kilometres outside Sidi Bouzid. More than 5,000 people attended the ceremony, which was under police surveillance to make sure that it did not turn into a major political demonstration. As Ali Moncef, a 26-year-old man from Sidi Bouzid who attended, told me: 'Our quiet presence at the funeral was already a political statement ... Many of us did not know Bouazizi or his family personally.'

On 6 January, cyber activists Slim Amamou, Aziz Amami, Sofiane Bel Hadj and Bullet Skan were detained in Tunis. The same day the 22-year-old Tunisian hip-hop artist Hamada Ben-Amor, known as El Général, was arrested in Sfax. A critic of the government, he had released a song called 'Mr President, Your People are Suffering' that attacked Ben Ali. Over the following days police reinforced their crackdown on demonstrators and fired on the protesters. More than 20 people were killed in Kasserine, Regueb and Sidi Ali Ben Aoun (Dégage 2011).

On 9 January, in a more pacific gesture, the government announced that it would invest US$5 billion in development projects that would employ 50,000 university graduates in the next few months. The next day Ben Ali promised to create 300,000 jobs over the next two years. That same day, police attacks on protesters in Regueb claimed several victims. 'We organised a peaceful demonstration, and suddenly the police arrived and attacked us,' recounted Khalifi, who was 21 at the time. 'As we fled a bullet fired by a sniper hit me on my left thigh ... I later learned that that was the same bullet that killed my friend Slimi. He was just 21 years old.'

On 11 January, the protesters in Kasserine fought so hard that they managed to drive the police and the military out of town. As Hafsia, a 34-year-old woman from Kasserine, recalled: 'For us Kasserinians January 11 was like an independence day … but we were still a bit afraid of what the regime would do in retaliation.' Walid, aged 29, added that:

> The problem we faced after the police and the military left was that there was no order in the city and we risked falling into a chaotic situation, so we quickly decided to establish voluntary neighbourhood associations to ensure the security of people and their property.

That same day Ben Ali replaced the minister of the interior, Rafik Haj Kacem, and announced the release of everyone who had been arrested during the protests. These measures were aimed at appeasing the young protesters, but 'it was too little too late', said 31-year-old Ali from Kasserine.

On 13 January, a curfew was declared for Greater Tunis, which includes Tunis, Ariana, Ben Arous and La Manouba, from 8.00 p.m. until 5.30 a.m. Ben Ali addressed the nation and promised to respond positively to popular grievances if the violence ended right away. He declared that he would not seek re-election in 2014.

> I have understood you all … I'm speaking to you because the situation needs radical change; yes, a radical change … I understand the unemployed, the needy, the politicians, all those demanding more freedom. I have understood everyone. But what is happening today is not the way Tunisians do things.

Ben Ali announced that he had ordered his security forces not to employ firearms against the protesters. For the first time in his 23-year presidency, he used colloquial Tunisian rather than Modern Standard Arabic (MSA) in parts of his speech. According to El Mustapha Lahlali, an Arabic scholar:

> By switching to dialect, Ben Ali may have been trying to appeal to a wider section of Tunisian society, especially those less

educated people who could not easily follow his speech in MSA.
He may also have wanted to remind his own people that he
is a Tunisian and try to bridge the social gap between himself
and the wider Tunisian public. The use of dialect could also
be interpreted as an attempt to bypass the middle-class people
taking part in the protests. (Lahlali 2011)

Many young people thought that this speech was orchestrated
by the regime to gain time and give the impression that the
majority of the people supported Ben Ali. Zied, a 21-year-old law
student from Tunis, said:

Five minutes after his speech we heard people on the streets
shouting 'Viva Ben Ali.' I looked carefully and saw that these
people were in rented cars and they were all from the RCD ...
They wanted us to believe that the people were with Ben Ali.
I quickly went to Facebook and everyone was noticing similar
situations in their neighbourhoods, the same rented cars full of
members of the RCD. Then we decided that we needed to come
out in force to counteract them. The UGTT had already called
for a strike and we all joined protests the next day, January 14.

On the night of 13 January, Slim Amamou, Aziz Amami, Bullet
Skan and others were released from jail. 'The police said that
we had been granted a presidential pardon and so we were free
to go ... We were not aware of what was happening outside as
we were completely cut off,' Slim Amamou explained. But they
soon rejoined the demonstrators, whose numbers had multiplied
several fold since they had been detained just a week before.

On 14 January, 'Ben Ali Dégage!' ('Ben Ali Go!') shouted thousands of young Tunisians gathered in front of the Ministry of the
Interior in the Avenue Habib Bourguiba in the centre of Tunis.
The UGTT had called for a national strike, and hundreds of thousands of Tunisians joined the demonstrations in Tunis, Sousse
and Sfax, the three largest cities in the country. In the beginning
the demonstration was very peaceful; people shouted 'Enough
is Enough', 'We Want Freedom' and 'Ben Ali Dégage'. But in the

afternoon the police started shooting tear gas canisters at the protesters. By 5 p.m. national television announced that Ben Ali would be leaving power in six months. The people wanted him to leave right away, so they continued shouting 'Ben Ali Dégage!' At around 7 p.m., Al Jazeera and France 24 announced that Ben Ali had left the country for exile in Saudi Arabia. According to Tarek, a 27-year-old from Menzel Bourguiba: 'Some people say they saw Ben Ali's plane in the air … Because the airspace was closed his was the only airplane authorised to fly that day. People say he flew out in a Tunisair plane because the military refused to fly him.'

Jasmine, Facebook or Tunisian revolution?

Many names have been given to the youth social movement in Tunisia. Some called it the 'jasmine revolution', others the 'Facebook revolution', or even the 'dotcom revolution'. Many Tunisians do not agree with these designations, however; they see them as appropriations and distortions of their revolution by the West. Zied, a 21-year-old law student from Tunis, commented:

> I think the name jasmine revolution came from Europe and was picked up by the foreign press. The jasmine flower is the symbol of the Tunisian tourism board, and the Europeans picked on that, that's what they know when they come as tourists … All they see about us is jasmine, couscous and camels, the exotic Tunisia … Why not just call it the Tunisian revolution? We say the French revolution and not … the baguette revolution, for example.

Indeed, many young Tunisians felt that the name 'the jasmine revolution' was inadequate to characterise their protests and experiences during that period. As Aïcha, a 24-year-old from Nabeul, pointed out:

> Jasmine is a beautiful flower with a good scent and symbolises beauty and peace. Our struggle was hard, there was a lot of blood, many people lost their lives for liberty and dignity … I don't like that expression; we Tunisians don't like that expression.[3]

79

Indeed, as Amin Allal and Vincent Geisser pointed out, 'this orientalist terminology with exotic accents ... emerges as a stereotypical representation of the "revolution", reproducing the same [Western] prejudices that have often led to neglect the repressive ... Benaliste regime'.[4]

Similarly, a young Tunisian commenting on Twitter asked: 'When are you going to get it that OUR revolution is NOT called the jasmine revolution?' (twitter.com@mostpurple). Another said adamantly: 'No to the postcard-like name "jasmine revolution", which is reductive and simplistic' (@Uyulaya).[5]

Many young people were equally uncomfortable with terms such as 'the Facebook revolution', 'the dotcom revolution', or 'the Twitter revolution'. While they acknowledge the role of the internet in helping them communicate, network and spread information, they complain that these expressions rob them of agency. Abdel Kader, a 26-year-old from Grombelia, explained:

> When people say 'the internet revolution' it is as if the internet did it all alone, or it was thanks to Facebook that this revolution happened. No, this revolution happened because of Tunisians. We used Facebook and Twitter and the blogosphere only as instruments to fight the regime of Ben Ali ... When you wage a war the praise is not for the effective weapons you used but for those who used them ... You don't call it 'the war of Kalashnikovs', do you?

Activists were concerned that catchy headlines could become a narrative and establish perceptions that differ from the reality. 'The Facebook revolution' or 'the Twitter revolution' might suggest that these media technologies *were* the revolution.[6] Ethan Zuckerman rightly asserts that 'any attempt to credit a massive political shift to a single factor – technological, economic, or otherwise – is simply untrue. Tunisians took to the streets due to decades of frustration, not in reaction to a WikiLeaks cable, a denial-of-service attack, or a Facebook update.'[7] Tunisian journalist Soufiane Ben Farhat[8] considers expressions such as 'the youth revolution' or 'the revolution of liberty and dignity' more appropriate to describe what happened in Tunisia in late 2010 and early 2011. Young Tunisians I spoke with, however, concurred that I should call this set of events 'the Tunisian revolution'.

The revolution that wasn't?

Following the elections of 2011, several analysts and observers have been debating whether the overthrow of Ben Ali and his replacement by an elected government was indeed a revolution. A revolution is defined as 'a process of change involving the mobilising of a mass social movement in order to radically transform the society'[9] whereas rebellions or revolts are 'aimed at removing particular rulers or regimes rather than bringing about significant structural changes in a society'.[10]

Examining the events in Tunisia, as well as in Egypt, over the course of 2012, various analysts considered that the electoral victories of conservative Islamist forces presented a potential risk of a return to autocratic regimes; in this sense, they argued that rather than revolutions, the social movements that marked the Arab Spring were simply national revolts or rebellions that did not significantly change the fundamental structures of power in these societies.

This is the view of Moroccan scholar Abdallah Balqaziz, who considers that what happened in Tunisia and other North African countries 'cannot be considered a revolution unless it carries society towards a more advanced political and socioeconomic system ... So far we do not know ... if the "revolution" will result in a cumulative process that is progressive rather than regressive.'[11] Balqaziz's statement is problematic because he seems to be making assumptions about what progress means for these societies.

Similarly, a report written by various academics in the UK and published by the London School of Economics Centre for the Study of International Affairs and Diplomacy (IDEAS), entitled *After the Arab Spring: Power shift in the Middle East?* (Kitchen 2012), states that there is little evidence to suggest that future historians will rank the events of 2011 in North Africa with those of the European revolutions of 1848–49 or the fall of the Soviet-backed regimes in Eastern Europe in 1989–91. Very few of the funda-mentals of socioeconomic and political organisation have been successfully contested and 'the post-revolutionary transitions ... are unlikely to deliver on the hopes that united the courageous protestors in their struggle,' the conclusion reads (Dodge 2012: 64).

Tunisians have a different view. For them, it took a revolution to topple the entrenched dictatorial regime of Ben Ali and most of what it represented to them. The political freedoms they are now enjoying constitute, for them, a major systemic change. Elections were held and Tunisians freely elected a new National Constitu-ent Assembly, which began the process of writing a new Tunisian constitution. Despite all the problems and challenges they face in the transition, these are already seen as major achievements for a country that has been buried under a 23-year dictatorship. More-over, as many young Tunisians pointed out, fundamental changes in the socioeconomic system do not happen overnight. They clearly stated that the revolution is not over; it is a long process that began in December 2011 and will continue, with twists and turns and ups and downs, until they are able to achieve economic stability, social justice and civil liberties. Imen, a 24-year-old woman from Sousse, emphasised that 'the revolution is in constant movement; each day it gains new contours and changes ... We are still in the revolution; we fought Ben Ali and we will continue for fight those who want to derail our efforts.'

What appears to be remarkable about these recent social move-ments is the younger generation's courageous drive to reclaim autonomy and political self-determination. Young protesters in Tunisia refused to continue living under a dictatorship they re-garded as serving the interests of a corrupt and cliquish elite, as well as those of Western countries. They not only succeeded in getting rid of the dictatorship but also began to believe in themselves, in the power of their generation, as agents of social change. They demanded better lives and collective ownership of the places where they live, work, think and play.[12] Nobody will convince them that theirs was not a revolution but only a short-lived uprising or revolt. Besides, it is still too early to tell what will come of these processes and how these events will be written in history. For the time being, Tunisians are living their revolution.

Social movements and 'new politics'

Studies of social movements help to shed some light on the youth-led revolutionary movement in Tunisia. Social movements are understood as collective groups 'acting with some degree of organization and continuity outside of institutional or organizational channels for the purpose of challenging or defending extant authority' (Snow et al. 2007: 11).

There is a large body of literature on social movements that extends over nearly a century, but the bulk of the writing and theorising is mainly focused on developments in Western Europe and North America and a little on South America. Mainstream social movement theory has not sufficiently engaged with the realities outside Western societies. Similarly, studies of non-violent political action have neglected African realities, perhaps with the exception of South Africa. The works of prominent scholars in this field, such as Gene Sharp (1973) and Peter Ackerman and Jack Duvall (2000) attest to this.

Iranian sociologist Asef Bayat (2010) has argued that Western theories have not merely ignored what is going on in places such as the Middle East and North Africa but have concluded that social movements do not exist in these contexts. Middle Eastern societies have been seen as monolithic and static, characterised by historical and political continuity rather than change. All non-violent political protest and rebellions taking place anywhere on the globe that do not conform to the theoretical framework based on dominant Western models and experiences have not been considered social movements. Bayat finds it problematic to make comparisons by taking one element as the 'norm' without questioning the 'original configuration'. Thus, he questions the ability of Western theories to address the complex sociopolitical and socio-religious 'social movements' taking place in the Middle East.

Indeed, these theories have failed to effectively account for and explain the intricate dynamics of protest and resistance movements in the non-Western world. As pointed out by Oliver et al. (2003), it is fundamental that the theoretical underpinnings and frameworks of the analysis of social movements and non-violent political action are able to consider a broader geographic and empirical base, 'breaking out of a preoccupation with Anglo-America and Europe and becoming truly global in its orientation' (ibid.: 17).

European and North American studies European studies have been framed mainly by the Marxist/Hegelian tradition of the philosophy of history and preoccupied with the constitutive structure and type of society in which social movements emerge, as well as with the movements themselves and their historical role. Most recent European literature has been focused on the 'new social movements'; that is, movements that have emerged in Western societies in the wake of the 1960s, such as environmentalism, the peace movement, second-wave feminism and animal rights. These post-Marxist new social movement approaches reject the primordial position of class and class struggle as agents of historical change (Crossley 2002).

The North American tradition adopted a more empirical approach to the study of social movements, focusing on particular examples such as the civil rights movement. Its main concern has been with the specific empirical conditions that facilitate and inhibit the development and flourishing of such movements. A significant paradigm shift in the American school occurred in the 1970s with the emergence of 'resource mobilisation' and 'political process' models that rejected the 'collective behaviour' model that saw social movements as being spontaneous, unorganised and unstructured (Marks and McAdam 1996; Morris 2000). The new theories, on the other hand, proposed a more explicitly political view of the movements, and assumed a close connection between institutionalised politics and the ebb and flow of social protests that shaped the dynamics of collective action (Marks and McAdam 1996: 250). The political process model devoted attention to the movement itself, using the concepts of 'mobilising structures', 'political opportunity' and 'cultural framing' to examine and help generate a better understanding of the origins of social movements, the power they generate, their energising cultural content and forms, and their eventual outcomes.

Critics have argued, however, that this model remains overly structural and ignores some crucial aspects of collective political action (Ferree 1992; Goodwin and Jasper 1999; Jasper 1998; Morris 2000). For example, political process theorists' assumption that political opportunities must precede collective action is misleading, argues Aldon Morris (2000), because mass action can burst forth precisely when the authorities close ranks and resort to harsh repression (ibid.: 447).

What these Western approaches have failed to take into account are the factors that give rise to collective action in the South. Non-Western social movements, and the Tunisian case is no exception, have emerged in response to the inequalities that prevail in the world political and economic order. The existing world order has played and continues to play a major role in shaping relations of power and patterns of inequality in these societies. Southern scholars such as Wignaraja (1993), Amin (1976; 1993), Kothari (1993; 2005) and Mamdani et al. (1993) have emphasised the outcomes of global capital on development by pointing to the structural effects of neoliberalism as crucial to an understanding of why more unified social resistance has not taken place in the South. Likewise, Lisa Thompson and Chris Tapscott's recently edited collection on citizenship and social movements in the South argues that access to resources in Southern states continues to be 'mediated by a range of national and global factors, which have an impact on the extent to which the poor are able to mobilize into collective action and extract concessions from the state' (Thompson and Tapscott 2010: 26). Social mobilisation in Southern countries is, therefore, primarily oriented towards the attainment of socioeconomic rights rather than more generalised human rights (Wignaraja 1993; Thompson and Tapscott 2010).

Moreover, Bayat contends that there have been social movements and revolutionary insurrections in the Middle East that have brought about open collective action against the establishment.

85

However, beyond these there are also unconventional forms of action that combine political activism with the practice of everyday life, which Bayat calls 'social non-movements'.[13] These non-movements involve 'collective actions by non-collective actors; they embody shared practices of large numbers of ordinary people whose fragmented but similar activities trigger much social change even though these practices are rarely guided by an ideology or recognizable leaderships and organizations' (Bayat 2010: 14). These types of non-movement have been completely off the radar of mainstream social movement theory because they do not fit into the prevailing conceptual frameworks and categories.

How to understand the Tunisian experience Despite its short-comings, some of the approaches in mainstream social movement theory can be used to understand the Tunisian experience because both Western and non-Western social movements have in common a desire to mobilise and fight in order to achieve a collective goal. In terms of what factors may trigger collective action, the resource mobilisation theory may help shed light on questions such as: how does a social movement emerge and obtain the resources necessary to develop new modes of action, organise itself and communicate its message and tactics to others? What makes it possible for participants to take the risks that collective action entails?

In Tunisia, street politics (Bayat 2010; 1997)[14] by groups that lack institutional power played a critical role. The actions of a large pool of informal workers together with unemployed and underemployed graduates with skills and experience in communication and the organisation of collective action (the skills many acquired through the *maisons des jeunes*) were a determining factor in the emergence and development of the uprising, as was young people's ability to form alliances across class boundaries and with other civil society groups, such as the UGTT and the Bar Association. Although it took longer for the resources of those formal groups to be committed to the struggle, their members, who were accustomed to taking collective action (e.g. strikes by trade unionists), were drawn in immediately. The internet was without doubt the protesters' most obvious resource, but others were equally important.

In terms of political opportunity, the relevant questions would be: why was Ben Ali's dictatorial regime no longer able to govern according to its old methods? How did its rule break down in the wake of popular defiance? In Tunisia, underlying factors included the economic crisis, massive unemployment, especially of young graduates, and the increasing isolation of the circle around Ben Ali, which alienated significant elements of the former ruling elite. Precipitating factors included police repression, heavy censorship and the absence of civil liberties. When protesters are able to ignore and confront the heavy hand of the state, further repression is seldom effective. People feel elated that it is possible to defy the powers that be and come to regard freedom as something they can seize for themselves.

Finally, cultural framing interrogates the ways in which social movements articulate their grievances and demands for change so that people from less educated or politically engaged groups can identify with them. How do culturally appropriate frames help people overcome their fear of social instability and chaos? How are divisions that exist within the society overcome, or at least set aside for the duration of the revolutionary upheaval? What happens when other elements seek to reframe the issues in order to gain advantage and shift the political agenda? The key to framing theory is that what matters is not the relative merit of different positions as they might be debated, but rather the appeal of different ways of formulating the whole problem.

In Tunisia, it is clear that 'Ben Ali Dégage!' was a key demand that all could endorse, as were the demands to end police brutality and rampant corruption; these grievances were widespread. As Aditya Nigam points out in relation to the Anna Hazare social movement in India, through 'a series of exposures of corruption in high places ... the movement gave voice to people who do not otherwise participate in politics. Once again, the feeling that the hard-earned money of the taxpayer was being squandered was palpable', leading to many Indians joining the movement (Nigam 2012: 171).

The lack of fully developed programmes and policies in these early stages of the transition might be advantageous for Tunisians since groups have divergent, competing or opposing interests. However, it may prove fatal when particular groups, such as the Salafists, seek to reframe the issues. An example of that is the Islamist versus secularist debates that have dominated political discourses in the post-revolutionary period, in which Islamists try to reframe the secularist movement as non-Muslim and even atheist, while secularists try to depict Islamists as conservative and retrograde.

Overall, the political process model presents serious limitations to our understanding of contemporary social movements. As pointed out by Indian political scientist Aditya Nigam, political science's preoccupation with parties, 'party systems', 'mobilisation', elections and governance has very little to offer that is relevant to an understanding of the 'political' today, particularly in making sense of the 'new revolutions of our times' (ibid.: 167). Political science and social movement theory have not been able to offer insights into post-national struggles that establish connections with movements beyond national borders and may make use of support structures and resources from outside the country (ibid.).

All these uprisings, despite their domestic roots, draw inspiration in some form or another from other movements, just as they, in turn, inspire movements in other parts of the globe. While some Tunisians claim to have been inspired by the Palestinian intifada of 1987 and 1993 (Bayat 2011), young Egyptians who poured out into the streets also followed the example of their Tunisian counterparts. Together they inspired rebellions across the rest of the region. These movements increasingly take the form of a virus that travels, at very high speed, across borders. This process of propagation is made possible by the new technologies of information and communication, particularly the internet. The internet has also opened avenues of horizontal communication through its social networks, obviating the need for a centralised organisation with a hierarchical command structure (Nigam 2012). 'Internet, through the exchange in real time ... has allowed the emergence of a spontaneous free and radical protest movement by a generation that's had enough.'[15]

Moreover, the solidarity networks that are established by the various youth movements though the virtual and real worlds are remarkable. Tunisian cyber activists were greatly supported by Anonymous, the secret group of international hackers that was instrumental in helping them break into key government websites and expose the regime. During the cyber war against the dictatorship, Egyptian activists also supported Tunisians. Similarly, Tunisian cyber activists played an active role in supporting their Egyptian colleagues in their fight against the Mubarak regime. Aziz Amami revealed that a couple of weeks prior to the protests in Tahrir Square, a group of Egyptian activists came to Tunisia to gain insights and knowledge from the actions undertaken by Tunisians during their revolution.

The links between these two groups were again apparent in November 2011 when young activists unhappy about the rule of Egypt's Supreme Council of the Armed Forces, which led the post-Mubarak transition, came out onto the streets to protest about the demands of the military for special powers and protections in the future Egyptian constitution. Young Tunisians staged protests in front of the Egyptian embassy in Tunis in solidarity with their Egyptian counterparts, who were being brutally attacked and murdered by the military. Tunisian cyber activist Slim Amamou, who took part in the protests in Tunis, stated that:

> the military rule in Egypt has to stop. We feel for the Egyptians and will continue to support them. Our revolution and the Egyptian revolution is one. They were first to support us [following] Sidi Bouzid's events. We have to show them support till the end.

Social movement theory has not looked closely at these post-national protests and revolutions, which at a profound level are providing new thinking about the political and its relationship with power. Older notions of politics may no longer seem workable, especially as a new generation brought up in the post-Cold War era takes centre stage. Twentieth-century shibboleths mean little to them and they are in continuous conversation across the globe and across 'ideologies' through the internet (ibid.: 173). In fact, most theorists recognise the limitations of current models and the need to reformulate them. They agree that the challenge for political scientists is to devise new and robust theoretical formulations of collective non-violent political action to understand contemporary social movements and political realities (Morris 2000).

Conclusions

The 29 days of protests led by the various groups of young people across the country constituted moments of great creativity, engagement and enthusiasm as well as of vulnerability and danger, as many ended up injured and some were killed. The complete disruption of social lives took students and teachers out of their classrooms, workers out of their jobs and many ordinary Tunisians out of their daily routines. Families were supportive of their sons and daughters who decided to take control of their destinies; mothers and sisters cooked for the protesters and fathers encouraged them to stand up for themselves. The young Tunisians' sense of agency and ownership of this process was very apparent as they criticised designations such as the 'jasmine revolution' or the 'Facebook revolution' as attempts to exoticise and westernise their revolution. And they do not doubt that this was indeed a revolutionary process that shook the very core of Tunisia's dictatorial regime and paved the way for deeper socioeconomic and political transformations.

Revolutions do not produce results quickly, and young Tunisians understand that it is a long process towards freedom, economic stability and security for all. The Tunisian revolution renewed questions and debates about theories of social movements and non-violent political conflict; with a few exceptions, these theories have failed to take account of Southern realities. The types of events, practices, relationships and organisational models displayed in these twenty-first-century youth movements offer potential new understandings of the link between power and politics, governors and governed, and young and older generations. Thus, it is imperative that academic theory on social movements and non-violent political conflict catches up with these new realities, which are taking place in the global South but are also influencing the North. The role of young activists in the post-Ben Ali political transition will be examined in the next chapter.

4 | Transition

Following the departure of Ben Ali on 14 January 2011, Tunisians began grappling with the complex process of transition to democracy.[1] The post-revolution transition entailed establishing institutions to manage the changeover to a new democratic political system. An interim government was immediately put in place to handle day-to-day affairs and to prepare the first democratic elections. This process brought to the fore not only the cleavage between those who held power under the old regime and the majority of the people, but also between the differing political tendencies within the revolutionary movement.

Major debates during this period centred on the timing and extent of political change. Young activists, civil society groups and left-wing parties advocated a maximalist approach that would completely dismantle the previous regime's institutional apparatus. Those seeking stability and continuity rather than revolutionary rupture supported a compromise that would maintain the former regime's institutions while undertaking some reforms. The first two interim governments, mainly composed of politicians connected to the old regime as well as some technocrats,[2] advanced the latter position.

Tunisian youth, who were the major players in the revolution, were disappointed by the course of the democratic transition and the results of the electoral process. Initially, many young people were delighted with their newfound freedom and optimistic about the future. But their lives changed very little after the overthrow of Ben Ali, and the issues that had sparked their protests did not seem high on the agenda of either the interim government or the emerging opposition parties. Their hopes for social transformation soon began to fade. They became increasingly worried that the revolution was being taken over by the older generation that was clinging to the politics of the former regime or driving the country into religious conservatism. Young people grew increasingly dubious about politicians' capacity to effect the socioeconomic and political transformation that was demanded by the majority of the population during the uprising. Instead, it appeared, they were setting out to preserve the existing political system, and the 'old guard' remained in a powerful position to influence the direction of the country.

This chapter examines the tensions and negotiations between the various political forces that occurred immediately after 14 January 2011. It analyses the formation and actions of the interim government and discusses young people's views of the key political and social developments that marked the post-revolutionary transition. Understanding the process of building a multiparty democracy in Tunisia involves surveying the new political landscape, the development of various political discourses, and both common and divergent visions for the new Tunisia. The youth have appeared largely disconnected from the debate over identity politics conducted by political parties; they seem to consciously reject 'politics as usual' and are choosing to remain outside formal traditional political structures. Instead, they engage in civil society associations and use street protest to continue pressing for change.

The new political landscape

During Ben Ali's regime, politics were completely dominated by the Rassemblement Constitutionnel Démocratique (RCD). The opposition parties had no significant political weight. Some legal opposition parties that had been manipulated by Ben Ali were derisively labelled 'loyalists' because they did not take a strong stance against the regime. Others, including the Parti Démocrate Progressiste (PDP), Ettakatol and Ettajdid, remained independent but were subject to severe political restrictions. Banned political parties, such as Ennahdha and the Congrès pour la République (CPR), were forced to operate from exile. Opposition figures who remained in the country, including militants of the radical left, blended into the few non-partisan spaces for political expression, such as human rights organisations, trade unions and other civil society groups.

After the fall of the dictatorship, banned opposition parties became legalised, and new political forces were established and authorised to join the electoral register. By the end of June 2011, the country had 94 political parties on its electoral list, and new political parties continued to be formed and to apply to stand for the National Constituent Assembly elections. Neji Zouairi, an Interior Ministry official, said on 24 June 2011 that: 'We are currently looking into 31 more applications for new parties ... [and] have rejected 118 applications in the past few months.'[3]

The myriad of political parties in Tunisia at the time created an impression of political pluralism, with some parties aligned along a left–right axis and others with clear religious orientations. Political analysts have divided Tunisia's political scene into three main blocs: the conservative modernist bloc, which includes several reconfigurations of the former RCD; the progressive modernist bloc, which includes political formations from the radical left, centre-left and centre-right; and the conservative Islamist bloc, ranging from moderate to extremist tendencies.[4] Some parties fall outside these categories or position themselves between them, but the schema is useful for analytical purposes. Moreover, the polarisation among these political blocs became quite marked during the 2011 election campaign and continues to structure public debate today.

The conservative modernist bloc The RCD was established in 1988 by Ben Ali as the successor to the Parti Socialiste Destourien (PSD) founded by Habib Bourguiba in 1964.[5] The PSD's single-party rule endorsed centralised state planning and effectively consecrated the fusion of party and state in Tunisia, adopting a policy of limited political pluralism. The RCD was the pillar of Ben Ali's regime and exerted near total control over parliament, state and local governments, and most political activity in the country. It was banned in March 2011 after the revolution and the departure of Ben Ali into exile in Saudi Arabia.

Several parties have emerged from the remnants of Ben Ali's party. Al-Moubadara (the Initiative) is led by Kamel Morjane, former defence and foreign minister under Ben Ali. Al-Waten (the Nation) was co-founded by Mohamed Jegham, former interior and defence minister, and Ahmed Friaa, the interior minister who was in charge of police and security in the final days of the revolution. Other new parties formed by former RCD members include the Parti de la Justice et de la Liberté and the Parti de l'Indépendance pour la Liberté. The largest and most successful party is Al-Moubadara, a centrist party that strongly supports the representation of former RCD members in post-revolutionary politics and won five seats in the National Constituent Assembly.

The conservative modernist bloc also includes the so-called loyalist parties that belonged to the legal opposition but were considered puppets of Ben Ali. Their main political role seemed to be to criticise independent political parties that opposed the regime. The loyalist parties fell into disrepute after the revolution because of the stances previously taken by their leaders. Some disintegrated into a number of political factions, most notably the nationalistic Parti de l'Unité Populaire, the Parti Social-Libéral, the Mouvement des Démocrates Socialistes, the Parti des Verts pour le Progrès and the Union Démocratique Unioniste.[6]

The progressive modernist bloc The progressive democratic parties in Tunisia can be divided into four main groups. On the extreme left are parties with former Stalinist or Maoist tendencies, such as the Parti Communiste des Ouvriers de Tunisie (PCOT) and Watad (the Democratic Patriots Party). Both of these parties, which are rooted in the radical left of the late 1960s, were banned under Ben Ali. This movement in Tunisia was represented by the Groupe d'Études et d'Action Socialiste en Tunisie (GEAST) and the journal *Al-Afaq* (*Perspective*), later *Al-Aml at-Tunusi* (*The Tunisian Worker*), which were interdicted under the dictatorship.

The nationalist left is led by the PDP and the CPR. The PDP

is a centre-left party founded in 1983 that was part of the legal opposition during the Ben Ali regime. Its founder, Ahmed Nejib Chebbi, now 68, was banned from running for president in 2009. The PDP defends an Arab nationalist approach in which religion may have a role to play in state politics. It is the only Tunisian political party whose secretary-general, Maya Jribi, is a woman; she has held this position since December 2006. The CPR, which was banned by Ben Ali and legalised after the revolution, is led by Moncef Marzouki, a well-known human rights activist. Marzouki failed in a bid for the presidency under the dictatorship in 2009 and was then forced into exile in France; he returned to the country after 14 January 2011.

The social-democratic left is represented mainly by Ettakatol, the Forum Démocratique pour le Travail et les Libertés, a centre-left party that was part of the legal opposition to Ben Ali's regime. Its founder, Mustapha Ben Jaafar, now 72, was also barred from running for president in 2009.

Finally, the centrist left is completed by the Pôle Démocratique Moderniste (PDM), a coalition of centrist political parties and independent personalities led by the Ettajdid Movement. Ettajdid was the old Communist party, which reinvented itself as a centre-left party. The PDM coalition is running a secular agenda to counter Islamist tendencies and argues that Islam belongs not in the state but in the private sphere. Initially, this coalition sought to unite all the major centrist opposition parties against the Islamists, but the larger parties, particularly Ettakatol and the PDP, preferred to run on their own.

Although other progressive parties were formed more recently and legalised after the revolution, these established parties have been the most influential on the Tunisian political scene. The progressive parties' agenda during the democratic transition was to protect the revolution against conservative forces that aimed either to preserve the foundations of the old regime or to introduce and enforce extremist forms of Islam in public, limiting civil liberties.

The conservative Islamist bloc The main Tunisian Islamist party, Ennahdha (Renaissance), is heir to the Mouvement de la Tendance Islamique (MTI), which was founded in 1981 by Rached Ghannouchi, Abdelfattah Mourou and others.[7] Inspired by the ideology of the Muslim Brotherhood, the MTI believed in the application of Islamic principles to all aspects of political, economic and social life. It rejected the 'cultural colonisation' of the Islamic world by Western influence and maintained that the Islamic code of conduct, as expressed in Sharia, should be the law of the land (Hamdi 1998). In 1988 the MTI became known as Hizb al-Nahda (the Renaissance Party, or Ennahdha) in an attempt to meet Ben Ali's requirement that religion must be separate from politics.[8] In the April 1989 legislative elections, the movement won about 13 per cent of the vote, although the party claimed that massive electoral fraud had diminished its actual share. From the early 1990s, Ennahdha was subjected to an intense degree of repression by the regime. The party was accused of conspiring to overthrow the government in 1991, and most of its political leadership went into exile in France and Great Britain. Following the revolution, Ennahdha positioned itself as a Islamist party seeking to accommodate Islam with democracy.[9]

Ennahdha is not alone on the Islamist stage. The Al-Aridha Chaabia (Popular Petition) party merged with the Parti des Conservateurs Progressistes and is led by Hechmi Hamdi. Despite the fact that the name of the party itself conveys seemingly incompatible conservative and progressive ideals, Hamdi believes that both concepts are embodied in the essence of his party ideology. In his own words: '[The Al-Aridha Chaabia] ... is conservative because it belongs to the Islamist orientation, advocating for the preservation of Arab Muslim identity. It is progressive because it adopts the leftist vision of the welfare state.'[10]

Religiously conservative Islamist groups have resurfaced following the revolution. The post-Ben Ali period has created new opportunities for individuals and groups to organise at the local level, including the Salafists. The Salafist movement is a fundamentalist trend within Sunni Islam that emerged during the 1970s; in Tunisia, most adherents appear to be non-violent political Salafists, although some sympathise with intellectual aspects of the jihadist ideology and may not rule out completely the possibility of jihad.

The Reform Front (Hizb Jabhat al-Islah al-Islamiyya al-Tunisiyya – Jabhat al-Islah for short, or JI) was established as an official political party in March 2012. Led by Mohammad al-Khoujah, the party follows a Salafist ideology, based on an ultraconservative interpretation of Islam. It calls for the adoption of Sharia in the Tunisian constitution. The JI has its origins in the Front Islamique Tunisien (FIT), which was created by Al-Khoujah and others in 1986 and was banned under the Bourguiba and Ben Ali regimes, leading to Al-Khoujah's imprisonment for an extended period of time under Ben Ali's presidency.[11] Members of the JI were reported to have taken part in a variety of Salafist demonstrations, such as the one at Nessma TV over the broadcast of the animated film *Persepolis* (see Chapter 6). But while the old FIT advocated for armed jihad, the newly re-emerged JI declared itself to be against waging jihad wars inside or outside Tunisia, and vowed to participate in the democratic process. As Al-Khoujah explained: 'It is no longer the time for armed jihad ... we believe Islam is a religion of democracy and freedom.'[12]

Another Salafist party is the Hizb ut-Tahrir (the Liberation Party), an ultraconservative political organisation that calls for the establishment of an Islamic caliphate[13] and Islamic law. The party was legalised in July 2012 as the third Salafist party to be recognised by the Tunisian authorities. The leader of the Liberation Party, Mohammad Ben Hussein, declared that their ultimate goal is to establish a powerful Muslim society with no dependence on, nor interference from, the West.[14]

The Ansar al-Shari'a in Tunisia (AST) is one of the most radical Salafist groups in the country, believed to be a jihadist Salafist movement. It gained prominence after the revolution by holding high-profile pro-Sharia rallies and demonstrations across the country. The AST possesses a strong media machine with its own media outlet, the Al-Qayrawan Media Foundation, as well as Facebook pages.[15] The AST favours an Islamic state under Sharia and sees secularist tendencies as a continuation of past attempts to drive religion out of the state. Despite its reputation as a jihadist group, the leader of the AST, Saifallah Ben Hussein, better known as Abu Ayadh, reportedly said that they would not engage in violent jihad. 'We restrain ourselves. We say this is to be done through preaching,' stated Abu Ayadh.[16]

The transitional coalition government

The former speaker of parliament, Fouad Mebazaa, who became the interim president upon Ben Ali's departure under the existing constitution, established the first transitional coalition government on 17 January 2011. Its mandate, in addition to continuing the national administration, was to set up the elections. Led by Mohamed Ghannouchi,[17] Ben Ali's former prime minister, the coalition government was composed of members of the RCD, the main party during the dictatorship, as well as members of the two opposition parties that were legal under Ben Ali, the PDP and the Ettajdid Movement, along with a few independent individuals. Ettakatol and the formerly banned political parties (Ennahdha, the CPR and others) were not represented in this interim government. The Union Générale Tunisienne du Travail (UGTT) had been invited to join the government but decided to stay out of it. 'We withdrew from the government on the appeal of our union,' said Houcine Dimassi, who had been appointed minister of training and employment. The UGTT and other political formations declined to join because members of the RCD were accepted in the interim government and controlled all the key ministries, such as interior, defence, foreign affairs and finance.

Ghannouchi's transitional government established three commissions: the High Commission for Political Reform; the Extortion and Repression Commission; and an Embezzlement Commission.[18] Concerns were raised about these commissions' ability to carry out reforms. They had no decision-making authority and were strictly advisory bodies. Not only were their mandates limited, but they also lacked the resources and personnel to undertake their tasks effectively (Paciello 2011). Mohamed Ghannouchi's government's approach to the transition was to gradually move away from the logic of revolutionary rupture towards a more peaceful democratic system based on the consolidation of existing state institutions to guarantee a return to law and order and to avoid a political and security vacuum (ICG 2011; Paciello 2011).

From the start, the interim government faced serious challenges. The young activists rejected it and gathered in protests in Kasbah Square[19] in the centre of Tunis. (Later these demonstrations were called 'Kasbah one'.) The youth refused to recognise any government that included members of the former president's political circle.[20] On 20 January 2011, invigorated by these protests, the opposition formed the 14 January Front, which included progressive left-wing parties, the UGTT and the Bar Association.[21] Led by the radical left, mainly the PCOT and Watad, this broad front echoed the youth protests in calling for the ousting of RCD members from the interim government and the dissolution of all major institutions inherited from the old regime, such as the House of Representatives, the Senate and the Supreme Council of Magistracy.[22]

On 11 February, a broad-based opposition group to the interim government was established, the Conseil National pour la Protection de la Révolution (CNPR). Political parties and groups that were not part of the 14 January Front, including Ettakatol and Ennahdha as well as 28 other organisations, joined together with the Front in the CNPR. This politically diverse coalition asked for official recognition by presidential decree, demanded decision-making powers, and called for the interim government's resignation.[23] Regional branches were established in all governorates.[24] In opposition to what was perceived as a move away from the objectives of the revolution by the interim government, the CNPR joined youth in a second set of demonstrations in February in Kasbah Square (known as 'Kasbah two'), demanding a total ban on the RCD, the full dismantling of the old regime's repressive security apparatus, and a complete break from the old political system by electing a National Constituent Assembly to write a new constitution.

At the same time, divisions arose among the progressive forces because some organisations that had stayed out of the coalition[25] opposed the idea of the CNPR operating as a sort of shadow government. They preferred it to function as a pressure group for open consultations and more inclusive participation in the political process.[26] Members of the CNPR defended the need for the opposition to exercise a decision-making role because, in the absence of a parliament, this was the only way to counteract the government's actions. In an interview with the International Crisis Group (ICG), one of the architects of the CNPR described this vision:

> We speak of the Council as the 'pilot' of the transition. That is to say, in very concrete terms, a Council would have the power of overseeing activities, of proposing changes to them ... [The Council] composed of all parts of civil society and of the opposition, and authorized by presidential decree ... [would have] a political role. A [transitional] government carrying out all of the ... day-to-day management of the state ... [would be] a technocratic government. (ICG 2011: 15)

The CNPR polarised political debate and exacerbated tensions between the interim government and the non-governmental opposition. The debate was structured as a conflict between those forces that sought to dismantle the foundations of the old regime and stay true to the objectives of the revolution and those forces that, alongside Ghannouchi's interim government, were willing to preserve the existing state institutions because they feared a political vacuum and the radicalisation of the street movement. Maya Jribi, leader of the PDP, one of the two opposition parties that took part in the interim government, justified its position:

> The transition must be made on the basis of the present. That means constitutional continuity, with the transition at the institutional level ... This revolution, although popular, did not provide a political direction. We must limit the damage and combine the political break with the past with the existing institutions.[27]

Following the Kasbah demonstrations, and in response to popular pressure, the first interim government was dissolved and a second, more inclusive government was appointed. It had better regional representation, included members of civil society groups, and was less dominated by members of the former regime, but it was still headed by Mohamed Ghannouchi. The opposition parties PDP and Ettajdid remained in the interim government and adopted a minimalist political agenda based on constitutional continuity (ibid.).

Further anti-government demonstrations in late February 2011 called for Ghannouchi's resignation. Young protesters voiced frustration over the slow pace of the transition and accused Ghannouchi of being too close to Ben Ali's regime and unable to effect much-needed changes.[28] As 37-year-old Hichem pointed out: 'The revolution has gotten rid of Ben Ali, but his regime is still in power ... The RCD is still commanding everything.' Other young people made a similar point metaphorically, saying that 'we cut off the head of the beast, but the beast is still very much alive'. The prime minister, Mohamed Ghannouchi, was finally forced to resign on 27 February 2011. Some of his ministers presented their resignations a week later, including those from the PDP and Ettajdid.[29]

The Caïd-Essebsi interim government Beji Caïd-Essebsi,[30] a former minister under Habib Bourguiba, replaced Ghannouchi as interim prime minister. Caïd-Essebsi appeared to be more neutral, as he had bowed out of active politics in 1991 and kept some relative distance from Ben Ali's regime. Soon after taking up his post, he announced the dissolution of Ben Ali's political police and security apparatus, which was a critical issue for the young protesters and the opposition parties. The transitional government also banned from participation in the elections all those who had at some time during the previous ten years held major positions in the RCD. This policy affected members of the interim and former governments, as well as their advisers and staff. Opposition party leaders refused to endorse it, arguing for a more extensive ban of former RCD members from political life. Former leaders and members of the RCD, however, argued that only a court decision could make them ineligible to participate in the forthcoming elections. They held demonstrations in Tunis to protest against the interim government's decision, calling it contrary to the principles of democracy.

Caïd-Essebsi accepted the CNPR coalition's core demand: elections for a National Constituent Assembly that would be empowered to draft a new constitution and then convene parliamentary and presidential elections a year later. In a speech broadcast live on Tunisian television, President Fouad Mebazaa vowed that there would be 'a new political system that definitively breaks with the old regime'. The president's announcement on 3 March of elections for a National Constituent Assembly on 24 July 2011 signalled the victory of the forces united around the CNPR.

Furthermore, in a significant move, the interim prime minister renamed the High Commission for Political Reform 'The Higher Authority for the Realisation of the Objectives of the Revolution, Political Reform and the Democratic Transition' (known in French as ISROR, and abbreviated to 'the Higher Authority'), led by Yadh Ben Achour.[31] The new name was symbolically important because it combined 'revolution', 'reform' and 'transition', demonstrating that the Higher Authority was attempting to go beyond the dichotomy between the position of the CNPR and that of the interim government. Although this compromise initially appeared acceptable to both sides, it led to the breakdown of the political coalition around the CNPR. No sooner had the CNPR won this victory over Ghannouchi's interim government than the coalition dissolved into fractious groupings. While major parties such as Ennahdha, Ettakatol and the CPR and some civil society associations joined the Higher Authority, other CNPR members, especially those of the radical left, were against this move.[32] They preferred the previous form of the CNPR because they did not recognise the legitimacy of the interim government that appointed the Higher Authority; they claimed that the sole source of legitimacy in Tunisia at that time was the revolution itself.[33]

While tensions persisted within the progressive modernist bloc[34] and between it and the conservatives, the project of the Higher Authority moved forward as a workable compromise. This new body was expanded to have both national and regional representation and brought together a variety of actors, including civil society groups and independents. Given the broad spectrum of its membership, the Higher Authority worked through numerous committees and tried to engage in an open, consultative process. Tensions between the right and the left and between Islamists and secularists were apparent, especially in relation to such contentious issues as the 'republican pact', which aimed to ensure that Tunisia would remain a republic and not an Islamic state, the postponement of the elections and funding for political parties. These conflicts led to the withdrawal of Ennahdha from the Higher Authority.

The debates within the Higher Authority were carried out among the political parties, with no direct engagement of the youth movement that had led the revolutionary uprisings either in the capital and other large cities or in the interior regions. The young people who had carried out the revolution did not have a place in the formal political arena and were dissatisfied with the process of political transition. The interim authorities privileged preparing for the elections over addressing profound socioeconomic grievances, which were among the main motivating factors behind the December–January uprising. Many young people became seriously disillusioned. They felt the hardships of joblessness in their everyday lives as the economic situation continued to deteriorate following the revolution. Labour unions frequently conducted strikes and demonstrations over wages, quality of life issues and access to jobs across the country. While President Mebazaa appealed for patience from those demanding better living conditions, Prime Minister Caïd-Essebsi expressed concern that the street protests and social unrest were undermining the government's efforts to encourage foreign investment.

Youth and the transition

Throughout its tenure, Caïd-Essebsi's interim government struggled to earn public trust, especially from the younger generation. Many perceived the interim authorities as acting too slowly on reforms and feared that former regime stalwarts could re-emerge and consolidate their power. A major source of anxiety for the young revolutionaries was that their movement could not negotiate directly with the interim authorities and impose the political and socioeconomic changes they regarded as essential. Street protests remained their primary strategy for putting pressure on the government. Asma Nouira stated this point clearly: 'The lack of revolutionary leadership and the late entry of the political parties into the revolution mean that there is no group able to negotiate political reforms in the revolution's name' (Nouira 2011).

After 14 January 2011, when political forces began to position themselves to play a role in the transition, a few young Tunisians were asked to join newly established governmental bodies. Most of those co-opted into government institutions were middle-class cyber activists who had gained international visibility during the uprising. Sofiane Bel Hadj was appointed to the Higher Authority, and Lina Ben Mhenni became a member of L'Instance Nationale pour la Réforme de l'Information et de la Communication (INRIC). While initially some saw these invitations as a genuine attempt to listen to the concerns of the younger generation and uphold the achievements of the revolution, they realised that their participation offered legitimacy to those institutions, given that the majority of the individuals who controlled those bodies were not directly linked to the revolutionary movement. Soon they became aware of their inability to effect any meaningful changes from within.

Slim Amamou's experience exemplifies this predicament. The 33-year-old cyber activist was the youngest member of the interim government and served as Secretary of State for Youth and Sport under both Ghannouchi and Caïd-Essebsi.[35] Freed after being jailed by Ben Ali's regime for his role in the cyber war, he accepted the appointment because he saw it as his 'duty and an opportunity to participate in rebuilding the country'. Many of his fellow cyber activists opposed his decision, feeling that these token appointments were intended to gain popular support for conservative endeavours. Amamou received several tweets attempting to dissuade him from serving, such as 'As a dear friend, I ask you @slim404 don't accept [the invitation] to collaborate with those who killed Tunisians, stay clean, stay a citizen' and '@slim404 I'm worried you are making the wrong choice here, my friend'. He defended his decision as a necessary compromise: 'It is a temporary government to set up the elections. I'm here to watch and report and be part of the decisions. Not to rule.'

Amamou was a breath of fresh air in a government whose ministers' average age was above 50. He tweeted live from government meetings, even reporting on his clash with his elders over his refusal to wear a tie to cabinet meetings. He persuaded some ministers to set up Facebook pages to make their agencies more accessible. On a more political level, however, Amamou was fully aware of young people's concern about the composition of the transitional government, as well as the importance of the government making an effort to address their immediate problems.

> From my first day, I was received by demonstrations against the interim government. I sympathised with them ... The protests were mainly against the inclusion of ex-RCD people in the government ... From the beginning, my work was to listen to people's demands and try to explain to them that this government's mandate was not to solve problems but to organise the elections. And that was the problem, because to properly organise the elections it was not enough to put in place an electoral code and voting booths; it was fundamental to create the proper context for the elections to happen in a suitable climate. People shouldn't have to vote under stress or fear but in full freedom. That's why it is important to try and resolve their problems ... That was the contradiction in the government's mandate.

The continuation of police violence from the old regime to the new interim government was one of Amamou's main concerns. 'I saw very early on [that] the main problem [was] ... the Ministry of the Interior, especially the police department. The ministry has been corrupt for years ... If there is a ministry that needs to change now it's this one.' The police department, too, 'needs deep reforms in the practices of its employees ... I spoke to the minister of interior [about this] ... but it is not simple,' he wrote on his blog.[36]

Despite the challenges, Amamou's work in the interim government helped produce some positive change. In addition to participating in the preparation of the electoral code, he was instrumental in pushing for the release of unpublished government data on youth unemployment and for the introduction of 'citizen journalism clubs' at youth centres across the country.[37] He took part in important discussions within the cabinet and expressed the hope that his contributions made some difference.

As a cabinet member, Slim Amamou sparked controversy for speaking his mind. For example, he made comments opposing censorship of pornography on the internet and supporting the legalisation of cannabis in the context of discussions about internet censorship.[38] Ahmed, a 59-year-old man from La Marsa, said:

> The young Secretary of State for Youth and Sport should focus on helping young people deal with unemployment and the difficult economic situation, but instead he is interested in the legalisation of drugs and of pornography on the internet ... That's wrong, and against Muslim ways.

Basti, a 25-year-old man, responded:

> Slim didn't say everyone should start smoking cannabis or watch pornography online ... He was just advocating for freedom of choice and freedom of the internet. And he is right, because the government should not decide for adults; the government has to allow people to make their own decisions ... In Tunisia a person can be sentenced to a minimum of one year in prison if found in possession of cannabis.

The conservative forces won when in May 2011 the courts ordered the Tunisian Internet Agency to block access to all sites with pornographic and 'adult' content. This decision was taken following a lawsuit arguing that these sites were contrary to Muslim values and posed a danger to youth. These sites had been available for a short period when censorship of the internet was relaxed following the fall of Ben Ali's regime.[39] Since this ruling, the issue has been widely discussed in the Tunisian blogosphere,[40] and many Tunisian youths see the reimposition of censorship as a major setback in their fight for freedom of expression and civil liberties.

This debate highlights the tensions that exist within Tunisian society in the post-revolutionary period. Young people's liberal views are confronting conservative values in a society that has relied on the state as the main arbiter of moral standards. How much freedom is too much? What is the proper role of the state? Who is responsible for morality?[41] These are only some of the questions that young Tunisians are trying to come to grips with in the post-Ben Ali era.

Although Slim Amamou thought that the third interim coalition government led by Caïd-Essebsi was committed to positive change, democracy and freedom, he was concerned by the fact that censorship of the internet was ongoing, police violence and brutality continued, and the elections were further postponed. These factors, along with pressure from friends and a sense that he had already done as much as he could, were the main reasons for his resignation from the interim coalition government in May 2011. His departure was welcomed both in the Tunisian blogosphere and by young people, who felt that formal politics did not offer space for youth interventions to effect much-needed reforms. When I spoke with Amamou in Tunis in June 2011, he appeared comfortable with his decision to leave and felt that he would be more useful to the revolution by fighting for freedom of expression and civil liberties outside the government. His new agenda was to work with young people and political parties to provide information about the electoral process so that youth would not be exploited in the elections. He wanted to make sure that voters were well informed and that the elections were free and transparent.

Amamou's decision to try to effect change outside governmental structures revealed the disconnect between the aspirations of his generation and formal politics. Indeed, some of the tensions between the transitional government and those who embodied the revolution were resolved only through pressure from the streets. Popular demonstrations eventually forced the interim government to retract some unpopular decisions, especially the political involvement of former RCD members in the democratic transition. However, various groups of young activists were unable to make positive progress towards many of their goals, and tensions between the interim government, opposition political parties and young protesters remained. In fact, those who created the revolution were not the ones who held power and control in the post-revolutionary transition.

Ahmed, a 20-year-old man from Grombelia, voiced an opinion that many of his peers shared:

> They changed Ghannouchi for Caïd-Essebsi, but that doesn't solve anything. Both of them are part of the same old style of politics of Bourguiba and Ben Ali ... They belong to the older generation and they will not bring about the change we need. The youth is not being heard; we are not sufficiently represented in the transitional government.

Aïcha, a 24-year-old woman from Nabeul, seconded his views, asking:

> Where is the youth in this transition process? What I see is the absence of the younger generation from the interim government ... They put a new young Secretary of State for Youth as if young people can only deal with youth stuff, which I find quite patronising ... Young people were in the forefront of this revolution but today they have been put aside. It is the older generation that is in the government and busy creating political parties.

Young people not only distrusted the interim government but also expressed scepticism about the troika government that was later established after the 2011 elections.

Youth's view on the banning of the Constitutional Democratic Rally Before it was banned, the RCD comprised almost 3,000 members, including senior politicians and their aides, civil servants, business people and many ordinary citizens. Immediately after Ben Ali's departure, one of the most hotly debated topics among Tunisians, and among young people in particular, was how to deal with the former members of the RCD, some of whom continued to hold positions of power and influence. In addition to having served as ministers in the interim government, many former RCD members continue to occupy important positions in the state administration, as well as in major businesses. Under Ben Ali, no one was able to succeed professionally without becoming a member of the RCD; the party dominated all aspects of political, economic and social life and there was no separation between the state and the party.

Young radicals wanted to see all former RCD members removed from the government and from politics altogether. Arfaoui, a 23-year-old woman from Bizerte, said:

> Although the RCD has been dissolved after the revolution, its members are still around and they use the disguise of being revolutionaries, democrats, etc. ... And they are now establishing new political parties ... They are putting on a different mask to continue holding power ... They all need to be out sooner rather than later.

In the same vein, 37-year-old Hichem, an architect from Tunis, expressed outrage that 'Tunisia currently has 24 regional governors, and, of those, 17 are former RCD members, even today! This is completely unacceptable! They should all be out and be forbidden to occupy political positions for a period of at least five years.' Many of the young men and women I spoke with believed that the transitional government was not doing enough because 'Beji [the prime minister] himself is protecting his RCD friends and making sure they maintain the power and benefits they enjoyed with Ben Ali'. Zeinab, a 24-year-old woman from Tunis, declared: 'We did not bring about the revolution for this.'

Some young people worried that if the RCD members were all removed at once, the country might collapse. As 31-year-old Nassir from Tozeur pointed out: 'The RCD was not just a political party; the RCD was the state. They not only constituted one-third of all Tunisians but also controlled everything in the country.' Some youths suggested that the new government should phase their withdrawal from political life, starting with the top former RCD members and gradually going down through the ranks as they prepare new people to replace them. Nizar, a 48-year-old man from La Marsa, concurred: 'Ben Ali's political regime was ... entrenched in all aspects of Tunisian society ... We need to find ways of changing the system without destroying the country. We will have to do it step by step.'

Others suggested focusing solely on the 'big fish', the master-minds of the regime, and forgetting about those in the lower echelons who joined the party because it was the only available avenue to upward mobility. Those at the top were trying to re-invent themselves by creating new political parties so they could hold onto power. Young people thought that they ought to be banned from political life, but not the ordinary Tunisians who happened to become RCD members. For example, 22-year-old Nourddine mentioned that one of his relatives 'worked for a state-owned company for many years, but he wasn't getting the promotion he thought he deserved. Only after he accepted the RCD membership card did he manage to get the promotion.' Nourddine's relative was hardly a committed party member. Still, it is difficult to untangle the self-interested motivations and outside pressures that led people to join the RCD. Many young people agreed that all former RCD members should be held accountable, in one way or another, because they benefited from the old regime and were silent about the oppression and repression of the majority.

Youth's disengagement from formal politics

Very few young people have become involved in formal political parties, and the voices of the younger generation remain absent from party politics. Young Tunisians expressed misgivings about the scramble to form political parties and were concerned about attempts by some political forces to profit from the revolution. They were sceptical about entities with such names as '14 January Front' and 'National Council for the Protection of the Revolution', as they believed that most of their members had not earned the right to those titles.

As 21-year-old Zied emphatically asserted:

Ben Ali has been in power for 23 years ... and the generation of our parents did not openly confront the regime and take him out ... Our generation made the revolution and got rid of Ben Ali, and now the older politicians are all running to create parties, taking advantage of the change we created but completely disregarding us.

Young people expressed similar concerns about the new political actors and groupings. Zeinab, a 24-year-old woman from Tunis, said: 'Many of the adults who are forming the new political parties have not participated actively in the revolution. They are seeing this moment as an opportunity to play a role ... but unfortunately many of them are in this for personal gain.' In the same vein, 48-year-old Nizar from La Marsa remarked that 'the rush to establish political parties and gain visibility in the political arena was a process of appropriation of the revolution by the adult population, especially the elites'.

Hichem, the 37-year-old architect from Tunis, was one of the few people who spoke about trying to establish a political party:

Here in Tunisia you are not allowed to get into politics before you are in your sixties. Yes, it's a joke, but you get the point ... All these people in the political parties are too old ... We tried to constitute a political party of the young revolutionaries ... but they found some technicality to block us out.

Explaining that 'ex-RCD people got authorisation to constitute a new political party and we did not', he exclaimed: 'Something is not right here!' Hichem sees himself as politically well informed and calls himself a 'Guevariste', a follower of Che Guevara.

In the Kasserine region, the regional coordinator of Watad is a 31-year-old man whom I met during my second visit to Kasserine in April 2012. Ayman is among the few who believe that in order to effectively intervene in the political process, the young activists have to enter the space of formal party politics. He comes from a very political family; his parents, aunts and uncles were active militants in left-wing parties. 'I know I am an exception, as the majority of youths do not want to be involved in political parties,' he acknowledged. But why aren't young Tunisians more involved? Commenting on his generation's distance from formal politics, Ayman stated:

The attitude of the youth against politics results from the Ben Ali regime's effort to smother young people's critical thinking and their interest in politics. The regime did not want to develop critical political minds that could challenge their policies and ideologies ... Moreover, the political culture developed by the RCD in the last 23 years was not an example most youths want to follow, and young people in this country don't have any experience of a pluralist and democratic political culture.

Many youths mentioned that their reluctance to enter the formal political arena stemmed from their experience of politics during the former regime; they associated politics with dishonesty and corruption. Young people saw their own political struggles as distinct from formal party politics. 'The majority of young people in Tunisia are not interested in politics,' declared 22-year-old Mahmoud from Metline. He continued: 'The revolution? Many of us don't see that as politics per se but a fight for our freedom and for better life opportunities, like jobs and freedom of expression on the internet.' Ben Ali's regime successfully compartmentalised Tunisian society to such an extent that many young people, especially in the more remote areas, do not even consider their protests during the revolution as a political activity.

The exclusion of the young from politics has continued into the current political transition (Collins 2011). Those in impoverished and remote regions perceive the current democratic transition to be a closed, elite-led process that is taking place mainly in the capital. The political transition is widely seen as lacking in transparency. Abidi, a 37-year-old man from Regueb, shared his views: 'We don't know what is going on in Tunis. These people are now playing politics and political parties ... but here we want jobs and bread, not "politicking".' Zarai, a 26-year-old woman from Sidi Bouzid, was equally sceptical about the transition process:

> I don't believe in the politicians. Some of them are the same ones from the time of Ben Ali. Here in Sidi Bouzid we started the protests, but politicians stay in Tunis and don't come here to talk to us to know what we want ... Like before, it is all done and decided in Tunis.

As Raouf, a 29-year-old man from Kasserine, avowed: 'We don't want to create political parties ... We don't want to "do politics"! We want to create associations to help young people, especially unemployed young people.'

Tunisian youth have been socialised in the *maisons des jeunes* (youth centres), which sponsor a variety of cultural and recreational activities and associations. Established by the Bourguiba regime in the 1960s, the youth centres are funded by the state and managed by the Ministry for Youth and Sport. These popular institutions exist all across the country.[42] According to Kamel Dridi, director of the *maison des jeunes* in Tinja, a northern town near Menzel Bourguiba, 'In Tunisia we have about 380 *maisons des jeunes* ... Here young people find a space to be themselves and express themselves through theatre, poetry and other activities that we offer.' As they socialise, train and enjoy the entertainment and cultural events, young people develop their talents in theatre, music, and information and communications technology. In the process, they develop a culture of association and collaborative work.

The regime's intention in establishing and supporting these youth centres appears to have been to occupy young people and divert them from conscious political action. But the regime did not take into account the possibility that this strategy could backfire, as young people congregated, learned organisational and communication skills, and developed a sense of solidarity that they could turn against the regime. Indeed, Dridi explained that:

> the majority of youths who participated in the revolution came from the associative movement developed through the *maisons des jeunes*. These centres helped youth to develop self-expression ... The internet clubs, which are very popular in our centres, provided youth with free access to the cyber world, and that played a major role in the revolution.

While they were not directly involved in party politics, young Tunisians were not apolitical. They developed their political consciousness in the streets and within civil society associations and institutions such as the *maisons des jeunes*, and that experience shaped the ways in which they organised themselves during the revolution and the transition period.

Youth's civic engagement

Tunisian youths have channelled their energy into creating associations as platforms to continue articulating their views and expressing their needs. Since the fall of the old regime, young people have established a wide range of associations. Some focus on political education and some on the creation of job opportunities. Others are primarily cultural and recreational.

The Young Independent Democrats The Jeunes Indépendants Démocrates (JID) was established in January 2011 by a group of university students. Zied, a 22-year-old law student, explained:

> A few days after the fall of Ben Ali, a group of us got together and decided to do something to counteract the massive disinformation and media unreliability that reigned during that

115

period, and we established JID as an association to help provide young Tunisians with more reliable information about the democratic transition.

JID works to offer young Tunisians accurate and up-to-date knowledge about current developments and how these might affect their lives. 'We are confused ... Many of us don't understand what is going on ... JID is putting in place a forum for discussion of issues regarding the revolution and the role that youth can still play in politics and within civil society in general,' asserted Hella, a 22-year-old JID member.

The association is run by an executive committee of 12 members, composed mostly of university students from disciplines as diverse as law, medicine, film studies, languages, computer science and sciences. JID is non-partisan; members of the executive committee cannot be affiliated with any political party. Aziz, age 20, emphasised that:

> although we do not support any political party, we do stand for
> certain principles and values, such as women's equality and
> freedom of expression ... Our association doesn't influence
> young people one way or another; we only offer elements for
> them to reflect upon, analyse, and come to their own con-
> clusions.

JID uses the internet as the main mechanism to reach its young audience. In addition to sponsoring discussion forums, the association synthesises information on political documents, concepts and institutions. In sum, it acts as a channel between young people and the political process.[43]

JID has hundreds of members in universities across the country. The executive committee carries out research, organises documentation, produces a web-based magazine and organises seminars. *Ikhtiar*, its internet-based document containing the platforms of the many political parties putting forward candidates in the elections, enables young people to learn more about the political parties and see which ones address the issues that concern them. JID also has a video programme, funded by UNESCO, that produces short documentaries by young people about their concerns, such as the revolution, employment, migration, education and music. JID organises conferences and workshops on various themes; the most recent considered the issue of funding for political parties. Talking about the future, Zied asserted that: 'JID doesn't want to be transformed into a political party. We only want to see young Tunisians well informed and well prepared to participate in the democratic transition ... This is an essential step for preserving and protecting our revolution.'

Sawty: Sawt Chabeb Tounes Sawty: Sawt Chabeb Tounes, meaning 'My Voice: The Voice of Tunisian Youth', is a non-profit, non-partisan association also established by a group of young Tunisians following the revolution. The association operates under the banner 'The future is in our hands!' Like JID, Sawty aims to provide objective information about democratic ideals and values, political parties and their manifestos, and the role of citizens in the transition process. It is guided by the principles of diversity and freedom of expression. As its website states: 'By engaging with a wide community of young students and professionals both within and outside our organisation, we take advantage of the wealth of ideas and experiences that enable us to broaden our thinking.'[44] The association operates through an informative and interactive website and holds conferences, workshops, interviews and public debates on a variety of topics aimed at creating a well-informed young electorate. It also establishes alliances with other non-governmental organisations, associations and civil society groups sharing similar principles.

Radio Sada Chaanbi in Kasserine Galvanised by the success of the revolution and the fall of Ben Ali's dictatorship, three young men in the west-central Tunisian town of Kasserine, 31-year-old Ali, 29-year-old Walid and 30-year-old Foued, created an online radio station for young Kasserinians, taking advantage of the fact that the region has more than 100,000 active internet users.

117

Teaming up with AVDN Flavius, another group of young people already working in the audiovisual field, they founded Radio Sada Chaanbi, which means 'the echo of Mount Chambi'. This refers to Jebel ech Chaanbi, one of the highest mountains in the country, which stands over Kasserine at over 5,000 feet. The regional commission for culture provided them with studio space and basic equipment, and they were licensed to operate by the governorate of Kasserine.

The main objective of the radio station is to create a platform that focuses on issues of interest to young people in Kasserine. It provides a forum for Kasserinians to communicate among themselves and develop their ideas for making the region more prosperous. Walid explained: 'We decided to focus on Kasserine because our region had been forgotten by the Ben Ali regime, and there isn't much information in the national media about what is happening here. That has not yet changed, so we decided to do it ourselves.' The programmes presented by Radio Sada Chaanbi address social, economic, political, historical and cultural issues of interest to Kasserinians, as well as offering music and sports. The radio aims to provide young people with reliable information and facilitate their participation in the socioeconomic, historical and cultural life of Kasserine, as well as in the political transition and the October elections. Ali explained that this was a vital task because 'there are a lot of rumours circulating and people are misinformed. Rumours often create trouble because this is a moment of a lot of uncertainty ... We want to give young people accurate information about politics and what is going on in Tunisia at the moment.'

The head of political programmes at Radio Sada Chaanbi is a very dynamic woman, 34-year-old Hafsia, who studied law and holds a diploma in audiovisual communication:

> My programme invites lawyers, politicians and other well in-
> formed people to come and explain things to young people. We
> also carry out debates and young people come to express their
> views about various issues ... We have a lot to learn. Tunisians

were cut off from politics during previous regimes, especially young people. We need to learn quickly to be able to make informed choices during the elections.

The radio station organises discussions where young people can share their experiences of the revolution. Another programme, also coordinated by Hafsia, deals with the psychological impact of the revolution on the residents of Kasserine. Some of the most violent confrontations between demonstrators and the police took place here, and many people were injured or killed. Hafsia and her colleagues believe that the people of Kasserine need healing. They need to 'tell their stories, and share their pain with others ... We work with psychologists in this programme,' she remarked.

During the afternoon I spent with the team at Radio Sada Chaanbi, we had interesting discussions and I watched them record their programmes. I also gave them a brief interview about my project and my visit to Tunisia, and to Kasserine in particular. The team aspires to start broadcasting on FM as well, but lacks the resources to do so. Unlike the capital, Kasserine is struggling to attract funding from international organisations and philanthropic institutions. Young people can rely only on themselves and on occasional and limited support from the regional governorate. However, the success of the radio broadcasts is already being felt in the region.

The Open Government initiative OpenGovTn was established in November 2011 by a group of young cyber activists as a nonpartisan initiative to achieve the objectives of transparency and a corruption-free government. Jazem Halioui, one of the young founding members of OpenGovTn, and his colleagues are pushing the transitional authorities in Tunisia to implement the concepts and practices of open governance. This doctrine holds that citizens have the right to access government documents and data to allow for effective public oversight. In its broadest sense, open governance opposes state secrecy.

The young activists behind this initiative want to make sure that the new constitution includes clear clauses to guarantee and protect the principles of open government in Tunisia. The initiative includes both open government and open data components. Halioui explained: 'We are giving the current government a chance to prove its good intentions ... because whether or not it implements effective open governance, we will fight for our rights.' OpenGovTn is fighting to get the government to implement new transparency procedures, 'for example, in making public the administration's budget, with all its details'. It also encourages the involvement of civil society in defining the modalities of good governance and transparency at various levels of state administration, from central government to municipalities. The movement has attracted more than 500 members, including 26 members of the National Constituent Assembly.

OpenGovTn launched a national campaign called '7ell' ('Open') aimed at raising awareness of open government concepts among both the public and decision makers. During the campaign the young people involved with OpenGovTn used social media, online magazines, radio stations and print media to disseminate information creatively about the open government principles. As a result of the enthusiasm and commitment of this campaign, in April 2012 the new National Constituent Assembly approved legislation favouring the public broadcast of the assembly's meetings. The campaign was equally successful in persuading the president and several members of the National Constituent Assembly to publicly support the initiative. These were major victories for OpenGovTn and for the democratic forces advocating transparency and good governance in Tunisia.

Conclusions

The younger generation that led the revolution was not sufficiently organised to articulate an alternative political discourse, stand on its own, and face the challenges of the democratic transition. Divisions among various groups of activist youths emerged during this period, as they did among more experienced political actors. The absence of a common enemy after the overthrow of Ben

Ali's regime diluted their collective force, and differing interests surfaced as the transition took its course. For the impoverished and unemployed youths of the interior of the country, the lack of jobs and regional economic imbalances are at the core of their battle against the establishment. Urban elite youths, on the other hand, focus their struggle on demands for individual civil liberties and freedom of expression in the real and virtual worlds. Aziz Amami, a prominent cyber activist from Tunis, stated that:

> Whatever the next leaders of the country do, I believe there will not be compromises on the question of individual liberties. And if that's not the case, people will immediately go back to the streets. The message is now clear: as long as our rights aren't respected, we'll never stop.[45]

His priorities differ markedly from those of unemployed youth in underdeveloped regions, which are focused on getting jobs and better living conditions, but they too think of going onto the streets as their primary form of political expression and engagement.

Even though young people exhibited distinct priorities during the transition, they all seem to oppose the idea of entering formal political structures. Young Tunisians continue to participate actively in street politics and civil society initiatives and contribute to building a democratic culture. Young people remain an important force to be reckoned with, even though they are struggling to find a place in this rapidly changing and somewhat confusing political environment. Will the activities of their civil society associations be enough to promote change and build a new political culture? Will their absence from formal politics allow conservative forces to annihilate the fragile but critical achievements of the revolution? Will they continue to go back to the streets every time their aspirations are not met? Or will they create new forms of effective political engagement and dialogue with those in power? Only time will tell how the new Tunisia will shape up and how effectively young Tunisians will be able to intervene in this process. The next chapter examines the elections and youth participation in the electoral process.

5 | Elections

Caïd-Essebsi's interim government decided to postpone the elections, initially scheduled for 24 July 2011, to 23 October 2011 because of delays in passing the new electoral law. This postponement worried many young people because it allowed the 'old guard' to prolong its control over the country. Despite the challenges it faced, the Higher Authority managed to move forward with the preparations for the elections. In April 2011, it passed a critical gender equality bill, declaring that men and women must be represented in equal numbers as candidates on electoral lists.[1] It constituted the Instance Supérieure Indépendante pour les Elections (ISIE) to guide and organise the electoral process. The ISIE carried out voter registration, organised training for poll workers, procured election materials, and set up the complex logistical arrangements required to guarantee credible, transparent and fair elections.[2]

On 23 October 2011, Tunisians elected 217 representatives to the National Constituent Assembly. This body was charged with appointing a new interim government, rewriting the nation's constitution to embody the aspirations of the revolution, and preparing for presidential and parliamentary elections in 2013. The decision not to hold immediate presidential and/or parliamentary elections and instead to elect a transitional National Constituent Assembly was greeted as a victory by young revolutionaries who demanded a fundamental break with the past. Indeed, the interim government's decision appeared to respond to the public's desire for radical political change based on a process of broad consultation.

These were the first free elections since independence, and Tunisians were expected to turn out in large numbers. Despite an intense campaign to persuade citizens to cast their ballots, however, the turnout – especially among youth – was significantly lower than anticipated. The sheer number of participating parties was one of the main challenges for the electorate. The progressive parties – socialist, liberal and democratic – failed to run together, thereby dispersing the votes of their supporters. This fragmentation provided a significant advantage to the Islamists. Ennahdha drew support from all the Islamist forces around it and won the largest number of seats in the National Constituent Assembly. With 89 seats and the support of smaller parties, it was able to form a new government.

This chapter examines youth participation in the elections and the significance of the low youth vote. It discusses the challenges young people faced in navigating the maze of political parties and describes their engagement in voter education during the electoral campaign. Finally, it considers the election results and the constitution of the coalition government. The main argument of this chapter is that young Tunisians' absence from the polls was due to their conviction that neither the established nor the emergent political forces would steer the country towards positive change. Campaign discourse turned on issues of identity, revolving around debates between secularism and Islamism, rather than addressing the key concerns of the revolution – unemployment, social justice and civil liberties.

Low voter registration

Despite their active participation in the revolution, the youth vote was significantly lower than initially projected. Young people's reluctance to register for the elections was a cause for concern. According to the ISIE, by 30 July only 23.5 per cent of Tunisia's 7 million eligible citizens had registered to vote, and the largest proportion of those registered were between the ages of 41 and 51.[3] That situation prompted the ISIE to extend the deadline a few weeks until 14 August 2011.[4] Although the numbers rose, nearly half of Tunisians of voting age, especially the young, chose not to register.

The number of political parties and candidates to choose from bewildered many young people. More than 100 parties were registered, and the 1,500 electoral lists they put forward included some 11,000 candidates.[5] The proliferation of parties with very similar messages made it difficult to distinguish between them. Most of the new political parties did not have clear political messages or concrete programmes of action, making it hard for the electorate to understand their positions. Several parties issued vague and general statements in order to present themselves as centrist. Young people saw most of the emerging political forces, especially those that rebranded the former Rassemblement Constitutionnel Démocratique (RCD), as opportunistic enterprises trying to cash in on the revolution. Those who had actively participated in the uprising were very distrustful of most political parties and decided early on not to take part in what they saw as a travesty.

Marouen, a 28-year-old man from Metline, explained that: 'I did not bother to register because I knew I was not going to vote ... I didn't believe the political parties were willing and capable of resolving the unemployment problem and sort out the economy ... It was all about them and not about the people.' Zeitouna, a 29-year-old woman from Le Kef, echoed his remarks:

> I too did not register and did not vote. I don't trust any of our politicians because politics is a dirty game ... They promise you many things they know they won't be able to do. It's all election 'bla-bla' to get people's votes ... All they care about is getting into power.

Houssem, a 28-year-old cyber activist from Kasserine, went so far as to say that: 'I knew the elections would be a charade because all these people who created parties were not involved in the revolution; they all wanted to replace Ben Ali and would end up doing the same thing.' Many young people I interviewed during my second visit to the country in 2012 shared similar views.

Young people's shift from fervent engagement in the revolution to apparent lack of interest in the elections may be attributed to a number of factors: their frustration over the marginalisation of critical issues such as unemployment; their alienation from the new political discourses that became prominent in the campaign; and their disapproval of politicians' heated competition for posts that conferred personal power and influence. Moreover, young people's disengagement may also have stemmed from their frustration with the interim government's failure to begin making much-needed changes. The socioeconomic situation in the country deteriorated further after the fall of the regime, and young people in particular were seriously affected by rising unemployment. Many of the grievances that brought them out onto the streets – unemployment, corruption, lack of freedom of expression, and exclusion from political decisions – were not addressed.

The political messages of the electoral campaign and the programmes of the political parties failed to effectively articulate the economic and social concerns that youth had presented during the revolution. According to Béatrice Hibou, Hamza Meddeb and Mohamed Hamdi, 'these economic and social considerations were set out hazily [in political party programmes] with general statements ... and without any analysis of the origin of this situation, systematic critiques of past options, or concrete proposals to address socioeconomic demands in depth' (Hibou et al. 2011: 92).

Instead, the new political forces prioritised debates on secularism and the place of religion in society. Mohammed, a 31-year-old from Tunis, affirmed that:

> The revolution was not about cultural or religious identity. Muslims, Christians and Jews[6] were together against Ben Ali and against lack of employment and civil liberties ... I remember being in the Avenue Habib Bourguiba on 14 January 2011 and hearing an isolated voice say *Allāhu Akbar* [Allah is great] after the news of Ben Ali's departure. That was the only time I heard the invocation of God during the entire period of protests.

The youth-led revolution was neither Islamist nor anti-Islamist; from its genesis, the movement did not treat religion as an issue.

To young people, both the old and new political parties appeared to be disconnected from the central issues that animated the revolution. When they entered the political scene, political parties debated with one another, rather than engage in dialogue with the young activists who had led the popular uprising. Established parties did not take the time to examine the broader socioeconomic situation and try to understand the new political reality in Tunisia. Conservative and Islamist parties saw the post-revolutionary moment as an opportunity to advance their anti-secularist and traditionalist agendas, while progressive and leftist parties used it to push forward their modernist and secularist ideologies.

Young people's sense of being neglected by politicians was especially evident in the poorest regions of the country. In Sidi Bouzid, Atef, a 22-year-old unemployed man, declared that nothing had changed for him, his family or his neighbours.

> We went out to the streets and drove Ben Ali out of power, but our life is not better. I took a bullet during the revolution that is still lodged in my body ... It was here in Sidi Bouzid that it all started, but we have not benefited from the revolution. We are worse off than we were before: unemployment is much higher now; factories are closing down, and those who had jobs have lost them. I don't know what the politicians in Tunis are doing.

Young people became very sceptical about the way in which the electoral process was being managed by the interim government. They believed that the revolution was theirs but the democratic transition was dominated by an older generation of politicians who were completely out of sync with the issues of the day. Some of my interlocutors were adamant that this amounted to a counter-revolution by remnants of the old regime, repackaged in new parties, to try to maintain the status quo with minor cosmetic changes. Political scientist Béatrice Hibou concurs with that view, remarking that Tunisia is indeed 'facing a conflict between the social movement [the revolution] and the [political] system, which seeks to perpetuate itself, though relieved of the most excessive forms of predation and repression. In the government, the administration, the justice system, it is largely the personnel of the former regime who are in place.'[7]

This realisation led some young activists to call for a boycott of the elections. Lina Ben Mhenni, a 27-year-old cyber activist, declared: 'I do not think we can start something new while keeping the old [RCD] elements. To talk of a revolution we have to break totally with the past and with the old regime.'[8] Indeed, she had no confidence in any political forces: 'The only thing that counts [for them] is getting elected, nothing else.'[9] Not all young revolutionaries agreed with this position, however. Another prominent cyber activist, 32-year-old Aziz Amami, warned that:

> If we don't participate in the process, we must be ready to accept the consequences. We have two choices: either we bring about change or we submit ourselves to it. Every citizen living in a free society has a right and a certain obligation to choose. The Constituent Assembly, in spite of its shortcomings, offers us this possibility.[10]

Facebook and Twitter were the main media through which the youth engaged in debates among themselves about the elections and the future of the country. On popular Facebook pages such as 'Tunis', which has more than 750,000 followers, they talked about how they were no longer listened to. One visitor to the Tunis page wrote:

> The young people who initiated the revolution and saw it to its conclusion are not represented in the political council and they have been let down by the political system and all the political groups and parties are not working on a solution for their problems or a better future for young people.[11]

Discussions on social media sites focused on the large number of parties with no clear political programme, the slow pace of change since the revolution, rising unemployment, distrust of politicians, and mounting tensions about the role of religion in post-revolutionary Tunisian society.

Ben Mhenni reported that a Facebook event was created on 25–26 July 2011 for young bloggers and internet users to register for the elections. More than 309 bloggers participated, some urging young people to take part in the elections and others calling for a boycott. One of the bloggers quoted by Ben Mhenni said:

> I registered my name on the electoral list. My family members, my neighbours and my friends did the same. We registered despite everything: despite the incredible number of political parties and their unconvincing political rhetoric, despite the lawlessness ... despite the high cost of living and deterioration of purchasing power, despite ... the continuing unemployment.

In response to other bloggers recommending that the youth neither register nor vote, one commented that to boycott the elections was to take a negative position and 'negativism and resignation do not build a country'. A spokesperson for Takriz addressed the Tunisian government, saying: 'You want elections? Give us justice, transparency, financial control on the parties, a less absurd electoral code and foreign controllers.'[12]

Despite their misgivings about the elections, many young Tunisians did not shy away from engaging in the electoral process through their associations.

Youth voter education initiatives

The election campaign was an opportunity for citizens to be educated about democracy and for political parties to present their programmes to the electorate. Young people were very active in civil society associations that sought to educate voters. Most importantly, they acted through their own associations to reach out to other youths, offering them the tools they needed to make informed choices. From the numerous initiatives organised by youth groups in various regions, I have selected four for detailed discussion.

The Citizen Bus The Citizen Bus project was established by a coalition of civil society organisations to promote democratic values in preparation for the elections. Those involved included the Union des Tunisiens Indépendants pour la Liberté, Sawt Chebeb Tounes (Voice of Tunisian Youth), Tounesa (Tunisian), ACT

Khammem ou Qarrer (Act, Reflect and Decide), Women and Dignity, and the Tunisian UNI group (itself a coalition). Realising that the population, especially youth, needed substantive knowledge about how to participate in democratic elections and to develop an understanding of the complex political landscape that emerged following the revolution, they organised three caravans of buses to go out across the country and meet potential voters in their neighbourhoods, workplaces, schools and marketplaces in order to promote the exercise of participatory citizenship.

The educational campaigns of the Citizen Bus were organised in two phases: the first focused on voter registration and the second on the importance of voting. Teams of trained activists, mainly young people, travelling in the buses organised presentations and discussions with various groups of people – young and old, men and women – across the country. They talked about the meaning of the elections, especially the role of the National Constituent Assembly in rewriting the constitution, as well as about specific electoral matters, such as who is eligible to vote, how and where to vote. They showed short videos on large screens on themes such as 'Why it is important to vote' and simulated the voting procedure using polling booths, ballot boxes and ballot papers. Music and other forms of entertainment attracted the crowds and kept them interested. The activists answered people's questions, distributed flyers with simplified information about the voting process in Arabic, and encouraged people to register and vote on election day.

The Citizen Bus project did not represent any party or political tendency. It took care to provide neutral information to the electorate and prepare them to vote freely for any party of their choosing. Between July and October, the caravans covered all the electoral districts in the country. The populace's response to this initiative was remarkable. The Citizen Bus trained hundreds of young activists, and its rallies attracted thousands of participants.

'Democracy in Action: Our Vote is Our Voice!' The Ali Belhouane Youth Cultural Club in Tunis undertook a project called

'Democracy in Action: Our Vote is Our Voice!' to teach Tunisians between the ages of 18 and 25 to become informed actors in the electoral process. Participants in this training programme were young men and women leaders who represented the different regions of the country. The five-week training programme conducted in the capital covered such topics as democratic culture, participatory citizenship, the electoral process, the role of the interim government and the task of the National Constituent Assembly, as well as strategies for mass mobilisation. Participants attended seminars and workshops presented by politicians, university professors, civil society activists and election experts. They also visited different neighbourhoods, state institutions, the headquarters of political parties, media organisations and major civil society groups. The young people came from diverse socioeconomic and political backgrounds, and the programme was non-partisan. When they returned home to their regions, these young men and women trained other youths and worked to motivate them to participate in the election.

Tarek, a 28-year-old trainer who was in charge of the cultural programme for the trainees, confessed that, despite being active in this initiative and encouraging others to vote, in the end he himself did not vote. 'I couldn't identify one single party that I felt represented my interests. The majority of the parties were externally funded and I was uncomfortable with that because they had to also represent the interest of their donors.' The fact that political parties could be beholden to their financial contributors made many other young people uncomfortable as well.

The Ikhtiar platform The Jeunes Indépendants Démocrates (JID) sought to provide young people with the tools they needed to exercise their agency as well-informed citizens during the democratic transition. It established Ikhtiar as a platform to present the different political positions and socioeconomic policies advocated by the parties. The website ikhtiartounes.org allowed potential voters to identify which political parties were closest to their own ideas and values.[13] By responding 'agree', 'disagree' and 'no idea' to a quick questionnaire with 30 main commitments espoused by political parties[14] in key areas such as the political system, human rights, institutional reform, the economy, transitional justice and the environment, young voters were able to match their political views to particular parties. The platform was opened to all Tunisians. The JID, together with the experts who designed the site, made sure that Ikhtiar was not a partisan internet tool. ikhtiartounes.org was one of the most popular websites of this kind during the campaign, with 70,000 visitors, and media reports were full of praise for this initiative.

My Voice youth debates In an attempt to set the political agenda and to bring forward the concerns of youth, the youth association Sawty: Sawt Chabeb Tounes (My Voice: The Voice of Tunisian Youth) organised debates and discussion sessions for young people with representatives of political parties and other personalities that focused on the younger generation's key concerns. For example, in April 2011 it hosted a debate on youth employment that brought students into dialogue with leaders of six political parties: the Forum Démocratique pour le Travail et les Libertés, the Parti Communiste des Ouvriers de Tunisie, the Parti Républicain, Ennahdha, the Parti du Centre Social and the Congrès pour la République (CPR). The students engaged political party leaders about their economic programmes and the steps they envisaged taking to alleviate the massive levels of youth unemployment. Party leaders explained their positions and tried to address youth's concerns. They mentioned such policy reforms as including the fundamental right to work in the new constitution, reforming employment laws, adjusting the definition of employment, and creating a national centre for employment. On a more practical level, they advocated encouraging small entrepreneurial projects, supporting young people in their job searches, reinforcing professional training and linking it directly to the needs of the job market, and putting an end to corruption and favouritism in the allocation of jobs.

While these ideas sounded sensible, many students who

attended the debate, and other youths I spoke to, saw them as empty promises that were not based on clearly articulated political and socioeconomic programmes. To be effective, such proposals had to take into account larger structural challenges, including the economy, reform of the educational system, migration policy, the national budget and the financial resources that the implementation of such measures would require. Ultimately, real reforms that would solve the unemployment problem would have to involve changes in Tunisia's current economic development model.

The rallies, training, internet tools, debates and discussions that youth associations organised during the electoral campaign certainly contributed to creating a better-informed and politically savvy young electorate. The fact that so many youths ended up not casting their ballots is, perhaps, a demonstration of their political education and a statement that they were expecting much more than what was being offered.

The political campaign

During the election campaign, questions of cultural identity and the debate between the values of religion and secularism overrode all the important and thorny issues regarding the economy, unemployment, justice and political reconciliation. Islamists emphasised their past histories of struggle. Ennahdha built its political campaign on respect for Islamic values, a return to morality and the ending of corruption, which it described as 'thieves holding public positions'. This message had broad appeal, since Ben Ali and his entourage had behaved like a mafia and had repressed Islamic values. With this message, Ennahdha hoped to be seen as representing a break with the past and as standing for moral righteousness.

The secularist parties became fixated on criticising Islamic extremism, while they remained oblivious to the need to better articulate the ideological underpinnings of secularism. The fact that the progressive bloc was divided into several political formations with similar programmes but no common way forward greatly limited their effectiveness. According to some analysts, the campaign waged by the progressive parties was less coherent than that of Ennahdha, which presented clear and simple messages, such as the promise to restore people's dignity by allowing them to profess their religion publicly. The progressive secularist movement tried to counteract the Islamists' position, but, as Salma, a 23-year-old law student from Tunis, pointed out: 'The left was not savvy in its approach against the Islamist discourse ... [and] ended up being seen as pro-Western and anti-Islamist ... That was not a good political stand to take in a country where the majority is Muslim.'

Political parties held rallies all over the country to disseminate their political agendas and persuade voters. Of all the political parties, Ennahdha managed to reach out most effectively. It opened offices in most districts and ran candidates in every governorate. Ennahdha was also reported to be the best funded party. It had enough money to distribute T-shirts, professionally printed pamphlets and flyers, and snacks and bottled water to the crowds at rallies. Its unprecedented level of financial resources led many Tunisians to wonder about the sources of its money. Some thought that its funds came from rich countries in the Persian Gulf, particularly Qatar and Saudi Arabia. Others thought that some wealthy members made large contributions and that many grassroots supporters made small donations. The party, however, never disclosed its funding sources.

There were several other allegations about the behind-the-scenes influence of money on the race. The Union Patriotique Libre (UPL), a new party founded by expatriate Tunisian businessman Slim Riahi, who made his fortune in the oil industry in Libya, was another big spender. Riahi, who used his own fortune to bankroll the campaign, had no previous history in politics, and his centrist party appeared to have no discernible political ideology. What it lacked in history and ideology was compensated for by exposure. The UPL outspent every other party in advertising and used its extensive resources to run a campaign that reached the country's most marginalised areas. Claims were made about Slim Riahi's close friendship with Imed Trabelsi, nephew of the former first lady, Leila Ben Ali, and the UPL was criticised as a neo-RCD party.[15] The Parti Démocrate Progressiste (PDP) also advertised heavily on billboards around the country in a full Western-style political campaign. Although it never disclosed its funding sources, wealthy businessmen from the former dictator's business elite allegedly financed its lavish campaign.

These allegations launched a debate about campaign financing and the role of foreign and 'tainted' money in the elections. Many young Tunisians worried that 'subtle forces were trying to pull the strings from behind the scenes, in part through political money'.[16] In response, the Higher Authority imposed rules limiting campaign spending and banning foreign contributions. While several parties reacted positively to these measures, Ennahdha decided to withdraw from the Higher Authority on the grounds that the commission was overstepping its mandate and such restrictions would make it impossible for the party to reach voters abroad.[17] Young voters were fully aware of these debates and the tensions between political forces, which deepened their disillusionment with politics and further alienated them from the electoral process.

The electoral campaign was also marred by reports of political parties trying to bribe voters with money and gifts. The French newspaper *Le Quotidien* claimed that the Tunisian election campaign was riddled with instances of direct or indirect vote buying, even comparing it with Bulgaria, where 'the buying and selling of votes is a true national sport'.[18] The wealthier parties did not hesitate to use their resources to fund pseudo-social service projects in order to be seen as Good Samaritans. Ennahdha is reported to have bought votes by paying for weddings – for example, they funded a group wedding for several couples in the town of Den Den – and by distributing free meat for the celebrations at the end of Ramadan. They appear to have also offered money to help people start small businesses, pay debts and so on. Amani, a 22-year-old computer science student from Kasserine, declared:

I did not vote. Initially I thought I would vote for Ennahdha, but after seeing how they operated I decided not to vote for them. They were buying people's votes; I saw it with my own eyes ... I couldn't find any other party to vote for because in the end they are all corrupt.

Several other parties on the left, centre and right faced similar accusations of vote buying. Even political parties without significant financial resources made small gifts. 'In order to find favour with the people, they have graciously [offered] ... 5 dinar [about US$3] charge cards for mobile phones'[19] to participants in their rallies. Ammar, a 27-year-old from Sousse, remarked:

I am not against elections and people exercising their choice, but my choice was not to vote because I found that most political parties were not honest with the voters; they bought people's votes and made promises they could not deliver ... When I realised that it was all a political game of money, influence and quest for power, I decided to stay out of it.

These corrupt practices discouraged many young voters who saw the political parties' programmes as full of empty promises rather than substantive proposals. With such weak political manifestos and meaningless slogans, vote buying and bribery became their main strategy to attract voters. After observing these problems, some of the young people who had registered and intended to participate in the elections decided not to cast their ballots. They became disillusioned with the electoral process because of the lack of serious political debate and the prevalence of dishonesty during the campaign.

Election day

On 23 October 2012, Tunisians cast their votes to elect 217 representatives to the National Constituent Assembly. Election day was marred by reported violations of electoral rules, although these incidents were not considered serious enough to compromise the legitimacy of the elections. On polling day, the ISIE decided to post a live map of voting irregularities and encouraged voters to send

SMS messages reporting any violations or logistical difficulties they faced or witnessed. Some parties continued the campaign beyond its official end, staging meetings and chanting slogans outside polling stations; some put up posters on unapproved sites. There were also cases of intimidation and attempts to influence voters. The voting process itself did not always go smoothly. There were several reports of polling stations that were understaffed and had long queues or closed early. Some were disorganised, leading to difficulties in finding the appropriate lists of voters and of eligible candidates. The disarray and delays reported at some polling places might have contributed to young voters leaving without casting their votes, albeit in relatively small numbers.

A number of university students registered to vote in their home districts during the summer vacation, but on election day they were at university in Tunis or in other major cities and were unable to cast their ballots outside their electoral district. Arwa, a 24-year-old student, stated that although she registered for the elections, in the end she did not vote because she was studying in a different city from her home town where she registered. She was initially thinking of voting for the CPR party, which she believed had a clear programme, but she was not 100 per cent convinced and decided not to vote. Although it was possible to change one's voting location, as the electoral commission amended the rules and announced that anyone with a national identity card would be able to cast a ballot, many young Tunisians, like Arwa, did not vote.

Despite being involved in the electoral process as a poll observer, 27-year-old Dhia abstained from voting because for him no political party was good enough. 'The results are what I'm worried about the most. Islamists are obviously the most popular and if they don't win, protests will be everywhere; people will think the elections were fake,' said Dhia. He also believes the National Constituent Assembly cannot possibly complete the work of writing a constitution within its one-year timetable, so the situation will keep getting worse and no significant changes will be made. Similarly, Hajer, a 22-year-old student, did not cast her ballot. She stated that: 'I am religious, but Islamic parties do not represent me. Contradictions in their speeches made me lose all faith in them.' Hajer preferred not to vote because she is not sure that politicians will stay true to their promises.[20]

Some young men and women who showed up to vote cast blank ballots because they could not bring themselves to support any of the parties that were standing for election. Asma, a 24-year-old student from Gabès, explained her rationale: 'Although I was not prepared to choose any of the political parties in the list I wanted to be able to exercise my right to take part in these historic elections ... The blank vote allowed me to do so without compromising my integrity.' It is clear that the vast majority of the young people who decided not to vote or to cast blank ballots did so deliberately, as an expression of their disapproval of the political system as a whole. Young Tunisians have little faith in politicians' willingness or ability to respond to their concerns regarding the state of the economy, unemployment and civil liberties.

Election results

Official results indicated that there were about 7,569,000 Tunisians who were eligible to vote. Of these, 4,123,602 (54.47 per cent) actually registered to vote, and only 3,205,845 of those registered cast their vote (77.75 per cent). An additional 496,782 people who had not registered ended up voting, making the total number of voters 3,702,627, which represents a 48.9 per cent turnout.[21]

Among that 48.9 per cent, the youth constituted a small proportion of the voting population as many young people abstained from voting. In addition to voters who failed to show up at the polling booths, blank or spoiled ballots accounted for 2.3 per cent and 3.6 per cent of the votes respectively.[22] The rate of participation appears to be surprisingly low, especially for young people who had turned out massively in protests against the regime. Also, there was the expectation that, because these were the country's first free and democratic elections after the longstanding dictatorship, people would turn out to vote in large numbers.

The significant levels of voter abstention from the elections may reflect the fact that the revolution clearly articulated political demands for freedom and democracy, with socioeconomic demands for jobs, development equity and a future for young people. However, ten months after the fall of the dictatorship, the interim authorities had failed to provide a sense of optimism about the future of the country. While Tunisians had achieved democratic freedoms, they felt that their socioeconomic demands were far from being addressed; not that they expected change overnight, but they had no trust in the willingness and ability of the interim government or of any of the existing political parties to address their concerns.[23]

In August 2011, the Institut de Sondage et de Traitement de l'Information Statistique (ISTIS or Statistic Data Processing Institute) conducted a national opinion poll with Tunisians from various regions and backgrounds that revealed that 70 per cent of them were dissatisfied with the performance of the political parties; 57 per cent could not name a political party they supported or liked; and over 60 per cent were dissatisfied with the economic situation of the country.[24] Indeed, many young people said they were disillusioned with the political parties and the system as a whole, and had little faith in the politicians' campaign promises about economic equity, prosperity and civil liberties.[25]

Ennahdha won 41 per cent of the total vote, and secured 89 (41 per cent) of the 217 seats in the National Constituent Assembly. Many of my interlocutors credited Ennahdha's victory to the older and more conservative people from the impoverished regions that were marginalised and repressed by the former regime. For them, voting for the Islamist party represented a real break from the past and the return of Islam to public life. But Ennahdha was also able to win the support of some young people, especially those from the interior areas of the country. During my visits to Kasserine and Sidi Bouzid, I met several young people who voted for Ennahdha; they resented both Ben Ali's assault on Islam and the underdevelopment of their regions.

How did Ennahdha win the elections? There is no doubt that religion played an important part in Ennahdha's victory, giving it a significant edge over other political parties. In a country that had been ruled by an autocratic regime, religion was a language that voters across the country could understand, trust and identify with. Ennahdha portrayed an image of its adherents as victims by highlighting the repression of its militants and the former regime's ban on the party, which provided it with unparalleled credibility. In fact, Ennahdha's leader, Rached Ghannouchi, has been quoted as saying that the Tunisian people voted for his party out of 'recognition of its oppression' as well as because it offered morality in politics and economics. As Ayman, a 31-year-old man from Kasserine, pointed out: 'For the majority of Tunisians religion is still the only source of morality. Non-religious people and non-practising Muslims are generally perceived as having no moral principles guiding their lives.' Voting for the Islamists was presented as a way of guaranteeing that those in power would govern with integrity and follow the moral principles of Islam.

Moreover, the generous financial support that Ennahdha reportedly received from Qatar and other countries in the Persian Gulf allowed it to reach out to voters in the remote and marginalised areas that had long been ignored by secularist regimes. People in these areas were terrified by the prospect of the return of the same corrupt political class, and for them Ennahdha represented the most wholehearted rejection of the old political order. Its financial resources enabled it to establish a strong organisation and conduct charitable projects to support voters, which many condemned as vote buying.

Equally critical was Ennahdha's ability to expand its membership substantially by reaching out to returned exiles, Muslim militants imprisoned by Ben Ali and underground pro-Islamist activists. Ennahdha gathered almost all the Islamist forces into its ranks and presented a united front to the electorate. 'We want to enter modernity as Muslims, not unbelievers,' said Rached Ghannouchi, driving home the perception that non-Islamist parties do not believe in Islam and that secularism is antagonistic to Islam.

Elections

The progressive secular parties played into this message. They ran their campaigns against Ennahdha, rather than explaining their own policy agendas. Arguably, they would have been better served by delivering a programmatic platform suggesting that they were just as clean and uncorrupted as Ennahdha, rather than the perceived anti-Islamist discourse they adopted. Their abstract rhetoric about modernity and secularism tended to alienate large sections of the population located in the marginalised central, western and southern regions. As Salma, a law student from Tunis, emphasised: 'The left failed to present a secular discourse that would make sense to the majority of Tunisians. They took a very Western approach by positing a complete dissociation between religion and the state ... and that did not work in their favour.'

Indeed, Tunisian secularists' critique of the Islamists was based on a reiteration of the modernist and secular discourse of Bourguiba that was continued by Ben Ali. They have not developed a strong critique of the old brand of secularism, nor have they distanced themselves sufficiently from the political projects that alienated many Tunisians in the past. In order to be acceptable and sustainable, Tunisian secularist discourse will have to break decisively from its perceived complicity with the West, and especially from French cultural influence. 'The Muslim middle class, who want the freedom to profess their religion, is not necessarily extremist. They needed to be reassured that society would respect their religion and who they are, and so far the secularist progressive bloc has not been able to do this,' argued Salma. She contended that the main challenge for the secularist movement in Tunisia was to try to inscribe a discourse dealing with human rights, women's rights and civil liberties within Arab Muslim traditions and references so that it could be understood and accepted by the masses.

Several young women and men agreed that, in particular, the dissociation of women's rights from Westernisation was essential to make the topic specific to Tunisia. Ennahdha was able to take advantage of this issue by reinforcing the idea that the secularist movement is anti-Islamic, heavily influenced by the West, and detached from the problems of the people. It also drove home the idea that secularists are bad Muslims, unbelievers and atheists.

Compounding their problems, the internal tensions and disagreements among the progressive parties espousing a secular agenda prevented them from presenting a united front to compete against the well-funded, well-organised and 'wronged' Islamists. Socialists, liberals and democrats were fragmented. The minor differences in their programmes confused the electorate and diluted their support. Some of the most prominent progressive candidates had trouble pointing out what distinguished them from their opponents in other progressive parties. Cherifa, a 21-year-old medical student from Tunis, analysed the situation:

> Despite sharing the same political views, my two best friends and I ended up voting for three different parties ... We did not discuss which parties we would vote for, and we only realised that after the fact ... Some progressive parties had very similar messages, but at the same time they were incredibly fragmented and that did not help them in the end.

Columnist Nizar Bahloul wrote in the Tunisian magazine *Business News* that while Ennahdha 'managed to penetrate the heartlands of Tunisia and the remote neighbourhoods ... [the progressive] parties were engaged in selfish wars, quarrelling over who should be heading the electoral list'.[26] These internal quarrels made a bad impression on voters, feeding into perceptions that progressives were disorganised, were motivated by personal ambition, and lacked clarity about what they stood for.

The fact that the progressive parties were less successful in raising funds and had insufficient resources to reach out to people in remote areas also hurt them. They were unable to communicate their vision to those who knew least about them and could not counteract the lavish gifts the Islamists were able to make to the electorate in the most impoverished areas of the country. All these factors combined to weaken the progressive parties and provide an edge to the Islamists at the ballot box.

Elections

Conclusions

The underlying reason for the low turnout among young people appears to be that the political discourse that guided them during the revolution was subverted by the elites that rushed into the political void created by Ben Ali's departure. The pragmatic discourse of the revolution that was centred on the disenfranchisement of youth and on their demands for jobs, better life conditions, social justice and freedom of expression disappeared during the electoral campaign. Instead, the dominant discourses adopted by the new and old political forces, both on the left and on the right, focused mainly on issues of identity, i.e. Islamism versus secularism or conservatism versus modernism.

This extremely polarised debate pitted the progressive and left-aligned parties that pushed for a modern and secular Tunisian state against the conservative and Islamist parties that vowed to bring Tunisia back to its cultural traditions and Islamic roots. Significantly, even these issues were often poorly articulated. Many observers became convinced that the campaign was motivated by personal ambitions and party quarrels and was conducted with complete disregard for the best interests of the majority of Tunisians. Young people felt equally let down by the quite different political forces that dominated the interim government and the electoral process and could not identify a political party that fully represented their concerns and addressed the socioeconomic predicament of most Tunisians.

While these factors contributed to the low youth turnout, youth associations played an important role in voter education during the electoral campaign. Young people cannot be discounted as irrelevant to the political process. They are focusing their energy on street politics and independent youth associations in a variety of areas, from culture, recreation and sport to social and civic activism.

Clearly, young Tunisians do not believe in the old political models but at the same time they have not yet been able to articulate a new model. And so, as the wave of mass struggles recedes, older animosities and conflicts between political parties resurface and occupy the political scene. In the meantime, young people are faced with the same framework of multiparty elections in which, once again, political parties step into the breach and play the same old game, completely disregarding the ideals that animated the youth revolution. But young Tunisians continue to put pressure on the tripartite coalition government to deliver on the issues that matter most to them. The following chapter considers the challenges and performance of the new establishment: the troika government and the National Constituent Assembly.

6 | New government, new constitution

Ennahdha's victory marked a new phase in Tunisia's transition to democracy. With 89 seats in the National Constituent Assembly (NCA), Ennahdha became the dominant party. The two runners-up were the Congrès pour la République (CPR), with 29 seats, and Al-Aridha Chaabia (Popular Petition), with 26 seats.[1] Having won a plurality rather than an absolute majority, Ennahdha was compelled to form a coalition government. Its leaders categorically refused to negotiate with Al-Aridha Chaabia, while Hechmi Hamdi, Al-Aridha Chaabia's leader, declared that he would stay in London and not return to Tunisia as long as Ennahdha remained in power.[2] Consequently, Ennahdha negotiated a coalition government with two centre-left parties, the CPR and Ettakatol, which was next in line with 20 seats. Together, the 'troika' built a strong majority with 138 of the NCA's 217 seats.

This chapter examines the initial challenges faced by the NCA as it set out to establish its role and mandates during the short transitional period leading to the presidential and legislative elections planned for the spring of 2013. The chapter also explores some of the main tensions within the coalition government and how such tensions impacted its performance and ability to deliver to the Tunisian people. The popularity of the government decreased substantially as it failed to even begin to tackle the pressing issues of economic stagnation, regional inequality and massive unemployment. An analysis of the role of the opposition parties in counteracting the government, especially Ennahdha's somewhat ambiguous Islamist agenda, is also carried out in the last sections of the chapter, which ends with a discussion of young Tunisians' views of the government, of the new constitution and of the future of the country.

The National Constituent Assembly: mandates and action plans

The first task of the NCA was to appoint the leadership of the troika government. Ennahdha took the post of prime minister. Rached Ghannouchi preferred not to take a public role and maintained his position as Ennahdha's 'intellectual supreme leader',[3] so the party nominated Hamadi Jebali,[4] its secretary-general, to occupy the position. Moncef Marzouki, head of the CPR, became president of the republic, while the founder and secretary-general of Ettakatol, Mustapha Ben Jaafar, was appointed speaker of the NCA.

The new administration was to be guided by the Law on the Provisional Organisation of Public Powers, known as the 'mini-constitution', which lays out the ground rules for the management of the country until the presidential and legislative elections of 2013. It was adopted by the NCA on 12 December 2011 with 141 in favour, 37 against and 39 abstentions from opposition delegates who decided to boycott it. The vote came after a tumultuous debate that saw thousands of people demonstrating outside the National Assembly building. The most controversial provision of the mini-constitution, which was drafted by a constitutional council led by Ennahdha,[5] was its substantial expansion of the powers of the prime minister and diminution of the authority of both the president of the NCA and the president of the republic. Ennahdha retained full control over the troika government, and Hamadi Jebali became the new 'super prime minister'. Anna Mahjar-Barducci,[6] a journalist and writer from Moroccan and Italian descent, emphasised:

> According to the 'mini-constitution', the new Tunisian prime minister is authorized to instate, modify or abolish ministerial posts as he pleases, after merely 'informing' the president. He is also allowed to appoint and dismiss top officials in public bodies, the civil service and the military. Moreover, if the president is temporarily incapacitated, the prime minister is to replace him for up to three months; whereas, if the prime minister is temporarily incapacitated,

the majority party is authorized to appoint one of its own members to replace him.[7]

Mahjar-Barducci stated that while Ennahdha's victory was won through a fair and transparent democratic process, its mini-constitution was engineered to ensure 'the party maximum power and shield it from political opposition'.[8] As many Tunisians have observed, Ghannouchi does not mask his power and dominance over the government, making his prime minister a mere spokes-person and executor of his decisions. The two other leaders of the troika have been relegated to symbolic roles.

Also contentious are the mini-constitution's articles VIII and IX, specifying who will be eligible to stand for president. These articles stipulate that candidates for president must be 'exclusively Tunisian, of the Muslim religion', the child of Tunisian parents, and at least 35 years old. Many in the opposition boycotted the vote because of the discriminatory nature of these articles, which exclude Tunisians with dual nationality as well as non-Muslim citizens. The country's population includes about 25,000 Christians and 1,500 Jews. This issue remains to be resolved in the new constitution.

The NCA initiated the process for drafting the new constitution in February 2012. Six working commissions of 22 members each were established to take up specific aspects of the constitution:

1 preamble;
2 general principles and amendments;
3 rights and liberties;
4 legislative and executive powers;
5 the judiciary; and
6 constitutional institutions, and regional and local public collectives.

The NCA is expected to finalise the new constitution within 18 months. Writing a new constitution raises a plethora of diverse and potentially divisive issues. The constitution will define the nation's identity, determine its form of government, and formulate its procedural laws.

In May 2012, Ennahdha promised that the new constitution would be ready by October 2012 and elections would be held in March 2013.[9] Many young people worried that the writing of the constitution would drag on for several more months and delay the 2013 elections. Khouloud, a 24-year-old woman from Sousse said:

> The National Assembly has not made much progress. We see some of the debates and they are not even tackling the serious issues ... Several months have passed and the process has not moved significantly. I don't know what to expect. I am tired of living in a provisional situation. Everything is provisional in this country: provisional government, provisional assembly, provisional constitution ...

Moreover, at the time of my visits, people were uncertain about the type of elections to be held in 2013, i.e. whether these would be parliamentary and presidential elections, or just parliamentary elections with the president being elected by parliament. All these aspects would certainly be defined in the new constitution, which was still in draft form at that time.[10]

In August 2012, the first draft of the new constitution was released, and Ennahdha's general rapporteur of the constitutional committee, Habib Khedher, declared that work on the new constitution would be finalised by February 2013. Following debates regarding the first draft, which was heavily criticised for failing to protect gender equality and free speech, a reworked second draft of the new constitution was finalised and open for public debate in December 2012. In early 2013, there were reports of members of the NCA travelling out to various towns and villages across the country to undertake a series of public consultations on the second draft of the constitution, to provide Tunisians with the opportunity to participate in the drafting process, and to promote a national dialogue about the new constitution.[11] According to Habib Khedher, as spokesperson of the NCA, the reports of the public consultations will then assist the NCA Joint Board for Coordination and Drafting in the revision and compilation process of the third, and hopefully last, draft of the constitution.[12]

Political tensions and weak performance of the troika government

Following its electoral victory and the establishment of the co-alition government with the CPR and Ettakatol, Ennahdha quickly managed to take control by forcing through a mini-constitution that deprived the president of his powers and enhanced those of the prime minister. Internal tensions within the democratic, socialist and progressive bloc, which won only a few seats in the NCA, did not permit a strong opposition to contain Ennahdha's tendency to monopolise power. The leaders of the other two parties in the coalition have been unable to combat or firmly stand against Ennahdha, perhaps because of competition be-tween themselves or perhaps in an effort to preserve the troika alliance with Ennahdha. However, as disagreements over particular issues have become more acute, party leaders have more openly disputed Ennahdha's rule. These power struggles have inhibited the formation and implementation of national policies, especially with regard to the economy, to curb regional imbalances and to reduce unemployment.

Tensions within the troika government were apparent from early on. A few months after the establishment of the coalition government, Prime Minister Hamadi Jebali made some contro-versial remarks about the return of the Islamic caliphate, stating: 'My brothers, you are at a historic moment ... in a new cycle of civilisation, God willing ... we are in the sixth caliphate, God will-ing.'[13] This declaration quickly rang alarm bells among Tunisia's progressive and secular parties and prompted Ettakatol to threaten to suspend its participation in the governing coalition. 'We do not accept this statement. We thought we were going to build a second republic with our partner, not a sixth caliphate,'[14] affirmed Khemais Ksila, then a member of the executive committee of Etta-katol. Ksila later resigned from Ettakatol's executive committee.

Ennahdha has been embroiled in other controversies since winning the elections. Souad Abderrahim, a prominent female member of Ennahdha, stated in a radio interview that single mothers are a disgrace to Tunisia, they 'do not have the right to exist', there are limits on 'full and absolute freedom', and one should not 'make excuses for people who have sinned'. Her comments angered many Tunisians, especially women's groups. In both cases, Ennahdha had to back down from these statements, downplaying their significance.[15] These instances have tended to reinforce the perception that Ennahdha engages in doublespeak, saying one thing publicly while saying something else privately to its followers.

The relationship between President Moncef Marzouki and Prime Minister Hamadi Jebali was reported to be fraught from the start, with open disagreements regarding many government activities. In July 2012, for example, the CPR and Ettakatol, the other parties in the troika, released official statements opposing the prime minister's decision to extradite the former Libyan prime minister, Baghdadi al-Mahmoudi. President Marzouki (CPR) has always opposed the extradition, arguing that Libya's new regime did not offer sufficient guarantees of a fair trial for Al-Mahmoudi. Meanwhile, Mustapha Ben Jaafar, president of the NCA and leader of Ettakatol, was credited with efforts to reconcile the president and the head of government to avert any further political tensions that would derail the democratic transition in Tunisia.[16]

The second half of 2012 was marked by a series of resignations of government officials, indicating growing divisions within the troika. Mohamed Abbou, secretary-general of the CPR, resigned from his post as minister of public service, alleging that Prime Minister Jebali restricted his authority to combat corruption and fully undertake his duties. In a similar fashion, President Marzouki's press secretary, Ayoub Messaoudi, and his economic adviser, Chawki Abid, resigned in June 2012.

Also in July 2012, there was the controversial dismissal of Mustapha Kamel Nabli, governor of the Banque Centrale de Tunisie (BCT), following disputes over who has the authority to set monetary policy, specifically the inflation target, which may be affected by monetary expansion. His firing divided members of the cabinet and the NCA, triggering heated debates between the government and the opposition, which accused the ruling coalition of seeking to control the BCT. The appointment of his successor, Chedly Ayari, was also controversial, with strong reactions from parliamentarians, technocrats and politicians. The appointment of 79-year-old Ayari has been strongly criticised by the opposition and by some within the ruling coalition because of his age and his links with the former regime. As a renowned economist, and having served as minister of planning under Habib Bourguiba, Ayari worked for various international financial institutions, including the African Development Bank, before being appointed as an adviser to former president Ben Ali. Ayari vowed to preserve the independence of the bank and the stability of the Tunisian dinar.[17]

In the same week, Houcine Dimassi, the finance minister and a trade unionist from the Union Générale Tunisienne du Travail (UGTT), resigned from his post. In his resignation letter, Dimassi denounced the government's spending policy for putting electoral victories above the nation's interests.[18] In an interview to *Business News* after his resignation, Dimassi stated that the prime minister was himself controlled by the party: 'Hamadi Jebali had always listened to me and understood me. But he also had his constraints, such as pressure from his party ... We have taken cabinet decisions that have never been implemented.' Asked what advice he had for the present government, Dimassi suggested to his former colleagues in the government, especially those from Ennahdha: 'When you think about elections, you must also think beyond them ... It is not enough to win the elections. You must also have a society that can be governed afterwards; government is supposed to govern and not react to street talk. It must reconcile [differences] without being dysfunctional.' In accepting Dimassi's resignation, the prime minister accused the finance minister of evading his responsibilities.

Moreover, in late August 2012, Yadh Ben Achour, chairman of the Higher Authority for the Realisation of the Objectives of the Revolution, Political Reform and Democratic Transition, announced that as a consequence of the ruling troika's failure to establish a new framework for the organisation, the Higher

Authority was ceasing its functions. Azad Badi, a member of the NCA, stated that: 'Most of the blocs in the Constituent Assembly think that the committee is no longer really needed, and saw no use in its continued existence.'[19] There has been, however, speculation in the Tunisian media that its dissolution might be connected to comments made by Higher Authority members against some of the provisions in the first draft of the constitution released for public debate in August 2012. Members of the Higher Authority decided to move on and form an independent civil society group, the Association of Experts of Democratic Transition.[20]

These tensions, and particularly the resignations of ministers from the smaller parties, have brought about discontinuity in the operations of the executive branch. The government has experienced paralysis in many areas, arguably because the parties have put their own interests above the task of governing and managing the post-electoral transition. The tensions seem also to have exacerbated the challenges faced by the Ennahdha-led government to implement much-needed post-revolutionary reforms and to demonstrate its capacity to lead the country in the right direction. Regional disparities, unemployment, rising prices for basic foodstuffs and widespread corruption strongly preoccupy the majority of Tunisians, but thus far the government has been unable to begin to tackle these problems seriously. The economic situation has not improved; in fact, some believe it has deteriorated since the elections. Popular discontent is again taking the form of angry riots, protests and sit-ins. There have been demonstrations against unemployment, high living costs and the troika government's broken promises.[21] Whenever government representatives travel into the regions, they are booed, and their presence often provokes clashes between those in support of Ennahdha and those critical of it.

During March 2012 alone, there were reports of about 15 daily sit-ins at government offices, 10 general strikes and 8 blocked roads throughout the country. In April 2012, twice as many incidents were reported. This trend continued in the following months. On 26 July 2012, the town of Sidi Bouzid, the cradle of the revolution, hosted street protests denouncing unemployment, low standards of living and water shortages, as well as the government's failure to address these problems. The water problem has exacerbated tensions in recent months; over the past six months, drinking water has been available for only a few hours in the evenings and occasionally has been cut off for the entire day across the region. The governor of Sidi Bouzid, Mohamed Najib Mansouri, is reported to have claimed that the failure of residents to pay their bills is the main reason for the water cuts. Some experts believe, however, that it is more likely that the local infrastructure is old and unable to sustain the increased consumption of water, especially during a hot and dry summer.[22]

The demonstrations culminated in attacks on the governorate headquarters and the local office of Ennahdha. Demonstrators threw rocks at government buildings, while the police responded by using tear gas to disperse protesters; several of them were beaten and arrested. There were reports of about 45 arrests in Sidi Bouzid. Samir Dilou, minister for human rights and transitional justice, has pointed out the difficulties of the troika government in striking a balance between protecting the protesters' human rights and fulfilling the state's duty to guarantee 'social order'.

The imprisonment of demonstrators was condemned by the UGTT, which called for a general strike in Sidi Bouzid a few days later.[23] Between 1,000 and 1,500 people joined the UGTT demonstrations in response to the arrests.[24] These events in Sidi Bouzid were considered by many analysts to be 'the culmination of an extended standoff, not only between the al-Nahda-led ruling coalition and Tunisia's main trade union federation, the UGTT, but also between those in power and those who are yet to see the revolutionary demands of "work, freedom, and national dignity" realised'.[25] In Sidi Bouzid, during events to mark the second anniversary of Mohamed Bouazizi's self-immolation, more than 5,000 people came out onto the streets to celebrate Bouazizi but also to express dissatisfaction with what they see as sluggish economic and social progress in the region since the revolution. 'Nothing has changed: no development, no employment. The revolution's goals are yet to be met. They're still mere slogans,' were the words of Nejib Bayaoui, coordinator of the regional office of the Front Populaire, to journalist Farah Samti. In the same article, Hedi Bouazizi, a cousin Mohamed Bouazizi, was reported to have stated that: 'We brought this freedom, but those in power are the ones enjoying it and not us.'[26] Following the speech of Mustapha Ben Jaafer, president of the NCA, some participants in the celebrations threw stones at the podium, aimed at Ben Jaafer, to show their discontent with the government and those in power. Ennahdha released a statement accusing leftist parties of being behind the incident and inciting violence against the government.[27]

On the economic front, since Ennahdha was elected to govern, the Tunisian economy has continued to flounder. While critics attribute the sluggish economic recovery to the weakness of the ruling troika and its lack of expertise in managing governmental and economic affairs, it is also true that current local, regional and international situations pose additional challenges. At the local level, political and economic demands have been increasing since the outbreak of the revolution. Social protests and labour strikes have also picked up since then. Regionally, the insecurity and instability created by the Libyan war have had a negative impact on Tunisia's economy because of the influx of refugees and the inability of Tunisian migrants to work in Libya. At the international level, economic growth has continued to slow down, with the Eurozone, Tunisia's largest trading partner, experiencing major economic contractions. Also damaging have been the heavy declines in tourism and in foreign direct investment (Arieff 2012). In October 2011, the International Monetary Fund (IMF) projected that the global economic crises would have a negative impact on Tunisia's economic growth prospects for 2012 (IMF 2011).

To tackle the country's economic situation, in May 2012 the troika government submitted two critical documents to the NCA: the Supplementary Finance Law for 2012;[28] and the government's programme for 2012. The programme detailed economic and social policies that, if implemented, would respond to some of the coun-try's basic economic needs, particularly regarding employment

153

opportunities and development in rural areas, which have suffered from marginalisation and deprivation since the time of Ben Ali's regime. According to an article by Lahcen Achy,[29] these two documents reveal an economic approach focused primarily on increasing expenditures, supporting regional growth and creating job opportunities during a recovery stage. In the start-up phase, set to begin in 2013, the government will concentrate on increasing the growth of gross domestic product (GDP) and will supplement its income with revenue from the recovery of state assets (confiscated money and property embezzled by Ben Ali and his family), from voluntary contribution campaigns, and from donations and foreign aid.[30]

While formulating these policies, the government has not been able to build consensus about their implementation. Instead, key officials, including the finance minister and the governor of the BCT, have resigned. The proposed economic development strategy seems to differ very little from the neoliberal agenda of the former regime. Furthermore, it does very little to alleviate the situation of many Tunisians from the marginalised regions who suffer from high levels of unemployment and a lack of investment. By relying on foreign and private investment, the government aims to provide 100,000 more jobs and predicts a GDP growth of 3.5 per cent for 2012.[31] Critics believe that such predictions are unrealistic, considering that Tunisia has experienced four consecutive quarters of negative growth.[32] And with levels of unemployment at 18.1 per cent in 2012, the aim to create 100,000 jobs will do little to abate social unrest in a country with over 700,000 unemployed people in an active workforce of 3.9 million.[33]

Moreover, the fact that the current government is still a transitional one, with its term ending once the new constitution is ready and elections are held, further complicates the situation, prompting proposals to adopt 'expansionary spending policies aimed at satisfying broad constituencies at the expense of structural reform, the results of which will only be felt in the medium and long term'.[34] As Lahcen Achy's analysis reveals, the government's programme for 2012 does not include clear plans for deficit reduction, and the promises of economic growth rates of just under 7 per cent in 2015 and 8 per cent in 2017 appear to be very elusive.[35]

It is no surprise that popular support for Ennahdha and the troika government has dropped dramatically and the government no longer has the space to manoeuvre it enjoyed before the elections. An opinion poll conducted by SIGMA Conseil in conjunction with Tunisian daily newspaper *Al Maghreb* in March/April 2012 showed widespread public discontent over the performance of the government regarding key problems. About 86 per cent of Tunisians think that the government has failed to alleviate unemployment, and 90 per cent consider the government unsuccessful when addressing inflation. Since financial corruption and bribery have historically been commonplace in the country's administrative system, the new government has charged special authorities with undertaking administrative reform and eradicating corruption. Still, 75 per cent of Tunisians find that the current government has failed in fighting these deeply rooted patterns.[36]

Ennahdha is clearly struggling to govern and manage the transition process. At its congress[37] held in July 2012, which was intended to clarify the party's strategy against a backdrop of political and religious tensions, Ennahdha reaffirmed its position as a centrist Islamist party. The gathering also aimed to reconcile different factions within the party, especially moderate and extreme Islamists, but it remains to be seen whether these efforts will bear fruit. Following the congress, Rached Ghannouchi, head of Ennahdha, declared: 'We are evaluating the performance of the government that has been in place for the past six months for information that could lead to a change of ministers or portfolios, even enlarging the coalition to include other parties.' Ennahdha sees such a move as a way of making the government, currently dominated by Ennahdha members, more efficient.[38] The future of Tunisia will depend largely on the way in which these economic and social challenges will be resolved.

Fractured and fragile political opposition

In the post-electoral transition period, the progressive democratic opposition to the Ennahdha government has remained weak and is not yet in a position to offer a viable alternative to the Islamists. Rather than lack of popular support, continuing disunity over the course of 2012 seemed to be the main problem of the opposition. On the left, as on the right, self-interested leaders and small groups have got in the way of possible agreements. In 2012, the opposition to the Islamists was still digesting its defeat in the 2011 elections and struggling to find innovative ways to reshape itself. It has appeared more preoccupied with combating extreme Islamism than with presenting sound alternative socioeconomic policies.

Whereas most Tunisian politicians have embraced broad free-market economic principles, they have also advocated that the government play a strong role in reducing economic and regional inequality and in boosting employment (Arieff 2012). While the opposition's lack of a strong alternative socioeconomic proposal could have been seen as stemming from disagreements between neoliberals and those who advocated a proactive government economic development policy, it may also have been an indication of the extent to which Islamism had defined the terms of debate and framed the 'political' at that particular time.

Despite the fact that the electorate would be well served by a strong opposition to keep the government in check, the progressive and secular forces are still fractured into several small party groupings. Opposition parties learned from the elections that unity is fundamental if they are to counter the government and challenge the Islamists in the 2013 elections, and efforts to establish political coalitions and work together have been undertaken since early 2012, but the process has often been hindered by egotism and clashes of personality among the leaders of political parties. Instead of forging stronger unity across the progressive bloc, new political coalitions of three or four parties emerged during the course of 2012.

In March 2012, three Tunisian progressive left parties announced the establishment of Al Massar (the Path of Social Progress), a coalition that united Ettajdid, the Parti du Travail Tunisien (PTT) and the Pôle Démocratique Moderniste. The coalition is led by Ahmed Brahim, head of Ettajdid. Attempts to broaden the Al Massar coalition by bringing in other progressive forces have failed as other alliances and groupings have been forged.

The Parti Démocrate Progressiste (PDP) along with two other centrist democratic parties, Afek Tounes and the Parti Républicain, established a coalition under the name of the Parti Républicain in April 2012. Mohamed Louzir, president of Afek Tounes, argued that unifying the opposition was the highest priority: 'This is a historic moment. Division does not serve Tunisia's best interests. Trust us, and we will not let you down.' In the same vein, Maya Jribi, secretary-general of the PDP, said that 'one of the goals of the revolution is equal opportunity for everybody' and vowed that the new Parti Républicain would work towards that objective.

A third political opposition coalition, known as Nida Tounes (Call of Tunisia), was created in June 2012. Led by 86-year-old former interim prime minister Beji Caïd-Essebsi, Nida Tounes is a centrist, liberal and unifying movement open to all political forces in the country. In his first speech as the new party leader, Caïd-Essebsi criticised the lax attitude of the government towards the abuses of the Salafists and called on members of the government to take responsibility for the recent events that have shaken Tunisian society. In a speech astutely punctuated by *suras* (verses) from the *Quran*, he insisted that 'there was no clergy in Islam' and that 'the Muslim Tunisian people do not need a government that behaves as a religious guardian or delivers sermons'.[39]

The party's openness to former members of the Rassemblement Constitutionnel Démocratique (RCD) did not sit well with many progressive politicians as it was seen as feeding into the perception that links were being kept with the previous regime. How Caïd-Essebsi integrates ex-RCD members will be key to the future of this coalition. Despite his advanced age and that of many of his supporters, Caïd-Essebsi insists that Nida Tounes will be a party of youth and will be open to all activists who oppose the current government but have no political party of their own. He believes that the only way towards a better future for the country will be a broad coalition based on a 'consensus' government run by a cabinet of technocrats.[40]

In October 2012, the Front Populaire was established as a coalition between the PTT, the Mouvement du Peuple, the Parti de la Lutte Progressiste, the National Democrats Movement Party, Watad (the Democratic Patriots Party) and a number of other parties on the left. Under the leadership of the PTT, the Front Populaire is trying to reframe the debate and present itself as an alternative to the polarisation between Islamists and secularists by focusing on socioeconomic needs and presenting itself as the coalition of the 'little people'.[41] It is unclear, however, how much political sway this Front Populaire will manage to have, because together these parties hold fewer than ten of the 217 seats in the NCA.[42]

Putting together coalitions constitutes just the first step. In order to seriously oppose Ennahdha and other Islamist groups, the progressive secular opposition needs to reach out to and attract two main constituencies: the young Tunisians who were instrumental in taking to the streets and overthrowing long-time President Ben Ali; and the people of the interior and the most disadvantaged regions of the country, who are more closely attached to Islam and who were alienated by the previous regime.

The young people who led the revolution reject the brand of politics carried out by political parties. 'In Tunisia, we live in the era of the old, not the young ... When I look at the Constituent Assembly, I see old people, old and incompetent. The deputies who don't have email, can't use the internet and don't speak three languages won't go far,' asserted 32-year-old blogger and activist Slim Ayedi.[43] These young Tunisians have decided instead to develop their activism through civil society organisations. In the midst of the economic crisis, however, youth have had to turn their attention from full-time activism towards making a living, and many have become consumed with just trying to survive.

Similarly, the opposition will need to deepen its roots in the interior and develop a discourse that attracts and speaks directly to the rural population. Opposition groups will need to shed their image of being pro-Western elitist movements based in the capital with few or no ties to populations from the interior and the most deprived areas of the country. They will have to adopt a rhetoric that speaks to people's attachment to Islam and local traditions as well as to their desire for progress, freedom of expression and civil liberties. But, most fundamentally, the opposition has to be able to put in place convincing and sound policies to resolve the economic imbalances and improve the lives of these Tunisians marginalised by the former regime.

Without a strong and united opposition, there will always be a risk that Ennahdha may rule unchecked and repeat the behaviour of the former ruling party, becoming a sort of Islamist dictatorship. Critics have pointed out that Ennahdha has already been running roughshod over the opposition, antagonising the unions and other civil society groups and showing little interest in building democratic institutions. Some analysts believe that the key to the next election will be the new voters, since more than 40 per cent of eligible voters, most of whom were young people, were not registered or did not vote in the October 2011 elections. Equally important will be the third of the electorate, about 17 per cent of voters, who voted for parties that did not win any seats in the NCA. Moreover, the rural population that overwhelmingly voted for Ennahdha appears to be increasingly disappointed by the government's performance, especially with regard to dealing with regional economic disparities and unemployment. Thus, there is room for a strong and savvy opposition to put pressure on and confront the party in power.

Ennahdha, the troika and the future of Tunisia

Young Tunisians hold differing opinions on whether Ennahdha is a political force capable of steering the country in a new direction. Some of my interlocutors thought that Tunisia is a Muslim country and that it is fitting that the new Tunisian government should have an Islamic orientation. 'Our people are proud of being Muslim,' said 23-year-old Jaafar from Metline. 'We need to move away from Ben Ali's repression of Islam that made us feel "uncomfortable" for being who we are ... Ennahdha can be good for Tunisia; they will respect our Muslim values and there will be more solidarity and respect among people,' he concluded. Ayoub, a 24-year-old man from Bizerte, acknowledged that he does not pray five times a day, but he believes that:

> the Islamist party will be good for Tunisia because after the departure of Ben Ali there was a lot of uncertainty ... Too many political parties all talking about the same thing, but Ennahdha has existed for many years and its message is clear: respect for Tunisia's Muslim values. Why is it bad to respect our own Muslim culture?

Some more conservative supporters of Ennahdha are disappointed because the party has not taken a firm stand on its religious beliefs. 'Ghannouchi, Jebali and others seem to be afraid of the left and the foreign governments. They are not being true to their religion and present themselves as moderate. I don't understand what it means to be moderate; you are either an Islamist or not,' asserted Ezzedine, a 35-year-old man from Sousse. Pro-Ennahdha youths have opposed the progressive parties' attacks on Ennahdha and the troika government. 'The left is not letting them do their work ... They have just been elected and need time. Tunisia is like a newborn baby and needs to learn to walk,' said Sumaya, a 34-year-old woman from Sidi Bouzid. In the same vein, 29-year-old Mootez from Monastir argued that 'the media is against the new government – they don't publicise the good things the government does, they only show the bad things. They don't want to see Ennahdha succeed ... The media is with the left.'

Other youths have more nuanced views. Hafsia, a 34-year-old woman from Kasserine, asserted: 'I am not against Ennahdha, but I am not sure because I don't know enough about what they really stand for ... We Tunisians are moderate people ... But I don't think I want a president who doesn't respect Islam.' Ali, a 31-year-old man from Kasserine, went further:

I am not sure what they mean by Islamist party. 'Islamist' is a new word, I think ... We are Muslims, not Islamists ... I believe that any political force in this country will have to take into account that we are a Muslim country; 90 per cent of Tunisians are Muslims ... [But] I don't see why a party needs to be 'Islamist'.

Now that they are in power, however, Ali believes they should be given a chance to govern: 'I am waiting to see how they perform and will judge them in the next elections.'

Those more critical of Ennahdha were concerned about blending religion and politics. 'The Islamists are using the mosque for politics ... We have to stay vigilant,' said 19-year-old Taoufik from Tunis. A young man from Kairouan remarked that: 'Normally, religious people do not create political parties. The fact that [Ennahdha] is a political party means that they are not honest.'[44] Critics fear that the country might become ultraconservative under the pressure of extremist groups. 'Ennahdha presents itself as a moderate party, but I don't trust them as their positions are contradictory; one day they want a caliphate, the next day they don't ... They are shifting according to the wind. I think they are also supporting the Salafists through the back door.'

The discourses focusing on the Islamic roots of Tunisian identity that dominated Ennahdha's campaign appear to have emboldened ultraconservative Muslims, the Salafists, to become more vocal and claim greater space in the country's political arena. As the Salafist movement thrives in the new atmosphere of freedom of expression, it has become more aggressive, launching violent attacks on those it perceives to be opposed to Islam, insulting its sacred figures and texts or violating its precepts and laws as they interpret them. In fact, while Ennahdha has presented itself as a moderate Islamist party and has vowed not to impose Sharia, Salafist groups have demonstrated in favour of instituting Sharia and establishing an Islamic state in Tunisia.

The Salafists have attacked a television station and a cinema that aired films they deemed blasphemous. In October 2011,

Nessma TV, an independent channel, broadcast Marjane Satrapi's Oscar-nominated animated film *Persepolis*,[45] set during the 1979 Iranian Revolution. The film contains a scene depicting God, which angered many in the country and drew thousands of pro-Islamist protesters onto the streets of Tunis. Nabil Karoui, head of Nessma TV, was taken to court and in May 2012 was found guilty of disturbing public order and attacking Muslim moral values. Karoui received a fine of 2,400 dinars (about US$1,500), a much lighter sentence than the prison term sought by religiously conservative politicians. Some Salafists in Tunisia even called for Karoui to receive the death penalty.

Several youths recounted that a group of extremist Islamists raided bars in the town of Jendouba and attacked men drinking alcohol. They also invaded brothels in Tunis on the grounds that prostitution violates Muslim values, although it turned out that some of the attackers were actually regular customers. Similar events took place in Sfax and other cities across the country. Many young Tunisians said they could not stand the sort of hypocrisy displayed by some Islamic extremist men, attacking brothels they patronise, preaching Islam but drinking alcohol, and calling for women to be virgins when they marry but sleeping around with unmarried girls. They worry about these extremists, in part because they attack aspects of youth culture that many young people value and enjoy. Young people criticise Ennahdha for not taking a firm stand against the Salafists, whose actions have gained greater visibility since Ennahdha's victory.

Indeed, according to various analysts, Ennahdha and its co-alition have not been able to deal with the problems posed by the Salafists. While Ennahdha has publicly opposed making Sharia the law of the state, it has been unable to distance itself from Islamic extremism. In March 2012, the Ennahdha-led government legalised openly Salafist political parties such as Jabhat al-Islah (JI, or the Reform Front) and Hizb ut-Tahrir (the Liberation Party), both strong advocates of the establishment of an Islamic state and the imposition of Sharia in Tunisia. Some critics have pointed out that the legalisation of Salafist parties would not have been possible without the firm support of Ennahdha.[46] The leader of the JI, Mohammad al-Khoujah, is reported to have appealed to the NCA to make Tunisia a true Islamic country, asking that 'Sharia be inscribed [in the constitution] as the sole source of legislation'. Ben Salah, a member of the party's political bureau, also stressed that 'separating religion and politics is a major mistake, since politics is the management of people's affairs'.[47]

In fact, the place of religion in public life has also been a point of contention in the debates within the government and NCA. While granting freedom of worship, in August 2012 the government submitted a draft bill by the NCA that emphasised the state's obligation to protect Islam as the official religion, and proposed to criminalise offences against 'sacred values'.[48] The proposed legislation criminalised any blasphemy of Islam, whether by statement, act or image, regardless of whether the expression was intended as a deliberate insult or an effort at irony or sarcasm. Offenders would be liable to prison sentences ranging from two to four years. The criminal law encompassed any religious offence, including insults, profanity, derision and mocking the 'sanctity of religion', which are forbidden in Islam.

As a professed centrist Islamic political party, Ennahdha's blasphemy law surprised some analysts. Indeed, despite public assurances that the state would remain neutral towards religion, Prime Minister Hamadi Jebali asserted that any publication of images of God or Islam's prophets would be considered 'a provocation [rather] than a matter of freedom of expression'.[49] Ennahdha's decision to prioritise political attention to anti-blasphemy legislation in the face of the country's ongoing and profound economic and social challenges is deeply troubling to young Tunisians who see this as a political concession to the Salafists.

Ennahdha seems to be having difficulties maintaining a balanced relationship between religion and politics. It has not preserved what Alfred Stepan (2012) calls the 'twin tolerations' that are the foundation of the separation between church and state. The first toleration, which concerns the relationship of 'religious citizens toward the state', requires that democratically elected officials are able to legislate and govern without being confronted by religious claims such as 'Only God, not man, can make laws.' The second toleration refers to the relationship of the state with religious citizens, who must, as a matter of right, have the freedom to express their views and values within society as long as they respect the law and other citizens' constitutional rights (ibid.: 89).

Nevertheless, some young Tunisians are not primarily concerned with Islamism as the single most important issue for the transition period. Most state that the majority of the Tunisian population are moderate Muslims seeking to respect their religion while preserving the social advances made since independence as well as the freedoms acquired with the revolution. Slim Amamou analysed the situation:

> I don't think Islamic extremism has a chance here in Tunisia
> ... Tunisian society is full of contradictions: people grapple
> with private and public positions and personal and collective
> interests ... They may say one thing in private but declare some-
> thing else in public. I don't think there is widespread support
> for a conservative, extremist-style Islamist politics in Tunisia.

Perhaps those contradictions stem from more than 20 years under a dictatorship that did not allow people the freedom to express themselves.

Many young Tunisians prioritise reducing youth unemployment, generating a more equitable process of economic development and advancing social justice as key actions for the new government. While the heavy-handed anti-religious practices of the Ben Ali regime tended to erode the country's attachment to secularism, the revolution seems to have, to a certain extent, reinvigorated the secular, liberal views of many in the younger generation.

However, the inability of the troika to govern effectively and address the critical socioeconomic needs of disaffected and unemployed young people makes them vulnerable to Salafist propaganda and recruitment. Moreover, Ennahdha's lack of clear positioning with regard to religion, advocating some tenets of

Islam but not others, has led to confusion among some young Muslims, who have become attracted to the more black-and-white positions of the Salafists.[50]

Islamic extremist groups have become savvier in using internet social networks and other media outlets to catch young people's attention and mobilise them. During my last research visit to Tunisia in June 2012, I noticed that more young Tunisian males had grown a beard, and in our conversations some tended to favour more conservative positions about Islam and women's veiling. It is hard to know the extent of youth's adherence to Islamic extremist ideas since the revolution, but there have been reports of Salafist riots including increasing numbers of young people.[51] This was the case in the attacks on the American embassy in Tunis in September 2012. Enraged Tunisians, many of them young, scaled the walls and smashed the windows of the building, then hoisted the black Salafi flag on the embassy's flagpole. They also torched the nearby American school, before being dispersed by the security forces.[52]

Mahmoud, a young Salafist interviewed by journalist Vivienne Walt, stated that the new government had betrayed devout Muslims like him, who then decided to embrace the Salafists. An accountant by trade, Mahmoud said that while he played a very active role during the revolution out of intense hatred of the dictator Ben Ali, he also joined the Salafist protests at Manouba University in November 2011 and at the American embassy in September 2012. He is critical of the new government, which he believes to have abandoned Muslim devotees in favour of good relations with the West. In his words, 'the government is pretending to be a revolutionary government, but it is not ... Instead of meeting the expectations of people who revolted against the dictatorship, they've adopted the easier option of executing the Western agenda.'[53] Mahmoud and other young Salafists have no interest in Tunisia's democratic process and the writing of a new constitution. Instead, they believe that Sharia law comprises all the rules by which people should be governed. 'Democracy is against the model we believe in,' said Mahmoud.[54]

Conclusions

Following the October 2011 elections, the new NCA formally appointed the new coalition government and initiated the drafting of the new constitution. But even before the actual writing process began, it was marred by tensions over mandates, competencies and deadlines as the various political forces represented fought to advance their agendas and counteract Ennahdha's drive to fully control power. The friction between Ennahdha and its troika allies soon became apparent and hindered the ability of the government to perform effectively.

The troika government's priorities are still not clear to most of my young interlocutors. While politicians show interest in constitutional questions about the status of women, the role of religion, the decentralisation of power and the specific functions of government, both revolutionary youth and the wider population want to see the government address the socioeconomic issues that guided the revolution.

Meanwhile, the political opposition remains divided and unable to appear as a strong counterpoint to the Islamists, who are becoming increasingly more conservative as the Salafists, aided by Ennahdha, are beginning to win political space – the legalisation of Islamic extremist parties such as the JI and the Liberation Party attest to this. Moreover, Ennahdha has also proposed and facilitated legislation that encroaches on existing women's rights and religious freedoms, which has been the subject of intense debates and strong reactions from the public. While the majority of young Tunisians appear to favour the separation of religion from the state, the old regime's repression of Islam, Ennahdha's ambiguous position and the debilitating socioeconomic crisis make unemployed and disaffected youths more vulnerable to Salafist ideologies.

There is no doubt that the issue of women's rights is a central one in the debates between secularism and Islamism in Tunisia. The next and last chapter of the book will examine this critical issue.

7 | Women's rights

The debate between secularists and Islamists about the place of Sharia (Islamic law) in the newly democratic state has made women's rights into a central and hotly contested issue. 'Women are at the core of Islamic law,' stated Monia Lachheb, professor of sociology at Manouba University in Tunis. Longstanding liberal and secularist critiques have linked Muslim women's inequality in relation to men to the foundations of Islamic religion. Consequently, discussions about the position of women in society have been wedded to polarising ideologies about identity politics and cultural nationalism. In the final analysis, these debates are not fundamentally about the women with whom they claim to be concerned; instead, women's rights and status in society are used as a pretext for struggles over religious versus secular ideologies. Muslim women's bodies have long been the terrain upon which wider battles of identity politics have been fought.

This chapter examines the context of women's civil society movements in Tunisia and young women's perspectives on current debates about women's rights. It begins with an examination of the contested issue of women's rights in Islamic law and the political and legal reforms with regard to women and family undertaken by the Bourguiba regime in the 1950s. The chapter then analyses the evolution of the feminist movement in Tunisia from independence to the post-revolution period, highlighting its diversity and women's activism during the transition. It shows that, although the reforms of women's rights began as part of a top-down, state-centred modernising project, women have become increasingly engaged in the debate and are now speaking for themselves.

Drawing on the interviews and focus groups I conducted in

2011 and 2012, the chapter presents the perspectives of a wide range of young women, highlighting their views about the actions of Islamic extremist groups aimed at forcing the imposition of Sharia in the new Tunisian state. Young women's thoughts about veiling and about women's rights to education, employment and self-determination indicate that, in contrast to male politicians whose concerns centre on morality and masculinity, women regard their ability to earn a livelihood and to be free from harassment and violence as the most salient issues.

Three main arguments guide the analysis in this chapter. First, Tunisia's long tradition of women's rights' reform, which dates from the late nineteenth century, paved the way for a strong feminist movement in Tunisia, which has grown significantly in the post-revolution period. Second, women's active participation in the revolution and the democratic transition attests to the strength of women's engagement in civil society, an important asset in a context where women's rights are often used as a political tool. Third, following the electoral victory of the Islamist party and the threats by Salafist groups to reverse women's rights, the Tunisian women's movement is trying to create a united front, beyond secularist versus Islamist divides, and to reframe the debate to focus on the issues that matter most to the majority of Tunisian women.

Sharia and women's rights

Sharia, an Arabic word meaning 'the path to be followed', refers to a set of legal injunctions collectively known as Islamic law (Doi 1984). The *Quran*, believed by Muslims to be the word of God, is the main source of Islamic law. The *Quran* comprises a series of ethical principles and guidelines rather than strict legal prescriptions. According to John Esposito (1982), the *Quran* is supplemented by other sources to form the basis for Sharia law. *Sunna* (tradition), which refers to the oral teachings and model behaviour of the Prophet Muhammad, is a primary source for Sharia. *Ijmaa*, a consensus of opinion among Muslim scholars, and *Ijtihad*, independent juristic reasoning, provide answers when the *Quran* and *Sunna* are silent. Reasoning by analogy, *Qiyas*, is a restricted form of *Ijtihad* through which precedents can be extended to cover new situations.

According to many Muslim scholars, while the first two sources of Sharia, the *Quran* and *Sunna*, are considered divinely inspired, the other three, *Qiyas*, *Ijmaa* and *Ijtihad*, are based on human reasoning that applies the principles of the *Quran* and the teachings of the Prophet. Amira Mashhour asserts: 'This proves that Sharia is not supposed to be static, but rather evolving, and that the role of *Ijtihad*, guided by the principles of justice, equity, and public welfare, is crucial in responding to changing social needs' (Mashhour 2005: 566). This position is held widely among Muslim scholars, although not by fundamentalists.

The conservative forces that dominate Islamist groups hold a position that allows no room for compromise, making gender equality and Islam mutually exclusive. As Rema Hammami points out:

> the choice offered to women is: either to remain attached to your religious heritage and accept that men and women are fundamentally different and therefore unequal; or to forsake your religious identity … for gender equality. In other words … women cannot lay claims to Islamic identity and gender equality at the same time. (Hammami 2012: 3)

Many Muslims, however, believe that Sharia is a wholly divine law with little or no room for interpretation or adjustment to social change (An-Na'im 1990), although what they consider to be Sharia includes a number of provisions not contained in the *Quran* or *Sunna*.

Some scholars argue that Bourguiba's Code du Statut Personnel (CSP), while essentially based on Islamic law and consistent with the spirit of the *Quran* and *Sunna*, offered a progressive model based on a modern and liberal interpretation of Islamic texts. Amira Mashhour emphasises that in the *Quran* 'men and women have equal religious duties, rewards, and punishments before God' (Mashhour 2005: 564). She argues that the discrimination against women enshrined in contemporary Muslim legislation, such as the penal codes regarding so-called 'honour crimes', is not inscribed in the *Quran* but 'actually run[s] against the spirit of Islam and justice' (ibid.: 564). She suggests that Bourguiba's project articulated a progressive and modernising discourse of women's rights within the framework of Arab Muslim cultural and religious traditions. Mashhour and other scholars maintain that the subordination of women is not based on Islam per se, but rather is the result of traditional, patriarchal, male-dominated social and political practices that aim to control and subjugate women. From this perspective, the Tunisian CSP can be seen as a model for achieving a common ground between Islamic law and gender equality through a process of liberal *Ijtihad* in relation to polygamy and women's rights to divorce, to be gainfully employed, and to represent themselves in civil society.

The feminist movement in Tunisia

Until the late twentieth century, Tunisia did not have an autonomous feminist movement. Male thinkers dominated the discourse of women's emancipation, from Tahar Haddad to Bourguiba and Ben Ali. Tunisian feminist scholars argue that until the 1980s, women's rights' reforms were largely promoted by men and were not aimed at radically transforming women's position. Rather, they encouraged women's emancipation and education as mothers, thereby upholding patriarchal family structures and men's spheres of influence (Ferchiou 1996; Charrad 2008; Zayzafoon 2005; Gilman 2007). While at the time of independence a few Tunisian women took positions on nationalism and women's emancipation, they did not develop women's movements and were mainly drawn from the educated, middle-class elite in Tunis (Jones 2010: 45). It was Habib Bourguiba who, in 1958, established the Union National de la Femme Tunisienne, the first nationwide women's organisation, as a vehicle for implementing his brand of state feminism. The reforms undertaken by Bourguiba, while popular and welcomed by women, did not emerge from a broad-based, autonomous women's movement.

In 1979, a group of left-wing feminist women formed the Club d'Études de la Condition des Femmes (Centre for the Study of the Condition of Women), which is also known as the Club Tahar al-Haddad, since it was based at the Tahar Haddad Cultural Centre in the medina[1] of Tunis. This women's studies centre engaged in various activities to promote women's rights and hosted talks and debates, including several presentations by Egyptian writer and feminist activist Nawal El Saadawi. In 1985, the centre created a monthly bilingual (Arabic and French) magazine, *Nissa* (*Women*), as a forum for discussing gender issues, but financial burdens and political tensions among the editorial board led to its demise in early 1987 (Jrad 1996). Also in 1985, members of the Club Tahar al-Haddad created a formal organisation, the Association Tunisienne des Femmes Démocrates (ATFD), which was finally legalised in 1989.

The legalisation of the ATFD marked a new chapter in Tunisia's feminist movement. Established and run by educated and professional leftist women, the ATFD has dedicated itself to the elimination of all forms of discrimination against women. It vows to fight for the transformation of patriarchal attitudes, the defence of women's rights, and the participation of women in all aspects of politics and civil society. In addition to its advocacy, the association operates a counselling centre for women victimised by domestic violence.[2] Through its actions, the ATFD has become a dominant force in Tunisia's feminist movement.

Established in 1989, the Association des Femmes Tunisiennes pour la Recherche et le Développement (AFTURD) is ATFD's research-oriented sister organisation. The AFTURD is formally affiliated with the larger women's research network, the Association of African Women for Research and Development, and participates in exchanges between women in the region. On a national level, the AFTURD sponsors forums on key women's issues such as inheritance, where ongoing research is presented and proposals for change debated.

These progressive women's organisations always had a difficult relationship with the regime. Ben Ali's dictatorship became very repressive of civil society and severely limited freedom of association and expression. The state instituted censorship committees that regulated the arts and popular culture as well as social and political activism. Women's rights activists were often silenced and their activities blocked. During the crackdown on Islamists in the 1990s, several pro-Islamist women militants were imprisoned for defying the regime's position on Islam, and the state police injured and harassed many more female activists. These notorious actions are part of what led young women to participate in the December 2010 to January 2011 uprisings that toppled the regime. Women's presence was felt on a variety of fronts: in the streets protesting loudly against the dictatorship; in cyberspace conveying to the world the events going on in the country; and in communities cooking and feeding street protesters, tending the wounded and consoling the bereaved.

Building on the revolutionary momentum, women created numerous civil society associations with diverse political orientations in the months immediately after the fall of the regime. The Association of Tunisian Women Lawyers was founded in March 2011 to improve the legal and juridical status of Tunisian women. This progressive, secular association works to inform women of their rights, guide them through the legal system, provide legal support, and develop research on women's rights and the legal system.

Nissa Tounsyat (the Association of Tunisian Women) was established in April 2011 as an autonomous association with Islamic tendencies but no affiliation with any political party. Its president, Ibtihel Abdulatif, explained that: 'For many decades, we Muslim women did not have an organisation that represented our views. The democratic feminists dominate the discourse of women's rights in Tunisia, but they do not take into account the views and needs of Muslim women like us.'

Arrhma: Association des Femmes Nahdaouis (the Association of Ennahdha Women) is an Islamist women's association founded in March 2011. While it is not the women's wing of Ennahdha, its members are all supporters of the Islamist party. The religious objectives of Arrhma are the promotion of the rights and obligations of Muslim women on the basis of the *Quran* and *Sunna*. Socially, it aims to support women, make them aware of their rights, within their interpretation of Islam, and develop networks of solidarity among Muslim women who have long been marginalised.

These associations, along with many others that sprang up across the country after the revolution, have been active in mobilising women to defend their interests, and have significantly transformed the landscape of the Tunisian feminist movement, not just in terms of the number of organisations but also in terms of their diversity of ideas. Over the years, feminist organisations in Tunisia have played an active role in trying to improve the rights of women, but women's associations that were instrumental in lobbying for the expansion of rights in the CSP during the 1990s are contending with Islamic extremism today.

The pre-revolution feminist movement, dominated by progressive left-wing women's associations, has been criticised by its Islamist counterparts as comprising elitist, middle-class women who are far removed from the experiences and aspirations of ordinary and poor women, who are more attached to Muslim traditions. It has also been accused of championing a Western brand of feminism that is alien to Tunisian society and culture. Similar debates occurred in Iran after the revolution of 1979, when women's fundamental rights in the public, familial and personal domains were undermined under the aegis of a return to Muslim values and traditions and a revival of an 'authentic' national identity (Shahidian 1998). Many women fought these incursions by appealing to the universality of human rights and opposition to patriarchal domination. Iranian conservatives, however, summarily dismissed the rhetoric of universality as a decadent, Western argument.

Non-Western advocates of women's rights have certainly had an ambivalent relationship with Western feminism. The debate between Western and non-Western feminisms has been a dominant feature of women's and feminist studies since the 1980s (De Groot 2010). The ideas and practices of feminism as enunciated and espoused by Western scholars and activists have been subjected to sharp criticism by non-Western feminists and gender studies specialists for postulating monolithic assumptions about the circumstances and aspirations of women in other contexts around the world (hooks 1981; Hull et al. 1982; Lugones and Spelman 1983; Amos and Parmar 1984; Crenshaw 1989). Some Western feminist theory has been charged with being ethnocentric for ignoring the specific experiences of women of colour and for homogenising women's experiences on the basis of Western perspectives and priorities, which it erroneously assumes to be universal. Critics in the 1980s have also taken issue with Western feminists' image of non-Western women as helpless victims of ethnic, cultural and religious traditions controlled by patriarchies. A prime example is the simplistic rejection of Muslim women's veiling as merely a form of patriarchal oppression (Saul 2003).

In response to this critique, feminist theorists have examined how Western understandings of women, gender and feminism have been entwined with colonial, class-based and ethnic histories (Mohanty 2003; Gunew and Yeatman 1993, Narayan and Harding 2000; Eisenstein 2004). Contested discussions about the potential of Islamic feminism, like discussions of race, class and gender, are now embedded in a range of historical, theoretical and social science research and analysis (Yamani 1996; Abu-Lughod 1998; Afshar 1998; Moghissi 1999; Mir Hosseini 2000; Wadud 2006; Badran 2009). Feminists have demonstrated that, over the centuries of European colonialism, women, both as a group and as a social category, have often been treated as passive symbols of national identity rather than being allowed to speak for themselves and act on their own behalf. Women have struggled to escape this symbolic function but have rarely been able to shed the definitions that others, both traditionalists and modernisers, have imposed upon them. The debates among Tunisians on the meanings and the ideological underpinnings of feminism and women's rights today generate possibilities for developing deeper and more nuanced understandings of contemporary women's struggles that may contribute to a reframing of the political debate on women's rights in a way that privileges women's priorities rather than the broader ideological views of political parties.

Women's rights and the secularism versus Islamism debate

Following its electoral victory in October 2011, Ennahdha reaffirmed its commitment to respect women's rights and vowed not to advocate for the imposition of Sharia as the law of the state. Since then, however, the struggle over the role of religion in government and society has become the most intensely divisive issue in Tunisia. Flourishing extremist groups led by Salafists who aim to promote the strict observance of religious law have conducted several street demonstrations in favour of instituting Sharia and establishing an Islamic state in Tunisia.

These conservative Islamic groups have been trying to scale back a number of the rights that are inscribed in the CSP of 1956. Ennahdha's ability to uphold its stated position of respecting rather than repealing the CSP is being hindered by its failure to take a firm stand against Islamic extremism. Ennahdha publicly calls for dialogue between Salafists and more moderate Islamists as well as with secularists, but many Tunisians believe that the party in power maintains a secret alliance with the Salafist movement. A division of labour seems to be at work, with Ennahdha taking a moderate stance to win the support of Western powers and some secularist groups, while the Salafists push a hard-line Islamist position.[3] In this way, Ennahdha publicly appears to be the voice of reason placed at the centre between Islamic extremists and secularists.

In July 2012, a parliamentary committee of the National Constituent Assembly (NCA), when considering the new constitution, proposed the very ambiguous Article 27 regarding women's rights. This stipulates that the state guarantees 'the protection of women's rights ... under the principle of complementarity to men within the family and as an associate of men in the development of the country'.[4] The proposed article provoked vigorous debate among Tunisians, because many saw it as undermining the equality of men and women. Women's rights activists took issue with the fact that the article defined women's place in society in terms of their relationship to men, emphasising complementarity, and therefore difference rather than equality. They feared that the article compromised existing rights enshrined in the CSP. More than 8,000 activists signed a petition addressed to the NCA, saying that 'the state is about to vote on an article in the constitution that limits the citizenship rights of women' and that women 'are citizens just like men' and 'should not be defined in terms of men'.[5]

Tunisian activists have been very vocal in defending women's rights. On 13 August 2012, thousands of people, both women and men, attended a march for women's rights on the occasion of Tunisian Women's Day. Despite being forbidden by the Ministry of the Interior to hold a march on Habib Bourguiba Avenue, political parties, non-governmental organisations, human rights groups and private citizens gathered together to chant slogans supporting women's equality and to march in an orderly fashion from the clock tower on 14 Janvier Square and along Mohamed V Street in the centre of Tunis. Some participants loudly exposed Ennahdha's hypocrisy and its inability to govern the country; they repeated chants from the revolution, such as the famous 'Dégage!' to demand change.

The march was characterised by remarkable unity and solidarity in support of women's rights. Tunisian women in veils walked beside unveiled women in jeans and short dresses, and many held signs demanding equality between men and women. For Tunisian women, the use of the veil is not the main issue; equality, self-determination and access to education and employment are far more central to their struggles. The march also showed solidarity between women and men; many men attended the event and marched alongside the women. Ben Ayed, who attended the march with his wife and two sons, said that he is trying to teach his children that there can be a balance between equality, democracy and development on one side and Islam on the other. 'There is a trend now in the Constituent Assembly ... to lessen the rights of the Tunisian woman. We are here ... to guard the rights of the Tunisian woman, and to keep them for the future generation,' asserted Ben Ayed.[6] The unity and solidarity displayed by Tunisians in this march demonstrate that secularist versus Islamist tensions result from politicians' manipulation of issues of identity: ordinary Tunisians are happy to coexist and respect each other's freedom of choice. That is why veiled and non-veiled women, men and women all marched together to protect women's rights.

Under pressure from civil society representatives, the NCA altered the clauses to remove the ambiguities over gender equality. The new draft of the constitution was released in December 2012.

The veil The hijab, the veil, has become an important symbol in the debate between Islamists and secularists, and serious conflicts have been sparked because of women wearing or not wearing it. During the dictatorship of Ben Ali, women were not allowed to wear the veil in educational or other government institutions. In November 2011, Manouba University in Tunis became the stage of fierce battles between Salafists and secularists. Several female students wearing the niqab (a black veil covering the full face and body)[7] were barred from attending class on the basis of previous laws about Muslim attire in educational institutions. While university officials accepted the wearing of the hijab, a veil covering only the hair and neck, they rejected the niqab because it appeared to obscure the student's identity.

The incident sparked demonstrations by pro-Islamist students, both male and female, claiming Muslim students' right to wear the niqab. Tensions grew as pro-secularist students, who comprised the vast majority, came out to demonstrate in favour of the ban on the niqab. As the conflict escalated, Salafist groups descended on the university to support the pro-Islamist demonstrators. They tore down the Tunisian national flag and replaced it with the Salafi flag, a black banner symbolically associated with jihadi Salafism. Khaoula Rashidi, a 25-year-old female student at the university, gained national acclaim for climbing the wall and attempting to take down the Salafi flag. The image of Rashidi pulling down the flag became one of the most iconic symbols of Tunisian women's fight against Salafism.

Ennahdha's position on the use of the veil in official institutions remains ambivalent. As a result of the November 2011 clashes at Manouba University, Habib Kazdaghli, the dean of the faculty of arts, became a defendant in a court case for allegedly slapping one of the female students wearing the niqab. Kazdaghli appeared before the first instance court of Manouba following a complaint lodged by the student. He was accused, by the public prosecutor, of 'violence committed by an official while carrying out his duties', which carries a potential five-year prison sentence.[8] While Kazdaghli completely denied the accusation as an attack on his freedoms, he stressed that it resulted from the fact that the student (who lodged the complaint) had been expelled from his faculty for a period of six months for refusing to remove her niqab. 'This trial is not just about me; it is aimed at all those who defend academic freedoms and who promote the respect of educational rules,'[9] Kazdaghli emphasised. Indeed, he has had the full support of the university's administration, of his colleagues and of the students' union. A formal statement in Kazdaghli's support was also issued by the university committee for the defence of university values and academic freedoms. The Union Générale Tunisienne du Travail and other secularist groups also expressed support for Kazdaghli.

Ennahdha has been conspicuously silent about this case and many other incidents of this kind. Assaults by extremist Islamists are becoming commonplace, and moderate secularist Tunisians are increasingly raising concerns about the behaviour of hard-line Islamists that goes unpunished.

Several young women I spoke with in major cities and small towns across Tunisia recounted stories of Salafists harassing girls in the streets for dressing in modern clothing and not wearing the hijab. 'My friend and I were walking down the street dressed casually in jeans and T-shirts when suddenly a group of Salafists began to berate us; they said we were not true Muslim women because we were not wearing the hijab,' asserted 22-year-old Rawya from Kairouan. Saida, a 26-year-old woman from Djerba, recounted that: 'Salafists can be physically violent against girls without the hijab ... They also call you bad names and say that you are women of ill repute.' These kinds of incidents have been reported across the country, although their frequency and the level of violence involved has varied. Appalled by these events, Aïcha, a 24-year-old from Nabeul, stressed:

> Bourguiba was the president who started freeing Tunisian women and Ben Ali continued that ... We don't want those gains to be reversed by the conservatism and extremism of the Islamists ... We don't want to be forced to wear the hijab ... We want a moderate society because extremes, in one direction or the other, are not good.

When I visited Tunisia in April and June 2012, I noticed that, compared with June 2011 when I first visited the country, there were many more women, especially young women, wearing the hijab. I also saw a few women covered by the niqab, which I do not recall having seen in 2011. Mouna, a 23-year-old also from Djerba, told me that she decided to start wearing the hijab after the revolution because she now feels 'free to respect my religion and obey the command of Allah that is written in the *Quran*. I wear the hijab out of piety.'

The connection between veiling and religious observance shapes many other women's thinking, even if they act differently. Kholoud, a 19-year-old from Monastir, told me that she intends to start wearing the veil after she gets married. 'Before marriage I won't wear the hijab because I want to enjoy my life, go out to the clubs with my friends and dance, and live a youthful life. But once I get married I want to devote my life to my family and to God.' To her, youth is associated with freedom from the constraints and responsibilities incumbent on married women. As 42-year-old Naima explained, women wearing the hijab are expected to conform more strictly to religious norms:

> To wear the hijab, young women have to trust themselves and

be sure that they will be able to behave 'properly' ... They cannot go out with boys and kiss or hug in public, they have to wear modest clothing covering the arms and legs, they have to be respectful, etc. ... The hijab should not be taken lightly as just a piece of clothing; it is a statement of piety.

During my first visit to Tunisia I befriended Rihem, a 30-year-old married woman enrolled in a PhD programme at the University of Tunis. At that time, like many modern women with young children, she was juggling family life with preparing for a profession. When I saw her a year later she explained that she had been grappling with the question of wearing the hijab. She said that she had always been religious but had never felt the need to display her piety in her attire, as so many Muslim women do. Now, after rereading the *Quran*, she was considering whether as a Muslim woman she ought to do so. Rihem felt unsafe in her society and believed that wearing the hijab would leave her free from negative judgements by radical extremists. Many women today are struggling with social pressure to conform to certain religious ideals in a climate full of tensions over the role of religion in public life. The increase in the number of women wearing the veil, or considering wearing it, may well be related to the pressure being exercised by Salafist groups, as well as by conservative husbands and relatives.

Notwithstanding these pressures, several young women refuse to be intimidated by the Salafists and will not wear the hijab. As Karima, a 25-year-old student from Sousse, commented:

I grew up in a Muslim family and have been educated as a Muslim but the hijab was not something the women in my family wore ... My grandmother wore the *safsari*[10] [a traditional Tunisian form of veil], which is different from the hijab, but my mother, my aunts and sisters never wore anything to cover their hair, neck or face. So, why should I wear the hijab today? I am comfortable being a Muslim woman without wearing the hijab.

During a focus group discussion in Kasserine with seven young men and three young women, a heated discussion erupted when one of the young women, a 22-year-old information and communications technology student, asked: 'Why is religion asking women to wear the hijab, or even worse the niqab, like in Saudi Arabia? Our religion is not promoting equality between men and women; I do not agree with those who want women to wear the hijab.' One of the young men, a 30-year-old pro-Islamist entrepreneur, considered her statement blasphemous. Raising his voice, he complained about what she had just said and threatened to leave the room. Most of the male participants sided with him, and the women felt intimidated by their strong reaction. As the atmosphere became tense, I intervened to try and calm down the situation, explaining that everyone is entitled to her or his opinion and that they should respect each other's views. Speaking in a more reasonable tone, the young men clarified their position. 'She should not have used that language. She cannot say that Islam is against women; she cannot say that Islam is wrong,' affirmed 27-year-old Ahmed. Bassem, who is 24, contended that: 'In Islam there are certain things that are not debatable; they are the word of God.' The young women remained in the room but did not engage in the discussion any more, as these two young men would not allow space for debate. What happened in the focus group in Kasserine is a microcosm of the sensitivities and tensions that have arisen around religion, politics and women's rights in Tunisia today.

Indeed, during my recent visits to the country I became more self-conscious about the clothing I wore, especially to interviews, given the charged atmosphere regarding the politics of women's attire. During a visit to the town of Regueb in the governorate of Sidi Bouzid, I requested an interview with 38-year-old El Hadj, a member of a Salafist group. While he agreed to be interviewed, he refused to speak to me unless I were wearing the hijab. After long negotiations in which I tried and failed to convince him to waive this requirement, I decided that I would rather comply for a few hours than forgo the interview, so I borrowed a veil from a local woman. In the interview, El Hadj stressed that in the view

181

of the Salafist movement the status of women in society is central to Sharia, and that the *Quran* and *Sunna* clearly state that true Muslim women must wear the veil. Explaining why he required me, a non-Muslim woman, to wear the hijab in his presence, El Hadj affirmed that Muslim men must not talk or interact with non-veiled women because men need to protect themselves from lustful gazes out of respect for the women's fathers, husbands or brothers, which is clearly stated in the *Quran*.

This conversation raised the issue of *awra*, the parts of the female body that must be kept hidden from the gaze of men. The female body is considered *awra*, which can also be understood as nakedness or being indecent and shameful when exposed to the outside world. According to the *Quran*, Muslim women should protect their *awra* by wearing the hijab and loose, long clothing. They can expose themselves only to their husbands, but they do not have to wear the hijab in the presence of direct male relatives – their fathers, sons and brothers – or other Muslim women.[11] The concept of *awra*, as El Hadj avowed, protects men from lustful gazes and sexual desires that might create problems of adultery and disrespect towards the woman's husband, father and brothers.

In a focus group session with veiled and non-veiled Muslim women in Tunis, a discussion of sexuality and women's bodies led to a heated debate. Some stated that the notion of *awra*, which is directly related to sexuality, placed the female body as the object of male desires and made it the cause of men's sins. As pointed out by Amira, a non-veiled 27-year-old:

A woman's beauty, her hair and her body, is considered as *awra* and thus indecent to be shown in public. If a man sees my hair or my curvy body he can be seduced, and that can lead into one of the biggest sins in Islam. So we, women, are regarded as the problem, not men.

Amira's view was contested by Olfa, a 32-year-old veiled woman from Tunis, who stated that:

Islam has never prohibited men and women from having sexual

contacts, but it imposes a code of conduct based on humility, modesty and respect for one another and for those around them. As a devout Muslim woman myself I cover my body, and personally I don't feel constrained or deprived in any way. On the contrary, in the street, no man will see my skin or touch me or try to abuse me ... at home I give myself permission to all sexual pleasures.

Indeed, several participants stressed that Islam encourages sexuality in the context of marriage. Unlike Christianity, which sees sexuality solely as a means of procreation, Islam allows sex for pleasure, both for men and for women. Amel, a veiled 33-year-old social worker, confirmed this: 'Our religion, the *Quran* and the Prophet's teachings are much more open to sexual pleasure because it encourages married couples to explore their sexuality. Sex is seen as spiritual.' Some non-veiled women found this portrayal of Islam inaccurate. They stated that practices such as oral sex, sodomy and intercourse during menstruation are prohibited in Islamic teachings. Karima, a 25-year-old from La Marsa, asserted: 'The fact that non-married Muslim women cannot have sexual relations before marriage, and Muslim men can, does not place Islam very high in the scale of a religion that encourages sexual pleasures equally for men and women.'

A number of veiled Muslim women stressed that, despite all the advances in modern society, women are still seen by men mostly as sexual objects. 'So why expose ourselves to satisfy them?' asked Nadia, a 30-year-old from Thala. Nadia continued to say that 'the hijab protects the honour of women and doesn't provoke undesirable sexual advances on the part of the opposite sex. I think that if women universally adopted the Islamic dress code, the rates of sexual harassment, kidnapping and rape would become more negligible.' Of course, this view was rejected by most of the non-veiled women. They considered it too simplistic to equate sexual harassment and rape with the way women dress and present themselves in public.

In Tunisia, as stated before, there has been greater visibility of Islamic extremism as Salafist groups have become more assertive. During my interview with El Hadj, the Salafist leader from Regueb, he argued that Sharia should be the law of the state, and claimed that he and his fellow Salafists will continue their jihad to make Tunisia a 'true' Muslim country. The pro-secular and some pro-Islamist women's organisations I worked with expressed concern in relation to the Salafists' extremist position on Sharia and women's rights. 'As Muslim women who are open to modernisation based on the Islamic law, we are against the extremism of the Salafists for whom violence is a legitimate form of imposing religion,' stated Atika, a 28-year-old pro-Islamist activist from Ariana. 'Salafists are giving a bad image to Islam, which is a religion of freedom, tolerance and democracy,' she argued.

The Ennahdha government has been severely criticised for its lax approach to curtailing Salafist assaults. Ennahdha has employed a very 'light touch' when dealing with the Salafist movement, and many people pointed to the yawning gap between Ennahdha's speeches and its actions. Ennahdha has failed to distance itself from the Salafists and has supported some of their positions, such as that on women's right to wear the full-face veil or niqab. Many Tunisian women, both secularists and Islamists, reject the niqab. As pro-Islamist Ibtihel Abdulatif asserted: 'The niqab is not part of Tunisia's Islamic tradition – Muslim women in Tunisia never wore it – the niqab is an import from the Gulf countries.' Zeynab Farhat, a secular activist from the ATFD, also expressed concern about Ennahdha's encouragement of the niqab because 'it takes away the identity of the woman in question; she becomes the "unknown" ... this becomes a way of controlling women's bodies'.

Secular groups complain that Ennahdha has engaged in doublespeak, sounding moderate in public while behind the scenes drawing upon a radical Islamist agenda that threatens Tunisia's progressive achievements. Indeed, many young women I interviewed believe that Ennahdha might be facilitating the rise of the Salafist movement and worry that Ennahdha might eventually adopt the Salafists' radical positions. This allegation does not appear absurd to experts in the field. According to Samir Amghar, a specialist in Islamic studies, it is not coincidental that Ennahdha takes an ambiguous position in relation to the Salafists. He stated: 'Ennahdha and the Salafists are not rivals. They move on different ground ... They are complementary ... There is an implicit division of work between Ennahdha and the Salafists. The latter assume positions that the former, Ennahdha, cannot afford to have.'[12] For Amghar, Ennahdha is trying to present itself as a moderate and non-radical Islamist party to avoid arousing concerns on the part of Western governments, but at the same time it is under pressure to address the concerns and aspirations of the extremist Islamic groups that voted for the party (Amghar 2011).

Pro-Islamist women's groups encourage women to wear the hijab and to conform to Islamic law, respecting the provisions of the *Quran* and *Sunna*. Amani, a 29-year-old member of a pro-Islamist women's association, stated that:

> the wearing of the hijab is part of the identity of the Muslim woman and is a personal act of worship. The *Quran* and the sayings (*hadith*) of the Prophet Muhammad insist that Muslim women must cover their hair and wear clothing that covers the contours of their bodies when they are outside their homes or in the presence of men.

Democratic and secular feminists find the use of the veil objectionable in principle and are opposed to it being imposed on women. At the same time, however, they believe that it should be the woman's choice to wear it or not. In 2011, Hélé Béji, a renowned Tunisian scholar, published *Islam Pride*, a controversial book about Muslim women and the wearing of the veil. While the author personally opposes the wearing of the veil, she believes that every woman should be free to make her own decision on this matter. Béji is very critical of types of feminism, which are most often found in Europe but are also represented elsewhere, that make no effort to understand the veil as an expression of feminism through which some Muslim women have chosen to enter and engage with modernity. She argues that the veil is a Muslim reaction against 'modernity as oppression. And if modernity has become oppressive, or experienced as such, then the recall of tradition resonates as a liberation' (Béji 2011: 50). In her view, modernity has failed women by not addressing a number of critical ills that affect them, particularly violence and sexual harassment. Feminists who fail to engage seriously with the problems faced by Muslim women in the context of modernity are limiting feminism to their own experiences and world views. 'If I denied them [Muslim women] this sovereign principle that resonates in any woman, I would weaken my own feminism ... I [would] limit the universal nature of women's sovereignty to only myself,' Béji concludes (ibid.: 108).

Women's right to education, employment and self-determination

All the women's associations I spoke with were committed to upholding women's rights to education, employment and self-determination. Latifa Araissia, president of the pro-Ennahdha women's association Arrhma, pointed out that:

> for Prophet Muhammad, women's rights are sacred, and he said to men: 'God orders you to treat women with respect because they are your mothers, daughters, your aunts.'
> Contrary to what Westerners think, in Islam women are not marginalised. There is a tradition of women's rights within Islam. For many centuries Muslim women have been involved in all areas of knowledge; before, there were Muslim women jurists (*fuqaha*), there were also those who recited the speech of the Prophet (*hadith*). Women were employed in a wide range of activities in trade, agriculture and the textile industry. This proves that women could work and achieve very high ranks even at the beginning of the Islamic era.

However, pro-Islamist associations tend to argue against full equality and to see women's roles as focusing mainly on their domestic responsibilities as mothers and wives, and, when extended to the public sphere, encompassing all-female and some gender-mixed settings but not male-dominated ones. In a focus group discussion with pro-Islamist women, many mentioned that having women working in male-dominated environments might lead to sins such as adultery and premarital affairs. Habiba, a 33-year-old primary school teacher in Tunis, stated that 'demands for women to work in men's settings under the pretext of modernism are very dangerous. The implications can be very serious, not to mention that they contradict sacred texts requiring women to stay home and to devote themselves primarily to the family.'

The ATFD and other secular women's associations are mobilising women to defend their rights and safeguard the CSP. At the same time, recognising the limitations of the CSP, they are demanding a review of the inheritance laws so that men and women are treated equitably. These women's organisations have also produced a substantial body of research on the situation of women in the country. They see this type of engagement as essential to preserving and improving the rights of women in Tunisia.

Many pro-Islamist women's associations are not comfortable with all the provisions of the CSP and favour some revisions. While there is incomplete agreement about which provisions need review, those on polygamy and adoption were mentioned as controversial, and most pro-Islamist associations oppose making any changes to the existing inheritance clauses.[13] As Ibtihel Abdulatif of Nissa Tounsyat explained:

> Sharia determines that the man should get more, precisely because of his social responsibility as protector. Men must look after their mothers, sisters, wives and daughters, and if we change the inheritance laws to be equal, then men may argue that they no longer have the means to protect the women ... In our society the majority of women still need men's protection.

Ibtihel's argument resonates with many poor women who fear that men may absolve themselves from their responsibility to protect the family if inheritance laws are changed. However, the inheritance issue directly relates to women's material position and their ability to be independent and access their legal rights.

In addition to espousing women's right to self-determination and full equality between men and women, the women democrats call for the complete separation of religion and the state. 'From the moment we start sanctifying our leaders we won't be able to continue to criticise them; that's why it is fundamental to separate religion from politics,' declared Ahlem Belhadj, president of the ATFD.

Polarising discourses are present in the NCA. Of the 217 members, 49 (23 per cent) are women; 42 of these represent Ennahdha and the other 7 are from secular parties. So many women were chosen because the law governing the elections mandated that all candidate lists had to include an equal number of men and women. But the women delegates have not been united. Meherzia Labidi, the female vice-president of the NCA, proposed in March 2012 the creation of an internal women's committee to allow women to collaborate across party lines. While the idea was never dismissed, such a committee was never developed. During important debates about the condition of women and their rights, female members tend to take the same stand as their party rather than uniting around women's interests. There have, however, been some modest signs of solidarity among women within the NCA. They have begun to forge informal connections with one another to ensure effective female leadership as they work towards increased parity in Tunisian politics. These tenuous and unofficial alliances have yet to produce concrete results.[14]

In terms of socioeconomic policy, unofficial proposals being circulated by Ennahdha militants suggest excluding women from the paid labour force and ensuring that they marry men who are breadwinners. This plan is based on the idea that male jobseekers should be given priority over female applicants, or even that men should be given some jobs now held by women in order to solve the male unemployment problem and create proper gender relations and family stability in one fell swoop. Employed men would be able to marry and support a dependent wife and children, while women would be consigned to the domestic sphere.

While this proposal sounds absurd to many, especially to

educated, middle-class people, it has some appeal for less affluent women whose opportunities are already restricted and who enjoy little support. Many young women are struggling to reconcile the demands of the workplace with their family responsibilities. Many employed women do not earn enough money to pay for domestic help and have little or no access to social services such as childcare for infants and pre-school-aged children or after-school programmes.

Members of Ennahdha have mentioned proposals that include subsidies for educated women who decide to stay at home rather than pursue professional careers. For example, Mounia Ibrahim, a member of the executive board and head of the Office of Women for Ennahdha, mentioned in an interview to the International Crisis Group (ICG) that the party was 'working on a social and economic agenda for women's rights, with, in particular, proposals for concrete measures, such as the implementation of a salary for housewives, so they can achieve financial independence' (ICG 2011: 25–6). Behind the idea of housewives' financial independence is the encouragement for women to stay at home rather than work outside the domestic arena.

For various reasons, some women are willing to consider the idea from a practical and sociocultural standpoint. Asma, a 29-year-old employed mother from Menzel Bourguiba, affirmed that:

> If they give money to stay home, I will take it. The money will give me some independence and I won't have to juggle work and children and the household chores ... Working women with no support end up doing two or three times more work than men. In fact, we have three full-time jobs: at the office, looking after the children, and taking care of the house and the entire family.

There is a similar proposition being floated by Islamists that is also unofficial but was discussed by almost everyone I met: that the prohibition on polygamy should be overturned because women find it difficult to marry since very few men have the financial stability required to support a family. If men who could afford it were allowed to have up to four wives, the thinking goes, the number of unmarried young women would be reduced, wealth would be spread among more people, and Muslim family values would be promoted. Most of the young women I spoke with strongly opposed the idea of reinstating polygamy under any circumstances, but a number of young men thought it was a good idea given the current socioeconomic situation. 'I think the important thing is that the man who has multiple wives has to be able to treat all of them fairly and with equal respect, and that is written in the *Quran*,' said Ali, a young unmarried man from Le Kef.

Despite their political differences, the pro-secular and pro-Islamist women's associations have more in common than some people may acknowledge. They are all in favour of women's freedom of choice, access to education and employment, and the right to self-determination. They disagree about the best process for achieving these aspirations, but all share the same goal: to protect and enhance women's rights in Tunisia. The president of the pro-Islamist group Arrhma, Latifa Araissia, emphasised that:

> We are open to meet with anti-Islamist women who have concerns about their freedom and about their daughters' professional futures. We want to reassure them that we are not against education and employment for women. We have aspirations for a just society where there is respect for the rights and duties inscribed in Islamic law.

Similarly, Monia Abed from the Association of Tunisian Women Lawyers pointed out that:

> Secular feminists need to connect better with the reality of women from the most deprived regions of the country. We cannot continue to be just groups of middle-class women ... I believe all Tunisian women agree with the universal principles of freedom and social justice, and together we need to find a strategy, contextual to the Tunisian situation, to improve the condition of women.

Conclusions

Today, Tunisians are grappling with the issue of women's rights within a context of severe socioeconomic difficulties and polarised political debates surrounding the place of Islam in the national identity. The discussion about the role of Sharia turns on the extent to which religion should be embedded in the laws and policies of the modern state. Women themselves are at the centre of these debates, not only as subjects of controversy but also, and even more importantly, as political actors. Whether Tunisia's legal achievements in granting civil and personal rights to women will be sustained and expanded depends on the capacity of the women's movement to find a common ground amidst the escalating conflicts between secularists and Islamic extremists. As Tunisians write their new constitution, the burgeoning women's movement, now deeply split along Islamist versus secularist lines, will have to put aside political differences to present a united front in their fight for emancipation.

Building a feminist coalition will require both women and men to reframe the debate on women's rights, sidestepping identity politics and finding a common ground despite their ideological differences. For example focusing on the issues most women care about: education and employment; more support with childcare and care of the elderly; the ending of harassment of and violence against women; and safeguarding women's right to self-determination. Women from various tendencies could come together around these issues, even though different groups might have different priorities. They all face the challenge of being heard and lobbying effectively for the most gender-sensitive constitution possible in the new Tunisia. Despite the current difficulties they face, many of my interlocutors pointed out that Tunisia has a solid tradition of reformist movements and will end up finding its own path towards democracy and human rights for all Tunisians. The reaction of many Tunisians against the proposed Article 27 of the new constitution, which forced the authorities to review and redraft it to state clearly the equality between men and women in the new constitution, certainly attests to this reformist tradition.

Conclusion

The path to constructing a new polity, capable of addressing both the individual grievances of Tunisians and their collective political and socioeconomic aspirations, has not been without obstacles. In the post-election period, Tunisia faces major challenges relating to an increasing polarisation between secularists and Islamists, particularly a rise in Islamic extremism, and a weak performance of the troika government with regard to setting the basis for improving the socioeconomic situation of all Tunisians. The presidential and parliamentary elections set for 23 June 2013 will hopefully put in place more permanent state structures to govern the destiny of the country. In the meantime, the younger generation of Tunisians who were instrumental in the demise of the dictatorship is still struggling to find its formal political role and develop a political culture different from old corrupt and self-serving models, and which responds to their future aspirations and vision for the country.

Youth and new political culture?

It is clear that young Tunisians who played a fundamental role in the overthrow of the dictatorship have not been integrated into political parties or taken an active role in formal politics. Young people remain politically engaged in the democratic transition through their own associations and civil society initiatives rather than by participating in formal political party structures. Despite their expressed scepticism about politics, young Tunisians have an acute political sense and gained tremendous political education during the revolutionary uprisings of December 2010 and January 2011. They organised mass protests and sit-ins, disseminating information via the internet, and articulated a political discourse of change that attracted many Tunisians. The revolution constituted an important laboratory for developing a new brand of active citizenship and political participation for the younger generation.

Ayman, the political coordinator of Watad (the Democratic Patriots Party) in the Kasserine region, believes that:

> Traditional political parties have been unable to provide a discourse and a political culture that meets the interests and aspirations of the youth, and that is why young people prefer to engage with civil society associations. The political parties need to step up and reform themselves to attract the younger generation.

Tarik, a 28-year-old from Menzel Bourguiba, believes that, rather than lacking a political culture, young Tunisians are consciously refusing to join in partisan politics. Their decision to stay away is a result of mature political deliberation. In his words: 'It is not that we don't know about politics. We know enough to decide that we don't want to join them [the political parties] and become dishonest and corrupt like many of them … It is our choice to do that.' Samir, a 27-year-old from Sousse, agrees: instead of parties finding ways to accommodate the youth, he argues, young people will develop a new political culture themselves. 'The youth is the future and we will steer the development of our own society … Just give us time.'

During the electoral campaign in 2011, many young Tunisian activists refused to be co-opted into and used by political parties of any ideology. Given their experiences of politics during the 23 years of Ben Ali's dictatorship, they became suspicious of politics and politicians and found little reason to trust the old parties or the new ones that emerged after the revolution.[1] It is clear that young Tunisians are questioning the relevance of 'politics as usual' as they struggle to find new ways to respond to the challenges they face amidst the opportunities generated by the revolution and the end of the Ben Ali dictatorship. They express a desire for radical change and a rejection of conventional political practices.

In a similar way, young Egyptians who gathered in Tahrir Square and successfully toppled Hosni Mubarak's regime have also not participated in formal politics. During the protests, various youth groups and individual activists effectively organised themselves in a horizontal fashion and were critical actors in the demise of the dictatorship. In Egypt, there was the April 6 Youth Movement, founded in 2008 mainly by people from an educated middle-class background, which also included members of the Kifaya (Arabic for 'Enough') pro-democracy movement that was established in 2005 (El Difraoui 2012). Another youth grouping was the 'We are All Khaled Said', a Facebook network named after the blogger who was brutally murdered by the Egyptian police in June 2010; and there was also the iconic figure of Wael Ghonim, the 30-year-old head of marketing for Google in North Africa and the Middle East, a democrat and activist who was secretly detained by the police in January 2011 (ibid.). Inspired by the events in Tunisia, all these youth groups played a central role and led the revolution against the Egyptian regime.

However, in the post-Mubarak period, they have been sidelined by the established political forces that took control of the political space. While a number of young Egyptians may belong to the youth leagues of political parties, they have very little political expression and appear to be there as token youth representation. Disappointed by the course of the democratic transition, many young activists have refused to be co-opted and manipulated by political parties, and have consciously distanced themselves from formal party politics. A young Egyptian activist whom I had a chance to interview during a youth conference in Addis Ababa in November 2012 stated that most young activists refuse to join the government or enter formal political structures because they would not have the space to effect meaningful change from within. They would end up tainted by or hostage of a political system driven by personal interest and greed, with no political autonomy – a system that, in their eyes, is becoming obsolete.

This scepticism towards established politics is also shared by activists of the Y'en a Marre youth movement in Senegal, which prevented the re-election of Abdoulaye Wade in the February

2012 elections. Having supported Macky Sall in the second round of the elections, Y'en a Marre's leaders declined invitations to join the cabinet or to transform the movement into a political party. Young Y'en a Marre activists pride themselves on being non-partisan and focusing on their national public campaign to create what they call a 'new type of Senegalese': one who is more socially and politically conscious and that assumes her or his responsibilities as a citizen to raise awareness and fight for a better life for the Senegalese people. They also vow to hold politicians accountable to those who elected them.[2]

Once the old regimes fall and the enthusiasm and energy of the street protests wane, the 'traditional' and more established political forces and practices quickly move in to occupy the institutional vacuum, reverting to 'politics as usual' even if there are some cosmetic changes. It is no longer the time of 'power to the people' and the politics of the street or the square. The young activists who participated in and led the revolution suddenly find themselves battling to define a new political role and to carve new spaces of intervention. They refrain from joining formal political parties and have to work around old political models that they despise, using street politics and civil society organisations as their institutional settings. As Aditya Nigam points out, after the protests and revolutions, these societies are 'living in an interregnum when the old forms of politics have become moribund and obsolete but new ones have not yet emerged ... Something, clearly, is waiting to be articulated in this relentless refusal of the political' (Nigam 2012: 175).

However, the rejection of 'politics as usual' and the search for new forms of political engagement are not limited to Africa, as movements such as the Indignados in Spain and Occupy Wall Street in the United States have also contested formal political order and have sought new forms of and locations for political organisation and participation.

Indeed, some analysts have suggested that the youth-led social movements of the twenty-first century are based on forms of mobilisation and political practices that call into question the very nature of 'the political' (ibid. 2012).[3] The traditional political system based on political parties with specific practices and relationships does not resonate with the young protesters. These recent youth movements reflect a generation's deep disaffection with 'normal' politics, and their striving to create a new 'political' by using both old models, such as assembly, consensus and autonomy, and new ones such as Facebook, Twitter feeds, YouTube videos, Instagram photographs and electronic messaging. Anthropologist David Graeber argued that the Occupy movement in the United States refused to accept the legitimacy of the existing political order and developed a strong anti-hierarchical and anti-authoritarian consensus-based type of politics.[4]

British philosopher Simon Critchley has suggested that young people's disconnect from current political culture stems from the dissociation of power from politics. He states that 'power is the ability to get things done, and politics is the means to get those things done,'[5] and democracy is the system that allows for power to be exercised by the people. Indeed, the principles of liberal democracy rest on the idea that citizens exercise their power through the ballot box to elect governments that will respect the will of the people and use that power on their behalf.

However, today we are witnessing a divorce of power from politics, as power has been seized not only by 'supra-national finance, trade and information platforms, but also by transnational organised criminal networks – human trafficking, drugs, weapons, illegal immigration'.[6] Devoid of power, politics remain localised in the nation state and respond to the interests of supra-national power, not to the will of the people. In this sense, 'sovereignty is outsourced' and democracy becomes a charade, as politics have no power but instead *serve* power. But Critchley reminds us that the separation between politics and power did not happen by chance but through the connivance of politicians who embraced free market capitalism as the engine of growth and personal gain.[7]

It is precisely this state of affairs that the younger generation is rebelling against. Young Tunisians, Egyptians and Senegalese have confronted corrupt and self-serving governments and dictators.

They have also denounced their governments' and political parties' dependency on Western funding for political campaigns and economic projects, which creates a culture of subservience to capital that undermines sovereignty and national interests. Young Europeans and Americans have also blamed the current economic crisis on politicians who are seen as being insufficiently accountable, corrupt and dependent on large corporations and supra-national businesses. This view extends across party politics: many in the Indignados movement claimed that there were few real differences between the two main parties – the conservative Partido Popular and the socialist Partido Socialista Obrero Español – and that they shared equal responsibility vis-à-vis the country's socioeconomic situation. Similarly, young Americans complained of the power of corporations over government and the control exercised by big money on election campaigns. In this regard, these social movements seem to be fighting to return power to the political arena, as young protesters question established credos and organise themselves differently, acting with transparency on consensus-based decision making and establishing horizontal and more equitable relationships within their movements.[8]

Like many young people around the globe, the young Tunisians I spoke to are convinced that the current system is not serving them and something new needs to happen. They appear to be fully aware of the situation and the challenges they face, and that they have a long road to travel. But they have vowed to carry on with the struggle and not allow the older generation to tarnish their revolution. They continue to put pressure on the authorities through street protests, sit-ins, exchanges on social networks and independent associations. But how, when and what kind of new political culture this generation will be able to create remains the big question.

Achievements and limitations of the Tunisian revolutionary movement

Tunisia gained international acclaim both as the spark that ignited the so-called 'Arab Spring' and as the first country to successfully institutionalise the 'revolution' through its universally commended 'free and fair' democratic elections in October 2011 (Shahshahani and Mullin 2012). However, this does not mean that either the political transition or democratic freedoms and equitable socioeconomic development will be achieved easily. As discussed throughout this book, the path to sustainable societal change is not linear but rather happens through complex processes of exchange and negotiation between diverse interests, tendencies, perspectives and ideologies. Tunisians are currently involved in such processes and trying to deal with a myriad of situations, both expected and unexpected, as they unfold. And the discussions highlighted above regarding the current challenges facing the democratic transition in Tunisia attest to this.

Despite this, it is possible at this point in the process to identify, and acknowledge, some of the revolution's achievements as well as its limitations thus far. A key lesson from Tunisia is undoubtedly that in the twenty-first century a revolution is still possible. For many decades the world had not seen any social movement of this magnitude that successfully toppled an entrenched and longstanding dictatorship. Whether the revolutionary process will be sustainable over the long term and whether it will translate into real change in power relations remains to be seen. But, as many of my Tunisian interlocutors emphatically stressed, the revolution has just begun and deep social change does not come overnight.

The spontaneous, leaderless revolution, unrestrained by the ideological framings of political parties, has indeed succeeded in putting an end to one of the most repressive and authoritarian regimes in the region. The sheer energy and determination of the younger generation, often deemed lost and apathetic, that were unleashed and channelled into the political arena were critical. Young unemployed graduates who sat doing nothing in street cafés; young cyber activists challenging internet censorship; young unemployed graduate women reduced to domestic chores or exploited in telemarketing call centres and factories; demoralised young graduate males relegated to occasional jobs on construction sites; and university students with little hope of joining the labour market – they all came out onto the streets to denounce their precarious situation, and to demand employment and better prospects for the future. The effervescent street demonstrations of the young people transformed the stale, everyday 'business as usual' situation in Tunisia into days of mobilisation and collective action that were often frightening and uncertain but also exciting. Young unemployed men and women from the most deprived areas of the country were joined by elite urban youths who rushed to Sidi Bouzid and Kasserine to support the uprisings.

The power and energy of the youth did not go unnoticed by many who knew them – their teachers, co-workers, parents, relatives, neighbours and friends – who, through trade unions, civil society organisations and opposition parties, attached themselves to the movement. The disconnects, grievances and discontent that guided the youth protests were felt deeply and shared by most Tunisians, and the collective force of this broad national coalition led to important political changes: the demise of the dictatorship and the dissolution of the Rassemblement Constitutionnel Démocratique that had ruled the country for over two decades.

While the rush of energy, excitement and engagement created in the days of the revolution could not be sustained over a long period, the new practices and understandings of citizenship from below that developed in the course of the uprisings continue to influence the relationship between state and citizens today. Indeed, at the moment of writing these lines (nearly two years after the events of January 2011), a Tunisian population that was once considered calm, docile and intimidated continues to sustain political protest in many cities and towns throughout the country, albeit more localised and smaller in scale. Ordinary Tunisians, on the right and on the left, Islamists and secularists, are becoming more assertive in voicing their discontent with the political and socioeconomic situation. They are holding the government accountable for creating the political conditions that will bring about stability and jobs and achieve economic growth. It is clear that the revolution provided Tunisians with a sense of empowerment to push forward demands for meaningful reform. Despite

Conclusion

199

the difficulties the country faces, freedom of expression is a reality in Tunisia today. Contrary to what happened under Ben Ali's authoritarian and repressive regime, Tunisians are openly talking politics and debating contentious political and social issues. There has been a pluralisation of the 'political' and ordinary Tunisians can freely voice their frustrations and challenge the state's monopoly of political discourse (ibid.).

Internet social networking sites were important tools of communication and mobilisation for young people involved in the revolution. Cyber activists and internet users were credited with having been instrumental in disseminating real-time information worldwide about the events in Tunisia during those days. But, at the same time, an important lesson to draw from Tunisia is that while social networking served the revolution well, the Tunisian government was also able to access and use it to track down protesters and political dissenters. Bloggers, cyber activists, journalists and politicians were detained as the authorities hacked Facebook, blogs and email accounts, forcing internet users to resort to proxies. Moreover, there is evidence today that ultra-conservative Islamic groups and other political forces are also making use of online social networks for mobilisation purposes; some Tunisians mentioned that young people are being recruited by Salafists through sophisticated cyber networks. This is a reminder that internet social networks can be exploited by a myriad of political forces and that cyber activists, especially in repressive regimes, may be vulnerable to retaliation.

Despite the fact that young people, from different backgrounds, were the precursors of this process, the movement was later transformed into a much broader coalition that extended beyond age, gender, political, socioeconomic, religious and ethnic divides. The coalition also helped to expand the initial demands for socioeconomic empowerment and freedom of expression to non-negotiable regime change. This national coalition was a key factor in the success of the revolutionary movement. On the other hand, the Tunisian experience also shows how difficult it was to maintain unity and sustain the mobilisation of such a coalition once the regime fell and the transition began. The absence of a clear common 'enemy' and the emergence of conflicting positions, perspectives and ideologies undermined the coalition. Traditional political forces, both old and new, scrambled to find a place in the political vacuum left after the fall of the regime; Islamist groups introduced a religious agenda, which prompted secularists to harden their positions; women's groups worried about the preservation and expansion of their rights; and the focus of the young revolutionaries became divided between basic socioeconomic rights such as employment (for the poor and unemployed) and more broader human rights such as civil liberties and democratic freedom (for the urban elites). However, both groups of young people withdrew from the political sphere after the revolution, rejecting any association with old-style party politics.

Although there have been twists and turns along the way, there is reason to believe that the social interactions between the various groups in the coalition during the uprisings and their shared experiences – the shared emotion of being part of the same crowds in the streets, the shared experiences of physical violence inflicted by the police, of political debates and engagement – may have deepened mutual understanding and enabled a better appreciation of one another's conditions, grievances and aspirations in ways that may resist the test of time. In this sense, the revolutionary uprisings constituted important laboratories for citizenship, unity and solidarity, and a hugely important step towards more inclusive politics. If, however, these experiences can be taken even further and harnessed for the establishment and consolidation of a new and more pluralistic political culture in Tunisia, especially by the younger generation, then the revolution will have triumphed.

In terms of the economy, and as Stiglitz reminds us, an important lesson from Tunisia is that it is not sufficient for governments to deliver reasonable economic growth, nor to simply follow the dictates of international financial markets. After all, gross domestic product in Tunisia increased by about 5 per cent annually over the last 20 years, and the International Monetary Fund and the World Bank often cited the country as one of the

better-performing economies in the region. Whereas these strategies may help get good bond ratings and please international
institutions and investors, they do not automatically translate into
job creation and increased standards of living for most citizens.[9]
That is why Tunisians came out onto the streets and overthrew
the regime. However, the failure of the troika government to
create an environment of political stability that will allow for
the implementation of much-needed economic reforms appears
to be one of the most significant limitations of the revolution so
far. Tunisians from the most impoverished areas of the country
continue to struggle as the economic situation deteriorates and
conditions worsen. The government's inability to tackle unemployment and unequal economic development has the potential to be
the critical factor in the unmaking of the revolution.

Moreover, and as discussed above, a thorny issue in Tunisia
today is the relationship between state and religion. It remains
to be seen how the Ennahdha-controlled government will be able
to politically frame and address the challenging balance of Alfred
Stepan's 'twin tolerations': first, that religious leaders cannot veto
the power of democratically elected representatives; and second,
that citizens are free to publicly practise their religion however
they choose provided they do not contradict the constitution. In
other words, how will Ennahdha balance its own religious beliefs
with the need to accommodate religious pluralism and freedom
of worship? If the Ennahdha-controlled government is capable of
developing a brand of political Islam that keeps it and everyone
else in the democratic game, in the process it might be able to
create a new model of Islamic democracy that does not involve
'the surrender of their religious identity, but keeps it integrally tied
to a firm respect for constitutional norms, liberties, and rights'.[10]

What took place, and continues to take place, in Tunisia is
being watched by many across the world as a possible model
of social transformation and political change or as a source of
revolutionary inspiration. And as time passes, more will be revealed about the processes of a historic event that is continuing
to unfold, but which has already had a tremendous global impact.

Afterword

I finished writing this book in December 2012, but just before it went to press a serious crisis arose in Tunisia following the assassination of Chokri Belaid, a renowned Tunisian human rights lawyer and political activist. Belaid was shot dead on 6 February 2013, outside his home in Tunis. Belaid was the leader of Watad (the Democratic Patriots Party) and an outspoken critic of Ennahdha. He had publicly denounced Ennahdha's political manoeuvrings and challenged the government to investigate and prosecute the violent acts of intimidation and violence carried out by religious extremist groups.

The struggle over Islam's place in government and society continues to be a divisive issue during the transition to democracy. Salafists are becoming increasingly violent in their quest to impose a strict interpretation of religion and enforce Sharia as the law of the state. The secularists, on the other hand, are increasingly afraid that such extremist positions will impinge on civil liberties and democratic freedoms, especially women's rights. The opposition and secular groups have accused the Ennahdha-led government of negligence in failing to counteract Islamic extremism. Chokri Belaid was, without a doubt, one of the regime's most vocal opponents.

This political assassination was an extraordinary event in Tunisian political history; nothing similar had occurred since 1952, when the founder of the UGTT, Ferhat Hachad, was assassinated. It was followed by the worst political and social unrest in Tunisia since January 2011, which seriously jolted the transition process. Outraged young people and people from various civil society groups came out into the streets to protest about the political murder. The Union Générale Tunisienne du Travail called nationwide strikes that paralysed the country. Growing unemployment and poverty, the sluggish economy, and the worsening security situation compounded this sense of grievance. Thousands of Tunisians from different social and economic backgrounds gathered for Belaid's funeral amid demonstrations that ended in violent clashes with the police. The massive participation in his funeral and the level of popular feeling surrounding it had never been seen before, prompting some analysts to compare it to the return of Bourguiba from exile in 1955 (Ben Hammouda 2013).

Many Tunisians called for the attackers to be brought to justice, and some demanded that the government resign. Supporters of the secular opposition pointed the finger at Ennahdha for Belaid's assassination. Ennahdha denied the accusation, instead blaming the murder on extremist Salafist militants, and vowed to find and prosecute the killers.

Ayman, a young cadre of Watad and comrade of Belaid with whom I spoke the day after the assassination, emphasised that:

> This situation is a result of Ennahdha's divisive politics that exacerbated tensions between Islamists and secularists ... They have been cosying up to the Salafists and allowing space for this sort of religious terrorism to take place ... This is an unprecedented act that opens up a new page in Tunisia's political life ... Chokri Belaid, a courageous and principled man, was killed just because he opposed Ennahdha. They forget that as a lawyer Belaid defended the Islamists who were prosecuted by Ben Ali.[1]

Belaid's murder brought to the fore serious fissures within the ruling party and the coalition government that led to the resignation of Prime Minister Hamadi Jebali. In responding to the crisis, Jebali tried to restore calm and assure the continuity of the political transition by proposing the formation of a new, non-partisan government of technocrats to lead the country until the parliamentary elections, now postponed until November 2013. Ennahdha vehemently rejected his proposal and accused him of not consulting with his party. Hamadi Jebali had no alternative but to resign from his post and from his party.

Another Ennahdha member, Ali Larayedh, was appointed to replace Jebali and to form a new government. Larayedh had served as interior minister in the troika government before being tapped for prime minister. The opposition, which supported Hamadi Jebali's efforts to constitute a broad-based non-partisan coalition government, did not endorse Larayedh's appointment. But he and his ruling Islamist party, Ennahdha, managed to secure the backing of their troika allies, the centre-left Ettakatol party and the secular Congrès pour la République. Ennahdha appears to have made some major concessions to keep them on board, entrusting key ministries such as the interior, defence, justice and foreign affairs to independents.

Indeed, the career diplomat and former ambassador to the United Nations Othman Jarandi was named foreign minister. Jarandi has strong ties with international bodies and the West. Judges Lotfi Ben Jedou and Rachid Sabbagh were made ministers of interior and defence respectively; Nadhir Ben Ammou became justice minister; and Elyes Fakhfakh of Ettakatol, an engineer, took the finance portfolio. Twelve members of Jebali's cabinet stayed on, including agriculture minister Mohamed Ben Salem and human rights minister Samir Dilou, both members of Ennahdha.[2]

According to Amine Ghali, programme director for the Tunis-based Kawakibi Democracy Transition Centre, the new government still faces a crisis of credibility. Some ministers who were considered ineffective in the previous government have been kept in their posts or were simply shuffled into new roles.[3]

Likewise, the opposition remains sceptical of Ennahdha's new inclusive government and its potential effectiveness. Some question whether the new independent members of the cabinet are in fact 'independent', or whether they are handpicked Ennahdha supporters.[4]

The situation in the country is still volatile as Tunisians struggle to find their way to a democratic and more equitable society. Once again it was the democratic movement, which remains in the streets, that exercised the power of veto over the troika transitional government; and young Tunisians came out in force.

Afterword

The popular demonstrations that followed Belaid's assassination brought down the government and exposed internal rifts within the ruling party and the coalition. It is still anyone's guess how the situation will unfold in the period running up to the elections. Only time will tell what kind of a future Tunisians will manage to build for themselves and for future generations.

Notes

Introduction

1 Bouazizi was born in Sidi Bouzid on 29 March 1984. His father, a construction worker who was employed mainly in Libya, died of a heart attack when he was three years old, and his mother later married his uncle. Along with his six siblings, Bouazizi went to school in Sidi Salah, a village 12 miles from Sidi Bouzid. He did not complete his baccalaureate (high school) degree, leaving school in his late teens.

2 The 2008 protests by Tunisian workers in the phosphate mines of Redeyef in Gafsa, and by unemployed youths in Skhira and Ben Gardane, were precursors to these 2010 events.

3 See Lina Ben Mhenni's report for Global Voices Online. Available at globalvoicesonline. org/2011/01/01/tunisia-lawyers-assaulted (accessed 15 February 2013).

4 Associated Press, World News (2011) '147 killed, 510 injured in Tunisian uprising, UN mission says'. *Toronto Star*, 1 February. Available at www.thestar.com/ News/World/article/931299 (accessed 15 February 2013).

5 See Manji and Ekine (2012), who argue that these events should be called 'African Awakening' as they first took place on the African continent (Tunisia, Egypt and Libya). In the same vein, Ali Mazrui (2012) suggests that 'Afro-Arab Awakening' more appropriately characterises the events that started in Tunisia in 2010. Mazrui points to the Sudanese popular uprisings against the military rule of General Jaafar Nimeiri in 1985 as a predecessor of these North African revolutions.

6 The name 15M stands for 15 May, the date on which the Indignados movement was established in 2011.

7 Salafism is a movement that emerged in the late nineteenth century as a trend in contemporary Sunni Islam and a reaction against the spread of Western and modernising values (which it saw as anti-Islamic). It has a missionary character revolving around the idea of 'moral re-armament' based on a literal reading of the sacred texts, inspired by Saudi Wahhabi ideology. It uses violence against those who do not observe Sharia as strictly as they interpret it. For more on the Salafist movement, see Meijer, R. (ed.) (2009) *Global Salafism: Islam's*

new religious movement. New York, NY: Columbia University Press.

8 With the exception of public figures, I have used pseudonyms to protect the identity of my interviewees. All quotations whose sources are not cited in the text or notes are based on interviews I conducted in Tunisia in 2011 and 2012.

9 My book *The Time of Youth: Work, social change, and politics in Africa* was published by Kumarian Press in the USA in August 2012. It includes case studies from Mozambique, Senegal, South Africa and Tunisia.

10 The United Nations and the World Bank define youth as those aged between 15 and 24, and the African Union definition of youth covers the age range 15–34. See United Nations 2007; World Bank 2007; and African Union 2006.

11 'History of Tunisia' on History World. Available at www.historyworld.net/wrldhis/plaintexthistories.asp?historyid=ac93 (accessed 15 February 2013).

12 See 'Union Générale des Travailleurs Tunisiens (UGTT)' in *Encyclopedia of the Modern Middle East and North Africa* (2004). Available at www.encyclopedia.com/doc/1G2-3424602775.html (accessed 15 February 2013).

13 Ibid.

14 'Tunisia: The protectorate (1881–1956)' in *Encyclopaedia Britannica*. Available at www.britannica.com/EBchecked/topic/609229/Tunisia/46621/The-protectorate-1881-1956 (accessed 15 February 2013).

15 Non-doctrinaire socialism is a more moderate and flexible socialism. Doctrinaire regimes are generally inflexibly attached to a practice of the theory without regard to its practicality.

1 Disconnections

1 Carpenter, J. Scott and David Schenker (2011) 'Tunisia on edge: the breakdown in Tunisia is an object lesson for similar police states'. Washington Institute. *The Cutting Edge*, 18 January. Available at www.thecuttingedgenews.com/index.php?article=31817pageid=13pagename=Analysis (accessed 18 March 2013).

2 On 7 November 1987, Ben Ali, a former army general and government minister, replaced Habib Bourguiba as president of Tunisia in what was dubbed a bloodless coup d'état. Ben Ali declared that Bourguiba was medically incapacitated and was unable to fulfil the duties of the presidency.

3 See Rogers, William (2011) 'Tunisia's economic problems still festering'. *Left Labor Reporter*, 20 April. Available at http://leftlaborreporter.wordpress.com/2011/04/20/tunisias-economic-problems-still-festering/ (accessed 25 February 2013).

4 Berthelot, Benoît (2012) 'Accro a l'usine qui l'empoisonne'. *Mashallah News*, 15 June. Available at http://mashallahnews.com/?p=8536 (accessed 25 February 2013).

5 Samir and other Kasserinians established in April 2011 the Forum for Citizenship and Equitable Development, a civil society association aimed at promoting a more equitable form of development for Kasserine and other economically distressed regions.

6 See 'Tunisie: un rassemblement de jeune diplômés chômeurs de la ville de Skhira tourne à l'affrontement avec les forces de l'ordre'. *Nawaat*, 4 February 2010. Available at http:// nawaat.org/portail/2010/02/04/ tunisie-un-rassemblement- de-jeune-diplomes-chomeurs- de-la-ville-de-skhira-tourne-a- laffrontement-avec-les-forces- de-lordre/ (accessed 25 February 2013); Ayad, Christophe (2010) 'Face au gâchis social, la Tunisie ose s'insurger'. *Tunisia Watch*, 22 December. Available at www.tunisiawatch.com/?p=3180 (accessed 25 February 2013).

7 All Tunisians between the ages of six and 15 are required to enrol in basic education, which covers the first nine grades, and at the end of this time students are awarded the Diplôme de Fin d'Études de l'Enseignement de Base (Diploma of Basic Education Studies). Secondary education lasts for four years and is aimed at preparing students for university or entry into the workforce. It is divided into two stages: one year of general education plus one year of pre-orientation, and two years of specialised education. It culminates in the baccalaureate diploma, a passport to higher education. The pass rate of the baccalaureate is not very high; on average, 60 per cent of students fail the baccalaureate examination each year.

8 ESSEC stands for École Supérieure des Sciences Économiques et Commerciales (School of Economic and Commercial Sciences).

9 Tunisia has a long history of labour migration to Europe. The first wave of migration took place in the 1960s when unemployed men in less developed regions migrated to France and Italy for work in car manufacturing and other industries.

10 WikiLeaks (2010) 'US embassy cables: Tunisia – a US foreign policy conundrum'. *Guardian*, 7 December 2010. Available at www.guardian.co.uk/world/us- embassy-cables-documents/217138 (accessed 10 March 2013).

11 See 'Corruption in Tunisia, part I: an economic success?' *Aftenposten*, 15 January 2011. Available at www.aftenposten. no/spesial/wikileaksdokumenter/ article3990364.ece (accessed 25 February 2013).

12 WikiLeaks, 'US embassy cables: Tunisia – a US foreign policy conundrum'.

13 See also WikiLeaks, 'US embassy cables: Tunisia – a US foreign policy conundrum'.

14 See Cole, Juan (2011) 'New wikileaks: US knew Tunisian gov. rotten corrupt, supported Ben Ali anyway'. *Informed Comment*,

16 January. Available at www. juancole.com/2011/01/new-wiki leaks-us-knew-tunisian-gov-rotten-corrupt-supported-ben-ali-anyway. html (accessed 25 February 2013).

15 'Tunisian police bans a demonstration against Sharon's visit'. *Arabic News*, 9 April 2005. Available at www.arabicnews.com/ansub/ Daily/Day/050409/2005040907.html (accessed 25 February 2013).

16 Saleh, Heba (2005) 'Ferment in Tunisia continues over lawyer's arrest'. *Financial Times*, 14 April. Available at www.ft.com/cms/s/0/087bd4de-ac82-11d9-bb67-00000e2511c8. html#axzz2Lvm6cCA8 (accessed 25 February 2013).

17 See Amnesty International (2008) 'Tunisia: submission to the UN Universal Periodic Review: first session of the UPR Working Group, 7–11 April 2008'. Available at www.amnesty.org/ en/library/asset/MDE30/011/2007/ en/925742b4-a71b-11dc-bf49-a1e 867231d5c/mde300112007en.html (accessed 25 February 2013).

18 Born in Tunis in 1899, Tahar Haddad was educated and became a scholar at the famous University of the Great Mosque of Zitouna. As a youth he became politically active, joining the Destourian Liberal Party in 1920 and in 1924 establishing the first Tunisian labour union movement, the General Confederation of Workers, with his friend Mohamed Ali El Hammi. Haddad's main cause

was women's rights, and he persisted despite being attacked for his revolutionary ideas and having his university diplomas revoked. Haddad's work paved the way for advocates of women's emancipation in subsequent years (Zayzafoon 2005; Mamelouk 2007).

19 The legal age of marriage was changed in May 2007 to 18 years of age for both men and women.

20 Bourguiba, Habib (1962) 'Les missions des femmes'. Speech delivered in Tunis on 26 December. For more on Bourguiba's speeches on women's rights, see Zayzafoon 2005.

21 In Bouzid, Dorra (2011) 'La nouvelle bourguibamania: le bienfaiteur toujours chéri de la patrie!' *Leaders*, 29 July. Available at www. leaders.com.tn/article/la-nouvelle-bourguibamania-le-bienfaiteur-toujours-cheri-de-la-patrie?id=5897 (accessed 25 February 2013).

22 Bourguiba's Neo-Destourian Party, which held power after independence, repressed all forms of dissent, including by conservative Islamists who were perceived as a threat to the modernisation of Tunisian society.

23 'State feminism' has also been used to refer to women's rights reforms in Australia, Canada and some Scandinavian countries, where women have a greater presence in legislative and executive bodies. Implicitly and explicitly the term amounts to a critique of the shortcomings of reforms that are enacted from

the top down rather than being advocated and advanced by an organised women's movement.

24 The Mufti is a Muslim legal expert who is empowered to give rulings on religious matters.

25 See *The New York Times*' article on Tunisia, updated on 12 November 2012. Available at http://topics.nytimes.com/top/news/international/countriesand territories/tunisia/index.html (accessed 25 February 2013).

26 See Merone, Fabio and Francesco Cavatorta (2012) 'The emergence of Salafism in Tunisia'. *Jadaliyya*, 17 August. Available at www.jadaliyya.com/pages/index/6934/the-emergence-of-salafism-in-tunisia (accessed 25 February 2013).

27 Amnesty International (2011) 'Tunisia'. In *Amnesty International Report 2011*. London: Amnesty Internation. Available at www.amnesty.org/en/region/tunisia/report-2011 (accessed 25 February 2013).

28 Ibid.

29 US Department of State (2010) *Country Reports on Terrorism 2009*. Washington, DC: US Department of State.

30 See Merone and Cavatorta, 'The emergence of Salafism in Tunisia'.

31 Ibid.

32 Quoted in ibid.

33 See also ibid.

34 'Jihad' means a struggle. It can be understood as a personal struggle in devotion to Islam, especially one involving spiritual discipline, but also as a collective struggle, i.e. a holy war waged on behalf of Islam as a religious duty.

35 Merone and Cavatorta, 'The emergence of Salafism in Tunisia'.

36 Ibid.

2 *Mobilisation*

1 See Meddah, Mohamed (2009) 'Tunisia: number of internet users reaches 2.8 million'. *StartUpArabia*, 29 January. Available at www.startuparabia.com/2009/01/tunisia-number-of-internet-users-reaches-28-million/ (accessed 18 March 2013).

2 See Internet World Stats. Available at www.internetworld stats.com/stats.htm (accessed 25 February 2013).

3 See Ryan, Yasmine (2011) 'Tunisia's bitter cyber war: Anonymous has joined Tunisian activists to call for end to the government's stifling of online dissent'. *Al Jazeera*, 6 January. Available at www.aljazeera.com/indepth/features/2011/01/20111614145839362.html (accessed 25 February 2013).

4 Stecklow, Steve (2011) 'Web's openness is tested in Tunisia'. *The Wall Street Journal*, 7 July. Available at http://online.wsj.com/article/SB10001424052702303544604576430041200613996.html (accessed 25 February 2013).

5 According to Slim Amamou, the power of Anonymous resides in its universality and its broad representation that goes beyond any existing criteria for distinguishing among human beings.

This common identity, or rather non-identity, allows its members to speak and act freely. See Slim Amamou's presentation about Anonymous for TED Carthage. Available at http://tedxcarthage. com/videos-2010/114-slim-amamou -anonymous (accessed 19 June 2011).

6 See 'Anonymous joins Tunisian cyber-activists in anti-censorship campaign'. *Emergency*, 7 January 2011. Available at http:// mrgnc.blogspot.com/2011/01/ anonymous-joins-tunisian-cyber. html (accessed 25 February 2013).

7 Quoted in Ryan (2011) 'Tunisia's bitter cyber war'.

8 See ibid.

9 Takriz has been an apolitical and independent network since its inception; its core values are freedom, truth and anonymity. Takriz is regarded by many youths as a voice of resistance against the establishment, and from 2000 onwards it was censored by the Ben Ali regime. With hundreds of active members online and offline, inside and outside the country, Takriz advocates freedom of speech and human rights in Tunisia. (See www.takriz.com.)

10 See McTighe, Kristen (2011) 'A blogger at Arab Spring's genesis'. *The New York Times*, 12 October. Available at www. nytimes.com/2011/10/13/world/ africa/a-blogger-at-arab-springs-genesis.html (accessed 25 February 2013).

11 Ben Mhenni cited in ibid.

12 See Lina Ben Mhenni's report to Global Voices Online. Available at http://globalvoiceson line.org/2011/01/01/tunisia-lawyers-assaulted (accessed 25 February 2013).

13 Yousfi, Hèla (2012) 'Tunisia's New Opposition'. *Le Monde Diplomatique*, November. Available at http://mondediplo. com/2012/11/03tunisia (accessed 25 February 2013).

14 In Tunis alone it is estimated that about 40,000 people came out onto the streets on that day.

15 The political parties legalised under Ben Ali's regime were: 1) the Parti Démocrate Progressiste (PDP); 2) the Ettajdid Movement; 3) the Forum Démocratique pour le Travail et les Libertés (FDTL or Ettakatol); 4) the Mouvement des Démocrates Socialistes (MDS); 5) the Parti de l'Unité Populaire (PUP); 6) the Parti Social-Libéral (PSL); and 7) the Union Démocratique Unioniste (UDU).

3 Revolution

1 See Lina Ben Mhenni's report to Global Voices Online. Available at http://globalvoiceson line.org/2011/01/01/tunisia-lawyers-assaulted (accessed 25 February 2013).

2 The Pirate Party is a small political party that strives to reform laws regarding copyright and patents and strengthen the right to privacy, both on the internet and in life in general. It also stands for the transparency of gov-

ernment and state administration. The Tunisian Pirate Party was established in 2010 by Shamseddine Ben Jemaa, Slim Amamou and Aziz Amami. Other Pirate Parties exist in Sweden, France, Austria, Denmark, Finland, Germany, Ireland, the Netherlands, Poland and Spain, and belong to the Pirate Parties International established in Belgium in 2010. The Tunisian party became one of the first branches of the Pirate Party movement in Africa.

3 According to French journalist Frédéric Frangeul, the expression was originated by Tunisian journalist Zied El Hani in a blog posted before Ben Ali's departure on *Jounaliste Tunisien*. Apparently the term had previously been used to refer to the events in 1987 that led to Ben Ali's presidency; see Malaponti, Olivier (2011) 'Révolution de jasmin?' *Mediapart*, 15 January. Available at http://blogs.mediapart.fr/blog/olivier-malaponti/150111/revolution-de-jasmin-o (accessed 25 February 2013).

4 See Amin Allal and Vincent Geisser (June 2011), 'Tunisie: Revolution du jasmin ou intifada? Movements'. Available at: http://www.mouvements.info/Tunisie-Revolution-de-jasmin-ou.html.

5 Frangeul, Frédéric (2011) 'D'où vient la "révolution du jasmine"?' *Europe 1*, 17 January. Available at www.europe1.fr/International/D-ou-vient-la-revolution-du-jasmin-375743/ (accessed 18 March 2013). See also

Le Monde (2011) '"Révolution du jasmine": une expression qui ne fait pas l'unanimité'. *Le Monde*, January 17. Available at www.lemonde.fr/afrique/article/2011/01/17/revolution-du-jasmin-une-expression-qui-ne-fait-pas-l-unanimite_1466871_3212.html (accessed 18 March 2013).

6 Allnutt, Luke (2011) 'Tunisia: can we please stop talking about "Twitter revolutions"?' *Tangled Web*, 15 January. Available at www.rferl.org/content/tunisia_can_we_please_stop_talking_about_twitter_revolutions/2277052.html (accessed 25 February 2013).

7 Zuckerman, Ethan (2011) 'The first Twitter revolution?' *Foreign Policy*, 14 January. Available at www.foreignpolicy.com/articles/2011/01/14/the_first_twitter_revolution (accessed 25 February 2013).

8 See Soufiane Ben Farhat's blog, which is available at http://soufiane-ben-farhat.space-blogs.net/blog.php?user=soufiane-ben-farhat&pagenum=7 (accessed 10 March 2013).

9 See online Sociology Dictionary. Available at http://sociology.socialsciencedictionary.com/Sociology-Dictionary/ (accessed 25 February 2013).

10 Ibid.

11 Balqaziz, Abdallah (2012) 'The Arab Spring: a 'real' revolution?' *Al-Monitor*, 12 January. Available at www.al-monitor.com/pulse/politics/2012/01/three-facts-to-consider-when-ana.html (accessed 25 February 2013).

12 Critchley, Simon (2012) 'Occupy and the Arab Spring will continue to revitalise political protest'. *Guardian*, 22 March. Available at www.guardian.co.uk/comment isfree/2012/mar/22/occupy-arab-spring-political-protest (accessed 25 February 2013).

13 Bayat contrasts these non-movements with the social movements taking place in the West, which are described as comprising three fundamental elements: 1) they must have an organised and sustained claim against the authorities; 2) they must undertake a range of action such as street marches, public meetings, establishing associations and issuing media statements; and 3) they must have 'public representations of the cause's worthiness, unity, numbers, and commitments' (Bayat 2010: 9). The non-movements taking place in the Middle East are unspoken, yet action-oriented. Their demands are made on an individual basis rather than through unified and ideologically driven groups. They are mainly horizontal, with no clear leadership structures, and their resistance takes place through the actions of everyday life rather than through activities such as meetings, lobbying and petitioning.

14 Asef Bayat describes street politics as 'a set of conflicts ... between an individual or a collective populace and the authorities, which are shaped and expressed in the physical and social space of the street' (Bayat 2010: 11). He also points out that social change in the Middle East is not undertaken by only the sociopolitical elites. Through street politics, the working poor, the unemployed and other disenfranchised groups play fundamental roles as agents of change.

15 See Marissal, Pierric (2011) 'The Indignants: a movement born on the web'. *l'Humanité*, 27 May. Available at www. humaniteinenglish.com/spip. php?article1782 (accessed 25 February 2013).

4 Transition

1 See also Lynch, Marc (2011) 'Tunisia's new Al-Nahda'. *Foreign Policy*, 29 June. Available at http://lynch.foreignpolicy.com/posts/2011/06/29/tunisias_new-al_nahda (accessed 25 February 2013).

2 'Technocrat' is a term employed to designate an official who is seen as qualified to make decisions because of his or her expertise in a field and is not primarily motivated by political considerations.

3 Toumi, Habib (2011) 'Number of political parties in Tunisia shoots to 94'. *Gulf News*, 25 June. Available at http://gulfnews.com/news/region/tunisia/number-of-political-parites-in-tunisia-shoots-to-94-1.827415 (accessed 25 February 2013).

4 Interviews in Tunis with Abdeljelil Bedoui from the Parti Tunisien du Travail, Mahmoud Ben Romdhane from the newly

established Nida Tounes party (the Call of Tunisia), and Hakim Ben Hammouda, economist and political analyst.

5 The PSD was a pillar of Bourguiba's regime and operated between 1964 and 1988. It played a pivotal role in the National Constituent Assembly of 1956 alongside the UGTT and UTICA (Union Tunisienne de l'Industrie, du Commerce et de l'Artisanat), the association for employers.

6 See Akacha, Shehrazad (2011) 'Across the political spectrum: the first democratic elections in Tunisia'. *The Majalla*, 21 October. Available at www.majalla.com/eng/2011/10/article55227007 (accessed 25 February 2013).

7 Rached Ghannouchi, the leader of the Ennahdha party, was in exile in the United Kingdom for more than 30 years and returned to Tunisia after the events of 14 January 2011. Abdelfattah Mourou, a well-known lawyer and Islamic politician who remained in the country, was jailed several times for speaking out against the regime. Mourou split from Ennahdha and later established the Alliance Démocratique, a centre-left party.

8 See Ibrahim, Sabir (2011) 'Tunisia: formation of the "Front of January 14" and its tasks'. *CUAfrica,* 25 January. Available at http://groups.google.com/group/CUAfrica/browse_thread/thread/a4330969eb3b3720/b50c413e024f67d0#b50c413e024f67d0 (accessed 25 February 2013).

9 For more on Ennahdha's ideology, see its website, www.nahdha.info/arabe/home.html.

10 Hechmi Hamdi is quoted in Ghribi, Asma (2012) 'Hechmi Hamdi elected as head of Party of Progressive Conservatives'. *Tunisialive*, 6 February. Available at www.tunisia-live.net/2012/02/06/hechmi-hamdi-elected-as-head-of-party-of-progressive-conservatives/ (accessed 25 February 2013).

11 Ajmi, Sana (2012) 'Reform Front Party: Tunisia's first Salafist party'. *Ramadan*, 11 May. Available at www.ramadan.com/news/reform-front-party-tunisias-first-salafist-party.html (accessed 18 March 2013).

12 Mohammad al-Khoujah is quoted in the article Zelin, Aaron (2012) 'Who is Jabhat al-Islah?' *Sada*, 18 July. Available at http://carnegieendowment.org/2012/07/18/who-is-jabhat-al-islah/cuxg (accessed 25 February 2013).

13 'Caliphate' means the 'dominion of a caliph (successor)' and refers to the first system of government established in Islam.

14 See YouTube video at www.youtube.com/watch?v=cRlHhydrToY (accessed 25 February 2013).

15 Zelin, Aaron Y. (2011) 'The rise of Salafists in Tunisia after the fall of Ben Ali'. *CTC Sentinel*, 1 August. Available at www.ctc.usma.edu/posts/the-rise-of-salafists-in-tunisia-after-the-fall-of-ben-ali (accessed 25 February 2013).

16 Abu Ayadh is quoted in the article Noueihed, Lin (2012) 'Radical Islamists urge bigger role for Islam in Tunisia'. *Al Arabia News*, 21 May. Available at http://english.alarabiya.net/articles/2012/05/21/215374.html (accessed 25 February 2013).

17 Mohamed Ghannouchi was prime minister of Ben Ali's regime between 1999 and January 2011. Regarded as a technocrat, he served as minister of finance (1989–92) and minister of international cooperation (1992–99).

18 See 'Tunisie: le gouvernement provisoire concrétise des décisions déjà annoncées'. *Tunisie Agence Presse*, 19 February 2011.

19 Kasbah Square is where the main government buildings are located in Tunis.

20 See Chick, Kristen (2011) 'Why Tunisia's interim government may not fly with protesters'. *Christian Science Monitor*, 17 January. Available at www.csmonitor.com/World/Middle-East/2011/0117/Why-Tunisia-s-interim-government-may-not-fly-with-protesters (accessed 25 February 2013).

21 Other political parties involved in the formation of the 14 January Front were the Trotskyist Ligue de la Gauche Ouvrière, the Unionistes Nassériens, the Ba'ath Party, the Parti du Travail Patriotique et Démocratique (PTPD), and the independent left. See also ICG 2011.

22 'Déclaration constitutive d'un Front du 14 Janvier'. Available at http://front14janvier.net/Declaration-constitutive-du-Front.html (accessed 15 May 2012).

23 See Chaker, Houki (2011) 'Les conseils pour la protection de la révolution'. *L'Observatoire Tunisien de la Transition Démocratique*, July. Available at http://observatoiretunisien.org/upload/file/HOUKICORR(1).pdf (accessed 25 February 2013); 'Tunisie: plusieurs partis et organisations appellent à la création d'un "Conseil national pour la protection de la révolution"'. *Tunisie Agence Presse*, 14 February 2011. Available at www.tunisiawatch.com/?p=4047 (accessed 25 February 2013). See also 'Déclaration Générale of the National Council for the Protection of the Revolution', 11 February 2011; ICG 2011.

24 The community vigilance and protection committees were transformed into regional councils for the protection of the revolution. Local leaders and members of civil society from various political tendencies composed the regional CNPRs.

25 Some of the organisations that refused to be part of the CNPR were the Association Tunisienne des Femmes Démocrates (ATFD), the Ligue Tunisienne des Droits de l'Homme (LTDH), the Conseil National pour les Libertés en Tunisie (CNLT) and the Syndicat National des Journalistes Tunisiens (SNJT).

26 See Chaker, 'Les conseils pour la protection de la révolution'.

27 Maya Jribi, Secretary-General of the PDP, in an interview with the ICG in Tunis in February 2011.

28 Willsher, Kim (2011) 'Tunisian prime minister Mohamed Ghannouchi resigns amid unrest'. *Guardian*, 27 February. Available at www.guardian.co.uk/world/2011/feb/27/tunisian-prime-minister-ghannouchi-resigns (accessed 25 February 2013). See also 'Tunisia: two ministers quit interim government'. *BBC News*, 28 January 2011. Available at www.bbc.co.uk/news/world-africa-1260 4730 (accessed 25 February 2013).

29 Five members of the government resigned with Ghannouchi. Two ministers who served under Ben Ali, Mohamed Afif Chelbi (minister for industry) and Mohamed Nouri Jouini (minister for international cooperation), resigned immediately. Two members of former opposition parties, Najib Chebbi (PDP) and Ahmed Ibrahim (Ettajdid), resigned a week later, along with Elyès Jouini (minister of economic and social reforms).

30 Beji Caïd-Essebsi, now 84, is a lawyer and served as a close aide to Tunisia's founding president, Habib Bourguiba. In the 1960s and early 1970s, he held a variety of government positions, including interior minister and defence minister. In 1978, he joined the Mouvement des Démocrates Socialistes (MDS), an opposition party, before being reappointed to the cabinet as foreign minister in 1981. Caïd-Essebsi served in parliament from 1989 to 1991.

31 Yadh Ben Achour is a Tunisian lawyer and well-known legal scholar who was formerly head of the law faculty at the University of Tunis. In January, Ben Achour was appointed to head a political reform commission charged with changing Tunisia's laws ahead of national elections. When this commission was restructured to become the Higher Authority, with about 130 members from various political groups, he continued as its head.

32 The Green Party also joined the Higher Authority, as did human rights organisations, the ATFD and the SNJT, which had all refused to support the CNPR. Ettakatol, the CPR and the Bar Association, among others, adhered to the Higher Authority. However, the radical left of the 14 January Front was divided: two of its founding political parties, Watad and the PTPD, agreed to join, while the PCOT and a number of other radical left-wing groups decided to stay out. The Ligue de la Gauche Ouvrière, the Mouvement du Peuple, the Ba'ath Party, the Parti de l'Unité Populaire and the independent left also refused to join the Higher Authority.

33 See Front du 14 Janvier, 'Notre position de la haute instance pour la protection de la révolution et de la transition démocratique'. Available at http://

front14janvier. net/Position-du-Front-du-14-janvier.de.html (accessed 15 May 2012).

34 Of the 28 organisations that joined the Higher Authority, 17 were previously with the CNPR; see Chaker, 'Les conseils pour la protection de la révolution'.

35 Mackey, Robert (2011) 'Tunisian blogger joins government'. The Lede (blog). *The New York Times*, 18 January. Available at http://thelede.blogs.nytimes.com/2011/01/18/tunisian-blogger-joins-government (accessed 25 February 2013).

36 Slim Amamou's blog, 'NoMemorySpace', continues to be available at http://nomemoryspace.wordpress.com (accessed 25 February 2013).

37 Stecklow, Steve (2011) 'Web's openness is tested in Tunisia'. *The Wall Street Journal*, 7 July. Available at http://online.wsj.com/article/SB10001424052702303544604576430041200613996.html (accessed 25 February 2013).

38 See 'Tunisie: Slim Amamou, secrétaire d'état à tête d'anarchiste?' *Tekiano*, 18 May 2011. Available at www.tekiano.com/ness/20-n-c/3767-tunisie-slim-amamou-secretaire-detat-a-tete-danarachiste-.html (accessed 25 February 2013).

39 See 'Tunisia's internet agency agrees to block porn'. *Information Policy*, 15 June 2011. Available at www.i-policy.org/2011/06/tunisias-internet-agency-agrees-to-block-porn.html (accessed 25 February 2013).

40 See, for example, the Tunisian website nawaat.org.

41 Churchill, Erik (2011) 'Give me my porno!' *Kefteji*, 6 July. Available at http://kefteji.word press.com/2011/07/06/give-me-my-porno/ (accessed 25 February 2013).

42 Every Tunisian town with more than 20,000 inhabitants has a youth centre. Small towns have youth clubs, which are affiliated to the youth centres. Itinerant youth clubs also visit small towns regularly.

43 See JID's website, www.jidtunisie.net.

44 Sawty's website is www.sawty.org/ (accessed 13 July 2011).

45 Amami quoted in Primeau-Ferraro, Rafaël (2011) 'Azyz Amami, a fearless activist'. *Tunisia Elections* (blog), 5 November. Available at http://tunisiaelection.blogspot.com/2011/11/azyz-amami-fearless-activist.html (accessed 25 February 2013).

5 Elections

1 Electoral lists name all the party's candidates for office.

2 Political parties disagreed regarding the postponement of the elections. The longer-established parties, particularly Ennahdha and the PDP, pushed to keep the initial date, while newly established parties supported the postponement, welcoming the additional months of preparation. Youth activists opposed the postponement because it would keep the interim government in power

longer. They wanted radical transformation as soon as possible and hoped that the elections would be a major step in that direction.

3 See Lerougetel, Antoine (2011) 'Low voter registration for the Tunisian Constituent Assembly elections'. *World Socialist Web Site*, 10 August. Available at www.wsws.org/articles/2011/aug2011/tuni-a10.shtml (accessed 25 February 2013).

4 See 'Communiqué of the Independent High Electoral Commission'. ISIE, 30 July 2011.

5 See Mahjar-Barducci, Anna (2012) 'Understanding the "Islamist wave" in Tunisia'. *Middle East Review of International Affairs*, 27 April. Available at www.gloria-center.org/2012/04/understanding-the-"islamist-wave"-in-tunisia/ (accessed 25 February 2013).

6 The Tunisian population is 99 per cent Muslim with a small Christian community of about 25,000, mainly foreign residents and a small group of native-born citizens of European or Arab descent. The Jews are the third religious group with about 1,500 members. See Bureau of Democracy, Human Rights, and Labor (2007) 'International Religious Freedom Report 2007: Tunisia'. US Department of State. Available at www.state.gov/j/drl/rls/irf/2007/90222.htm (accessed 25 February 2013).

7 Béatrice Hibou quoted in Lerougetel, 'Low voter registration for the Tunisian Constituent Assembly elections'.

8 Ben Mhenni, Lina (2011) 'Tunisian elections: beware, beware, my hunger and my anger'. *Guardian*, 22 October. Available at www.guardian.co.uk/comment isfree/2011/oct/22/tunisian-elections-2011-tunisia1 (accessed 25 February 2013).

9 Quoted in Schipper, Jannie (2011) 'Tunisia's elections: failing to grab the youth vote?' *Radio Netherlands Worldwide*, 17 October. Available at www.rnw.nl/english/article/tunisias-elections-failing-grab-youth-vote (accessed 25 February 2013).

10 Quoted in Primeau-Ferraro, Rafaël (2011) 'Aziz Amami, a fearless activist'. *Tunisia Elections* (blog), 5 November. Available at http://tunisiaelection.blogspot.com/2011/11/azyz-amami-fearless-activist.html (accessed 25 February 2013).

11 Quoted in Schipper, 'Tunisian elections: failing to grab the youth vote?'

12 Quoted in Ben Mhenni, Lina (2011) 'Tunisia: time to register for elections'. *Global Voices*, 25 July. Available at http://global voicesonline.org/2011/07/25/tunisia-time-to-register-for-elections/ (accessed 25 February 2013).

13 Similarly, the 'Tunisian Vote Compass' was created by Radio Netherlands Worldwide, VU University Amsterdam and Tunisian academics to help people find their way through the jungle of parties and guide them to the party that best matched their political convictions. See Schipper,

'Tunisian elections: failing to grab the youth vote?'

14 Only 25 political parties participated in the JID Ikhtiar platform, although all were invited.

15 See Ryan, Yasmine (2011) 'Tunisian newcomer spends big on campaign'. *Al Jazeera*, 21 October. Available at www.aljazeera.com/indepth/features/2011/10/201110217015351417.html (accessed 25 February 2013).

16 Kirkpatrick, David (2011) 'Financing questions shadow Tunisian vote, first of Arab Spring' *The New York Times*, 22 October. Available at www.nytimes.com/2011/10/23/world/africa/tunisia-election-faces-financing-questions.html?pagewanted=all (accessed 25 February 2013).

17 Ibid. See also Arieff, Alexis (2011) *Political Transition in Tunisia*. Washington, DC: Congressional Research Service, 20 September.

18 *Le Quotidien* quoted in Davies, Lizzy (2011) 'Tunisian election press round-up: dirty tricks?' *Guardian*, 20 October. Available at www.guardian.co.uk/world/blog/2011/oct/20/tunisian-elections-2011-tunisia (accessed 25 February 2013).

19 Ibid.

20 The stories of Arwa, Dhia and Hajer were quoted in Samti, Farah (2011) 'Tunisian youth losing faith in election'. *Tunisia Live*, 15 October. Available at www.tunisia-live.net/2011/10/15/tunisian-youth-losing-faith-in-election/ (accessed 25 February 2013).

21 See Martín, Jorge (2011) 'Tunisian Constituent Assembly elections: Ennahda victory prepares further uprisings'. *International Marxist Tendency*, 7 November. Available at www.marxist.com/tunisian-constituent-assembly-elections.htm (accessed 25 February 2013). See also the article 'Mais où en est la révolution tunisienne?' *Le Monde Libertaire*, Special Issue No. 43, 22 December 2011. Available at www.monde-libertaire.fr/international/15196-mais-ou-en-est-la-revolution-tunisienne%E2%80%88 (accessed 9 March 2013).

22 Mahjar-Barducci, 'Understanding the "Islamist wave" in Tunisia'.

23 See Martín, 'Tunisian Constituent Assembly elections: Ennahda victory prepares further uprisings'.

24 The pdf version of the ISTIS report of this poll is available at www.istis-tunisie.com/medias/Rapport-Sondage-situation-politique.pdf (accessed 25 February 2013).

25 Mahjar-Barducci, 'Understanding the "Islamist wave" in Tunisia'.

26 Bahloul, Nizar (2011) 'Il faut fêter la défaite'. *Business News*, 24 October. Available at www.businessnews.com.tn/details_article.php? t=523&a=27275&temp=3&lang (accessed 25 February 2013).

6 New government

1 It is noteworthy that the three parties that received the largest numbers of seats are all led by men who lived in exile during the Ben Ali regime and returned only after the revolution. Rached Ghannouchi, Ennahdha's leader, lived in London as a political refugee from the early 1990s. Moncef Marzouki, the CPR's leader, moved to France in 2002 in order to continue his political activism against the regime. Hemchi Hamdi, the founder of Al-Aridha Chaabia, is a London-based Tunisian tycoon.

2 Tensions between Ghannouchi and Hamdi stemmed from their time in exile in London. Hamdi had been a member of Ennahdha but was expelled following disagreements with Ghannouchi. He established Al-Aridha Chaabia (Popular Petition) as an electoral list to stand in the October elections. After the elections he became secretary-general of the Parti des Conservateurs Progressistes (PCP). See Hassassi, Hend (2011) 'Animosity between Ennahda and Aridha Chaabia'. *Tunisialive*, 28 October. Available at www.tunisia-live.net/2011/10/28/animosity-between-ennahda-and-el-aridah-el-chaabiah/ (accessed 25 February 2013).

3 See Schneider, James (2011) 'Tunisia's new government takes shape'. *Think Africa Press*, 18 November. Available at http://thinkafricapress.com/tunisia/new-government-takes-shape (accessed 25 February 2013).

4 Jebali, a Islamic militant and activist, was a political prisoner during the Ben Ali regime and spent more than a decade in solitary confinement. He then left the country and was exiled in London alongside other Ennahdha militants.

5 Ennahdha had originally agreed that the constitutional council would be headed by a member of the opposition, but when it made this appointment it disavowed its previous commitment and appointed Habib Khedher, a lawyer and politician who served in the party's legal affairs office.

6 Anna Mahjar-Barducci has published an autobiography in which she stresses the diversity among Muslims in her extended Moroccan family. She apparently says that the 'loss of identity' that immigrants experience in Europe leads some to embrace Islamic fundamentalism, which she regards as an assumed identity. She has published journalistic articles on Islam and cultural politics.

7 Mahjar-Barducci, Anna (2012) 'Understanding the "Islamist wave" in Tunisia'. *Middle East Review of International Affairs*, 27 April. Available at www.gloria-center.org/2012/04/understanding-the-"islamist-wave"-in-tunisia/ (accessed 25 February 2013).

8 Ibid.

9 Churchill, Erik (2012) 'Shaping Ennahda's re-election

strategy'. *Foreign Policy*, 27 March. Available at http://mideast.foreign policy.com/posts/2012/03/27/ennahdas_re_election_strategy_takes_shape (accessed 25 February 2013).

10 Shirayanagi, Kouichi (2012) 'Constituent Assembly members disagree on scheduling an end to their mandate'. *Tunisia Live*, 25 March. Available at www.tunisia-live.net/2012/03/25/constituent-assembly-members-disagree-on-scheduling-an-end-to-their-mandate/ (accessed 25 February 2013).

11 See Samti, Farah (2013) 'NCA seeks national dialogue over draft constitution'. *Tunisia Live*, 7 January. Available at www.tunisia-live.net/2013/01/07/nca-seeks-national-dialogue-over-draft-constitution/ (accessed 25 February 2013).

12 Ibid.

13 Quoted in Zelin, Aaron Y. (2011) 'Ennahda's tight rope act on religion'. *Foreign Policy*, 18 November. Available at http://mideast.foreignpolicy.com/posts/2011/11/18/ennahdas_tight_rope_act_on_religion#.TslRrwH_PTs.twitter (accessed 25 February 2013).

14 Ibid.

15 Ibid.

16 'Tunisia: The troika staggers but remains standing'. *The Maghreb Daily*, 2 July 2012. Available at http://en.lemag.ma/Tunisia-The-Troika-staggers-but-remains-standing_a1832.html (accessed 9 March 2013).

17 Ayari was also chief execu- tive officer of the Arab Bank for Economic Development in Africa (Banque Arabe pour le Développe- ment Économique en Afrique or BADEA) based in Khartoum. In January 2010, Ben Ali appointed Ayari as a senator. See also 'Tun- isia appoints controversial bank governor'. *Agence France-Presse*, 24 July 2012. Available at www. google.com/hostednews/afp/article/ALeqM5joa4GNFe2lViF-DXIDUyrOJd_lXA?docId=CNG. 00f85530b16770d544cdf094dd 88ca8a.321 (accessed 9 March 2013).

18 Bahloul, Nizar (2012) 'Tuni- sian finance minister quits, warns of economic crisis'. *Business News* (Tunisia), 30 July. Available at http://m.al-monitor.com/pulse/politics/2012/07/houcine-dimassi-tunisia-is-prepa.html (accessed 25 February 2013).

19 Ivey, Kevin (2012) 'High Authority for the Achievement of the Revolution's Objectives dissolves'. *Tunisia Live*, 25 August. Available at www.tunisia-live. net/2012/08/25/high-authority-for-the-achievement-of-the-revolutions-objectives-dissolves/ (accessed 25 February 2013).

20 Ibid.

21 Tajine, Synda (2012) 'Tuni- sia's new government confronts rising discontent'. *Business News* (Tunisia), 7 June. Available at http://m.al-monitor.com/pulse/politics/2012/06/tunisia--the-broken-promises-of.html (accessed 25 February 2013).

22 See Barrie, Christopher

(2012) 'Tunisia: Al-Nahda's failures lead Sidi Bouzid to rise again'. *Alakhbar*, 17 August. Available at http://english.al-akhbar.com/node/11211 (accessed 25 February 2013).

23 Samti, Farah (2012) 'Arrested protesters in Sidi Bouzid reportedly released today'. *Tunisia Live*, 15 August. Available at www.signalfire.org/?p=20333 (accessed 9 March 2013).

24 Ben Aziza, Med Amine (2012) 'People protest the arrest of demonstrators in Sidi Bouzid'. Demotix, The Network for Freelance Photojournalists, 14 August. Available at www.demotix.com/news/1388045/people-protest-arrest-demonstrators-sidi-bouzid#media-1387902 (accessed 9 March 2013).

25 Barrie, 'Tunisia: Al-Nahda's failures lead Sidi Bouzid to rise again'.

26 Samti, Farah (2012) 'Festivities mask disillusionment in birthplace of Arab Spring'. *Tunisia Live*, 17 December. Available at www.tunisia-live.net/2012/12/17/festivities-mask-disillusionment-in-birthplace-of-arab-spring/ (accessed 25 February 2013).

27 Masrour, Amira (2012) 'Leftist parties suspected of role in Sidi Bouzid disturbances'. *Tunisia Live*, 18 December. Available at www.tunisia-live.net/2012/12/18/leftist-parties-suspected-of-role-in-sidi-bouzid-disturbances/ (accessed 25 February 2013).

28 The Supplementary Finance Law 2012 was published on 18 May 2012 in the *Tunisian Official Gazette* No. 39 of 2012.

29 Achy, Lahcen (2012) 'Ennahda proposes big spending to stimulate Tunisia's economy'. *Al Monitor*, 18 April. Available at www.al-monitor.com/pulse/business/2012/04/tunisian-economy-weak-performanc.html (accessed 19 March 2013).

30 Ibid.

31 See Barrie, 'Tunisia: Al-Nahda's failures lead Sidi Bouzid to rise again'.

32 Ibid.

33 Ibid.

34 Ibid.

35 Achy, 'Ennahda proposes big spending to stimulate Tunisia's economy'.

36 Ghribi, Asma (2012) '100 day poll shows growing discontent with government performance'. *Tunisia Live*, 4 April. Available at www.tunisia-live.net/2012/04/04/100-day-poll-shows-growing-discontent-with-government-performance/ (accessed 25 February 2013).

37 The congress was the party's first since it came to power in October 2011 and was the first in the country for 24 years. About 25,000 Ennahdha militants attended the four-day event, which was opened with readings of verses from the *Quran*.

38 'Tunisia coalition's main party hints at reshuffle'. *Agence France-Presse*, 13 July 2012. Available at www.google.com/hostednews/afp/article/ALeqM5gjm8E1dAa7VYCtz5KizQp_

u3qBGg?docId=CNG.935d1b154999 fdc4e7033c8566526fc6.511 (accessed 9 March 2013).

39 Tajine, Synda (2012) 'Tunisia's most intimidating statesman creates new party'. *Al Monitor*, 21 June. Available at www.al-monitor.com/pulse/politics/2012/06/beji-caid-essebsi-why-is-he-so-s.html (accessed 25 February 2013).

40 Ibid.

41 Yousfi, Hèla (2012) 'Tunisia's new opposition'. *Le Monde Diplomatique*, November. Available at http://mondediplo.com/2012/11/03tunisia (accessed 25 February 2013).

42 Borders, Kane (2012) 'New coalition aims to provide stronger opposition to Ennahdha'. *Tunisia Live*, 13 August. Available at www.tunisia-live.net/2012/08/13/new-coalition-aims-to-provide-stronger-opposition-to-ennahdha/ (accessed 25 February 2013).

43 Ayedi is quoted in 'Tunisia has a weak opposition'. *Manila Bulletin*, 5 July 2012. Available at www.mb.com.ph/articles/364691/tunisia-has-a-weak-opposition (accessed 25 February 2013).

44 Quoted in Collins, Nicholas (2011) *Voices of a Revolution: Conversations with Tunisia's youth. Findings from focus groups with young Tunisian men and women conducted March 11 to 24, 2011*. Washington, DC: National Democratic Institute in collaboration with EMRHOD Consulting, Tunis, p. 11.

45 The film was also awarded a prize at the 2007 Cannes Film Festival, and at the 2008 French Césars (the French equivalent of the Oscars).

46 See Prince, Rob (2012) 'Tunisia's Salafists: brownshirts of the Arab Spring'. *Colorado Progressive Jewish News*, 3 June. Available at http://robertjprince.wordpress.com/2012/06/03/tunisias-salafists-brownshirts-of-the-arab-spring/ (accessed 25 February 2013).

47 'Tunisian Islamist party says religion, politics are one'. *Agence France-Presse*, 8 July 2012. Available at: www.google.com/hostednews/afp/article/ALeqM5h4ubyDCouIWqN9EQWt_2Ocb407Ng (accessed 25 February 2013).

48 Ghribi, Asma (2012) 'Heated debate over the place of religion in first Arab Spring constitution'. Available at www.tunisianloverats.com/threads/heated-debate-over-the-place-of-religion-in-first-arab-spring-constitution.2190/ (accessed 9 March 2013). See also 'Tunisia blasphemy bill threatens free speech: HRW'. *Agence France-Presse*, 3 August 2012. Available at www.google.com/hostednews/afp/article/ALeqM5iVZHjYo5k7pFnUkmf412-mVXqeCA?docId=CNG.3012aa257 93d245b04367a928a3d5bf9.351 (accessed 25 February 2013).

49 Quoted in Blitt, Robert C. (2012) 'Tunisia: springtime for defamation of religion'. *Jurist Forum*, 13 August. Available at http://jurist.org/forum/2012/08/robert-blitt-tunisia-defamation.php (accessed 25 February 2013).

50 Ibid.

51 Walt, Vivienne (2012) 'After protests, Tunisia's Salafists plot a more radical revolution.' Time World, 21 September. Available at http://world.time.com/2012/09/21/after-protests-tunisias-salafists-plot-a-more-radical-revolution/ (accessed 25 February 2013).

52 Ibid.

53 Ibid.

54 Ibid.

7 Women's rights

1 The medina is the old city centre.

2 I did not come across any particular legislation on the issue of violence against women.

3 Prince, Rob (2012) 'Tunisia's Salafists: brownshirts of the Arab Spring'. *Colorado Progressive Jewish News*, 3 June. Available at: http://robertjprince.wordpress.com/2012/06/03/tunisias-salafists-brownshirts-of-the-arab-spring/ (accessed 25 February 2013).

4 See Article 27, the draft Tunisian Constitution of August 2012.

5 'Tunisia activists braced to fight for women's rights'. *Agence France-Presse*, 11 August 2012. Available at http://english.ahram.org.eg/NewsContent/2/8/50142/World/Region/Tunisia-activists-braced-to-fight-for-womens-right.aspx (accessed 25 February 2013).

6 Radford, Megan (2012) 'Thousands of Tunisians celebrate Women's Day'. *Ramadan*, 14 August. Available at www.ramadan.com/news/thousands-of-tunisians-celebrate-womens-day.html (accessed 10 March 2013).

7 The niqab was never traditionally worn in Tunisia, but women in the Persian Gulf countries generally wear it.

8 Prince, Rob (2012) 'Tunisia culture wars: the case of Habib Kazdaghli, Dean of the University of Tunis-Manouba'. *Open Democracy*, 26 July. Available at www.opendemocracy.net/rob-prince/tunisia-culture-wars-case-of-habib-kazdaghli-dean-of-university-of-tunis-manouba (accessed 25 February 2013).

9 Quoted in 'Tunisia university dean to face trial over veil row'. *Agence France-Presse*, 4 July 2012. Available at www.modernghana.com/news/404519/1/tunisia-university-dean-to-face-trial-over-veil-ro.html (accessed on 25 February 2013).

10 The *safsari* is a traditional Tunisian form of veil worn mainly by elderly women outside their home. Not many women wear the *safsari* today. Elderly women dress modestly and generally cover their hair with a scarf.

11 See Surah al-A'raf (verse) 31 of the *Quran*.

12 Quoted in an interview conducted by Tunisian researcher Samir Bouzidi and published in Bouzidi, Samir (2012) 'Qui sont les salafistes tunisiens?' *Kapitalis*, 18 March. Available at http://kapitalis.com/fokus/62-national/8876-qui-sont-les-salafistes-tunisiens.html (accessed 25 February 2013).

13 The rules of inheritance under Sharia law determine that a female's portion is generally half

the amount a male would receive under the same circumstances.

14 See Joline, Courtney (2012) 'Women in the Constituent Assembly and the potential for cross-party collaboration'. *Tunisia Live*, 2 July. Available at www.tunisia-live.net/2012/07/02/women-in-the-constituent-assembly-and-the-potential-for-cross-party-collaboration/ (accessed 25 February 2013).

Conclusion

1 Nigam (2012) offers a perceptive analysis of how recent popular movements across the Arab world and in India differ, and indeed dissent, from conventional forms of politics that exist in both Western and non-Western societies.

2 See Y'en a Marre press conference in March 2012. Available at http://nomadicwax.com/democracyindakar/2012/03/01/senegals-elections-2012-march-1st/ (accessed 25 February 2013). See also Perdigao, Yovanka (2012) 'Transcending tradition: Senegalese youth make themselves heard: the Y'en a Marre movement is changing Senegal's political landscape'. *Think Africa Press*, 19 September. Available at http://thinkafricapress.com/senegal/youth-lead-way-y-en-marre-wade (accessed 25 February 2013).

3 See also Graeber, David (2011) 'Occupy Wall Street's anarchist roots'. *Al Jazeera*, 30 November. Available at www.aljazeera.com/indepth/opinion/2011/11/2011112872835904508.html (accessed 25 February 2013); and Critchley, Simon (2012) 'Occupy and the Arab spring will continue to revitalise political protest'. *Guardian*, 22 March. Available at www.guardian.co.uk/comment isfree/2012/mar/22/occupy-arab-spring-political-protest (accessed 25 February 2013).

4 Graeber, 'Occupy Wall Street's anarchist roots'.

5 Critchley, 'Occupy and the Arab spring will continue to revitalise political protest'.

6 Ibid.

7 Ibid.

8 Ibid.

9 Stiglitz, Joseph (2011) 'The lessons from Tunisia's fallen autocracy'. *The Moscow Times*, 8 February. Available at www.themoscowtimes.com/opinion/article/the-lessons-from-tunisias-fallen-autocracy/430572.html#ixzz24ZcXkCBT (accessed 25 February 2013).

10 Driessen, Michael (2012) 'Cooperating modernities in Tunisia?' *Contending Modernities*, 15 June. Available at http://blogs.nd.edu/contendingmodernities/2012/06/15/cooperating-modernities-in-tunisia/ (accessed 25 February 2013).

Afterword

1 Author's telephone interview with Ayman, 7 February 2013.

2 See Amara, Tarek (2013) 'Independents take senior roles in Tunisia's new

Islamist-led government'. *Reuters*, 8 March. Available at www. reuters.com/article/2013/03/08/us-tunisia-government-id USBRE9270Q420130308 (accessed 10 March 2013).

3 See Fahim, Kareen (2013) 'Tunisia includes independents in new cabinet'. *The New York Times*, 8 March. Available at www.nytimes.com/2013/03/09/world/africa/to-ease-crisis-tunisia-includes-independents-in-new-cabinet.html?ref=tunisia (accessed 10 March 2013).

4 See Amara, 'Independents take senior roles in Tunisia's new Islamist-led government'.

References

Abu-Lughod, Lila (ed.) (1998) *Remaking Women: Feminism and modernity in the Middle East*. Princeton, NJ: Princeton University Press.

Ackerman, Peter and Jack Duvall (2000) *A Force More Powerful: A century of non-violent conflict*. New York, NY: Palgrave.

African Development Bank (2011) 'Tackling youth unemployment in the Maghreb'. Economic Brief. Tunis: African Development Bank.

African Union (2006) *African Youth Charter*. Addis Ababa: African Union.

Afshar, Haleh (1998) *Islam and Feminisms: An Iranian case study*. Basingstoke, Hampshire: Palgrave.

Alexander, Christopher (2010) *Tunisia: Stability and reform in the modern Maghreb*. New York, NY: Routledge.

Allal, Amin (2010) 'Réformes néolibérales, clientélismes et protestations en situation autoritaire: les mouvements contestataires dans le bassin minier de Gafsa en Tunisie en 2008', *Politique Africaine*, 117: 107–25.

Amghar, Samir (2011) *Le Salafisme d'Aujourd'hui: Mouvements sectaires en Occident*. Paris: Michalon.

Amin, Samir (1976) *Unequal Development*. New York: Monthly Review Press.

— (1993) 'Social movements at the periphery'. In Wignaraja, Ponna (ed.) *New Social Movements in the South: Empowering the people*. New Delhi: Vistaar Publications.

Amnesty International (2009) *Behind Tunisia's 'Economic Miracle': Inequality and criminalization of protest*. London: Amnesty International.

Amos, Valerie and Pratibha Parmar (1984) 'Challenging imperial feminism'. *Feminist Review* 17: 3–19.

An-Na'im, Ahmed Abdullahi (1990) *Toward an Islamic Reformation: Civil liberties, human rights, and international law*. Syracuse, NY: Syracuse University Press.

Arieff, Alexis (2011) *Political Transition in Tunisia*. United States Congressional Research Service Report, 20 September 2011. Washington, DC: US Department of State.

— (2012) *Political Transition in Tunisia*. United States Congressional Research Service Report, 18 June 2012. Washington, DC: US Department of State.

Badran, Margot (2009) *Feminism in Islam: Secular and religious convergences.* Oxford: Oneworld Publications.

Bayat, Asef (1997) *Street Politics: Poor people's movements in Iran.* New York, NY: Columbia University Press.

— (2010) *Life as Politics: How ordinary people change the Middle East.* Stanford, CA: Stanford University Press.

— (2011) 'A new Arab street in post-Islamist times'. *Foreign Policy*, 26 January.

Beau, Nicolas and Catherine Graciet (2009) *La Régente de Carthage: Main basse sur la Tunisie.* Paris: Editions La Découverte.

Béji, Hélé (2011) *Islam Pride: Derrière la voile.* Paris: Gallimard.

Ben Hammouda, Hakim (2012) *Tunisie: L'économie politique d'une révolution.* Brussels: De Boeck.

— (2013) 'Chokri Belaid: le symbole et la trace!' Unpublished paper.

Ben Romdhane, Mahmoud (2011) *Tunisie: État, économie et société: ressources politiques, légitimation et régulations sociales.* Paris: Editions Publisud.

Bessis, Sophie (1999) 'Le Féminisme Institutionnel en Tunisie'. *Femmes du Maghreb. Clio* 9(1): 93–105.

Boubakri, Hassen (2004) 'Transit migration between Tunisia, Libya and Sub-Saharan Africa:

Study based on Greater Tunis'. Paper read at the Regional Conference on Migrants in Transit Countries: Sharing Responsibility for Management and Protection, 30 September–1 October 2004, Istanbul.

Bourdieu, Pierre (1993) '"Youth" is just a word'. In Bourdieu, Pierre *Sociology in Question*, translated by Richard Nice. London: Sage Publications, pp. 94–102.

Brand, Laurie A. (1998) *Women, the State, and Political Liberalization: Middle Eastern and North African experiences.* New York, NY: Columbia University Press.

Charrad, Mounira M. (2001) *States and Women's Rights: The making of postcolonial Tunisia, Algeria, and Morocco.* Berkeley, CA: University of California Press.

— (2008) 'From nationalism to feminism: family law in Tunisia'. In Yount, Kathryn M. and Hoda Rashad (eds) *Family in the Middle East: Ideational change in Egypt, Iran, and Tunisia.* Abingdon, Oxon: Routledge, pp. 111–35.

Collins, Nicholas (2011) *Voices of a Revolution: Conversations with Tunisia's youth. Findings from focus groups with young Tunisian men and women conducted March 11 to 24, 2011.* Washington, DC: National Democratic Institute. Also available at www.ndi.org/files/conversations-with-tunisia-youth-apr-2011.pdf (accessed 18 March 2013).

Crenshaw, Kimberle (1989) 'Demarginalizing the intersection of race and sex: a black feminist critique of antidiscrimination doctrine, feminist theory and antiracist politics'. *University of Chicago Legal Forum* 139: 139–67.

Crossley, Nick (2002) *Making Sense of Social Movements*. Buckingham: Open University Press.

Curtiss, Richard H. (1996) 'Women's rights: an affair of state for Tunisia'. In Sabbagh, Suha (ed.) *Arab Women: Between defiance and restraint*. New York, NY: Olive Branch Press, pp. 33–7.

de Groot, Joanna (2010) 'Feminism in another language: learning from "feminist" histories of Iran and/or from histories of Iranian "feminism" since 1830'. *Women: A Cultural Review* 21(3): 251–65.

Dégage (2011) *Dégage: La revolution tunisienne*. Livre-Temoignages. Tunis and Paris: Editions du Parimoine and Editions du Layeur.

Dhillon, Navtej and Tarik Yousef (eds) (2009) *Generation in Waiting: The unfulfilled promise of young people in the Middle East*. Washington, DC: Brookings Institution Press.

Dodge, Toby (2012) 'Conclusion: the Middle East after the Arab Spring'. In Kitchen, Nicholas (ed.) *After the Arab Spring: Power shift in the Middle East?* IDEAS report. London: London School of Economics and Political Science, pp. 64–8.

Doi, Abd ar-Rahman I. (1984) *Shari'ah: Islamic law*. London: Ta-Ha Publishers.

Eisenstein, Zillah (2004) *Against Empire: Feminisms, racism, and the West*. London: Zed Books.

El Difraoui, Asiem (2012) 'No Facebook Revolution – but an Egyptian youth we know little about'. In Asseburg, Muriel (ed.) *Protest, Revolt and Regime Change in the Arab World: Actors, challenges, implications and policy options*. Berlin: Stiftung Wissenschaft und Politik/German Institute for International and Security Affairs, pp. 18–22.

Esposito, John (1982) *Women in Muslim Family Law*. Syracuse, NY: Syracuse University Press.

— and Natana J. DeLong-Bas (2001) *Women in Muslim Family Law*. Syracuse, NY: Syracuse University Press.

Ferchiou, Sophie (1996) 'Féminisme d'état en Tunisie: idéologie dominante et résistance féminine'. In Bourqia, Rahma, Mounira Charrad and Nancy Gallagher (eds) *Femmes, Culture et Société au Maghreb. II: Femmes, pouvoir politique et développement*. Casablanca: Afrique Orient, pp. 119–40.

Ferree, Myra Marx (1992) 'The political context of rationality: rational choice theory and resource mobilization'. In Morris, Aldon D. and Carol McClurg Mueller (eds)

Frontiers of Social Movement Theory. New Haven, CT: Yale University Press, pp. 29–52.

Gilman, Sarah E. (2007) 'Feminist organizing in Tunisia: negotiating transnational linkages and the state'. In Moghadam, Valentine M. (ed.) *From Patriarchy to Empowerment: Women's participation, movements, and rights in the Middle East, North Africa, and South Asia*. Syracuse, NY: Syracuse University Press, pp. 97–119.

Goldstone, Jack A. (2011) 'Understanding the revolutions of 2011: weakness and resilience in Middle Eastern autocracies'. *Foreign Affairs* 90(3): 8–16.

Goodwin, Jeff and James M. Jasper (1999) 'Caught in a winding, snarling vine: the structural bias of political process theory'. *Sociological Forum* 14(1): 27–53.

Gunew, Sneja and Anna Yeatman (eds) (1993) *Feminism and the Politics of Difference*. Boulder, CO: Westview Press.

Hamdi, Mohamed E. (1998) *The Politicisation of Islam: A case study of Tunisia*. Boulder, CO: Westview Press.

Hamid, Shadi (2011) 'The rise of the Islamists: how Islamists will change politics, and vice versa'. *Foreign Affairs* 90(3): 39–47.

Hammami, Rema (2012) 'Gender equality and Muslim women: negotiating expanded rights in Muslim societies and immigrant contexts'. Paper presented at the tenth anniversary of the Prince Claus Chair, The Hague, The Netherlands, 28 November.

Hatem, Mervat F. (1992) 'Economic and political liberation in Egypt and the demise of state feminism'. *International Journal of Middle East Studies* 24(2): 231–51.

Hibou, Béatrice (2004) 'Fiscal trajectories in Morocco and Tunisia'. In Heydemann, Steven (ed.) *Networks of Privilege in the Middle East: The politics of economic reform revisited*. New York, NY: Palgrave Macmillan, pp. 201–22.

— (2006) *La Force de l'Obéissance: Economie politique de la répression en Tunisie*. Paris: Editions La Découverte.

— Meddeb, Hamza and Hamdi Mohamed (2011) *La Tunisie d'Après le 14 Janvier et Son Economie Politique et Sociale*. Copenhagen: Euro-Mediterranean Human Rights Network.

Honwana, Alcinda (2012) *The Time of Youth: Work, social change and politics in Africa*. Sterling, VA: Kumarian Press.

— and Filip De Boeck (eds) (2005) *Makers and Breakers: Children and youth in postcolonial Africa*. Oxford, Trenton, NJ and Dakar: James Currey, Africa World Press and Codesria.

hooks, bell (1981) *Ain't I a Woman?: Black women and feminism*. Cambridge, MA: South End Press.

Hull, Gloria T., Patricia Bell Scott and Barbara Smith (eds) (1982)

References

All the Women are White, All the Blacks are Men, but Some of Us are Brave. Old Westbury, NY: The Feminist Press.

ICG (2011) *Popular Protest in North Africa and the Middle East (IV): Tunisia's way.* Middle East/North Africa Report No. 106, 28 April. Brussels: International Crisis Group (ICG).

IMF (2011) 'Mideast outlook varies markedly across region'. IMF Survey Online, 26 October. Washington, DC: International Monetary Fund (IMF).

Jasper, James M. (1998) 'The emotions of protest: affective and reactive emotions in and around social movements'. *Sociological Forum* 13(3): 397–424.

Joffé, George (ed.) (2012) *Islamist Radicalisation in North Africa: Politics and process.* Abingdon and New York: Routledge.

— (ed.) (2013) *Islamist Radicalisation in Europle and the Middle East: Reassessing the causes of terrorism.* London and New York: I.B. Tauris.

Jones, Alyson (2010) 'Playing out: women instrumentalists and women's ensembles in contemporary Tunisia'. PhD dissertation, University of Michigan.

Jrad, Neïla (1996) *Mémoire de l'Oubli: Réflexion critique sur les expériences féministes des années quatre-vingt.* Tunis: Cérès Editions.

Kallander, Amy Aisen (2011) 'Tunisia's post-Ben Ali challenge: a primer'. Middle East Research and Information Project (website), 26 January.

Kausch, Kristina (2009) *Tunisia: The life of others. Project on freedom of association in the Middle East and North Africa.* Working Paper No. 85. Madrid: Fundación para las Relaciones Internacionales y el Diálogo Exterior.

Kilani, Mohamed (2011) *La Révolution des Braves.* Tunis: Impression Simpact.

Kitchen, Nicholas (2012) *After the Arab Spring: Power shift in the Middle East?* IDEAS report. London: London School of Economics and Political Science (LSE).

Kothari, Rajni (1993) 'Rethinking development and democracy'. In Wignaraja, Ponna (ed.) *New Social Movements in the South: Empowering the people.* New Delhi: Vistaar Publications.

— (2005) *Rethinking Democracy.* New Delhi: Orient Longman.

Lahlali, El Mustapha (2011) 'The Arab Spring and the discourse of desperation'. *Arab Media & Society*, 14 (Summer).

Lugones, María C. and Elizabeth V. Spelman (1983) 'Have we got a theory for you! Feminist theory, cultural imperialism and the demand for "the woman's voice"'. *Women's Studies International Forum* 6(6): 573–81.

Mamdani, Mahmood, Thandika Mkandawire and Ernest Wamba dia Wamba (1993)

'Social movements and democracy in Africa'. In Wignaraja, Ponna (ed.) *New Social Movements in the South: Empowering the people*. New Delhi: Vistaar Publications.

Mamelouk, Nadia (2007) 'Anxiety in the border zone: transgressing boundaries in *Leïla: Revue illustrée de la femme* (Tunis, 1936–1940) and in *Leïla: Hebdomadaire tunisien indépendant* (Tunis, 1941)'. PhD dissertation, University of Virginia.

Manji, Firoze and Sokari Ekine (eds) (2011) *African Awakening: The emerging revolutions*. Oxford: Pambazuka Press.

Marks, Gary and Doug McAdam (1996) 'Social movements and the changing structure of political opportunity in the European Union'. *West European Politics* 19(2): 249–78.

Mashhour, Amira (2005) 'Islamic law and gender equality: could there be a common ground?: A study of divorce and polygamy in sharia law and contemporary legislation in Tunisia and Egypt'. *Human Rights Quarterly* 27(2): 562–96.

Mazrui, Ali (2012) 'Between the Arab Spring and the African Awakening: an Afro-Arab renaissance'. Unpublished essay, May 2012.

Mir-Hosseini, Ziba (2000) *Islam and Gender: The religious debate in contemporary Iran*. London: I. B. Tauris.

Moghissi, Haideh (1999) *Feminism and Islamic Fundamentalism:*

The limits of postmodern analysis. London: Zed Books.

Mohanty, Chandra Talpade (2003) *Feminism without Borders: Decolonizing theory, practicing solidarity*. Durham, NC: Duke University Press.

Morris, Aldon (2000) 'Reflections on social movement theory: criticisms and proposals'. *Contemporary Sociology* 29(3): 445–54.

Murphy, Emma C. (1999) *Economic and Political Change in Tunisia: From Bourguiba to Ben Ali*. London and New York: Palgrave Macmillan and St Martin's Press.

Narayan, Uma and Sandra Harding (eds) (2000) *Decentering the Center: Philosophy for a multicultural, postcolonial, and feminist world*. Bloomington, IN: Indiana University Press.

Nigam, Aditya (2012) 'The Arab upsurge and the "viral" revolutions of our times'. *Interface* 4(1): 165–77.

Nouira, Asma (2011) 'Obstacles on the path of Tunisia's democratic transformation'. Carnegie Endowment for International Peace. *Sada*, 30 March.

Oliver, Pamela E., Jorge Cadena-Roa and Kelley D. Strawn (2003) 'Emerging trends in the study of protest and social movements'. In Dobratz, Betty A., Lisa K. Waldner and Timothy. Buzzell (eds) *Research in Political Sociology. Volume 12: Political sociology for the*

21st century. Stamford, CT: JAI Press, Inc., pp. 213–44.

Olson, Parmy (2012) *We are Anonymous: Inside the hacker world of LulzSec, Anonymous, and the global cyber insurgency*. New York, NY: Little, Brown and Company.

Paciello, Maria Cristina (2011) *Tunisia: Changes and challenges of political transition*. Mediterranean Prospects Technical Report No. 3.

République Tunisienne (2001) *Majallat al-Ahwal al-Shakhsiyya/ Code du Statut Personnel*. Tunis: Imprimerie Officielle de la République Tunisienne.

Sadiki, Larbi (2002) 'The search for citizenship in Bin Ali's Tunisia: democracy versus unity'. *Political Studies* 50(3): 497–513.

Saul, Jennifer Mather (2003) *Feminism: Issues and arguments*. Oxford: Oxford University Press.

Shahidian, Hammed (1998) '"Islamic feminism" encounters "Western feminism": towards an indigenous alternative?' Paper presented to the Feminism and Globalization Seminar, Illinois State University, 12 February.

Shahshahani, Azadeh and Corinna Mullin (2012) 'The legacy of US intervention and the Tunisian revolution: promises and challenges one year on'. *Interface* 4(1): 67–101.

Sharp, Gene (1973) *The Politics of Nonviolent Action*. Manchester,

NH and Westford, MA: Extending Horizons Books and Porter Sargent.

Singerman, Diane (2007) *The Economic Imperatives of Marriage: Emerging practices and identities among youth in the Middle East*. Working Paper No. 6. Washington, DC and Dubai: Wolfensohn Center for Development and Dubai School of Government.

Snow, David A., Sarah A. Soule and Hanspeter Kriesi (2007) 'Introduction'. In Snow, David A., Sarah A. Soule and Hanspeter Kriesi (eds) *The Blackwell Companion to Social Movements*. Oxford: Blackwell Publishing, pp. 1–16.

Stepan, Alfred (2012) 'Tunisia's transition and the twin tolerations'. *Journal of Democracy* 23(2): 89–103.

Stryker, Cole (2011) *Epic Win for Anonymous: How 4chan's army conquered the web*. New York and London: Overlook Duckworth.

Thompson, Lisa and Chris Tapscott (2010) 'Introduction: mobilization and social movements in the south – the challenges of inclusive governance'. In Thompson, Lisa and Chris Tapscott (eds) *Citizenship and Social Movements: Perspectives from the global south*. London: Zed Books, pp. 1–34.

Torelli, Stefano M., Fabio Merone and Francesco Cavatorta (2012) 'Salafism in Tunisia: challenges and opportunities for democratization'. *Middle East Policy* 19(4): 140–54.

United Nations (2007) *World Youth Report 2007: Young people's transition to adulthood: progress and challenges*. New York, NY: United Nations.

Wadud, Amina (2006) *Inside the Gender Jihad: Women's reform in Islam*. London: Oneworld Publications.

Wignaraja, Ponna (ed.) (1993) *New Social Movements in the South: Empowering the people*. New Delhi: Vistaar Publications.

World Bank (2007) *World Development Report 2007: Development and the next generation*. Washington, DC: World Bank.

— (2008) *For a Better Integration into the Labor Market in Tunisia*. Washington, DC: World Bank.

Yamani, Mai (ed.) (1996) *Feminism and Islam: Legal and literary perspectives*. Reading, Berkshire: Ithaca Press.

Zayzafoon, Lamia Ben Youssef (2005) *The Production of the Muslim Woman: Negotiating text, history, and ideology*. Lanham, MD: Lexington Books.

Zlitni, Sami and Zeineb Touati (2012) 'Social networks and women's mobilization in Tunisia'. *Journal of International Women's Studies* 13(5): 46–58.

Index

11 September 2001 attacks, 43
14 January Front, 100, 112
'7ell' campaign, 120

Abbou, Mohamed, 149
Abbu, Mohammed, 66
Abdel Kader from Grombelia, 80
Abderrahim, Souad, 148
Abdulatif, Ibtihel, 172, 184, 187
Abed, Monia, 42, 190
Abid, Chawki, 149
Abidi from Regueb, 114
abortion, legalisation of, 38
Achour, Habib, 22
Achy, Lahcen, 154-5
Ackerman, Peter, 83
ACT Khammem ou Qarrer
    organisation, 128-9
adoption, regulation of, 187
adultery, 187
Al-Afaq journal, 95
'African Awakening', use of term, 5
African Development Bank, 26
Agence Tunisienne d'Internet
    (ATI), 49
agriculture, decline in, 23
Ahmed from Grombelia, 109
Ahmed from Kasserine, 181
Ahmed from La Marsa, 107
Aïcha from Nabeul, 59, 62, 79, 109
Al Jazeera, 3, 57, 58, 73, 79
Al-Nahda party *see* Ennahdha
    party
alcohol, attacks on drinkers, 162
Algeria, 15; imports from, 24, 64

Ali Belhouane Youth Cultural
    Club, 129-30
Ali from Kasserine, 32, 77, 117-18,
    160-1
Ali from Le Kef, 190
Amami, Aziz, 50, 52, 56, 57, 89, 121,
    127; detention of, 76; released,
    78
Amamou, Slim, 50, 52-3, 56-7, 89,
    105-9, 164; detention of, 76;
    released, 78
Amani, a women's association
    member, 185
Amani from Kasserine, 134-5
Amel, a social worker, 183
Amghar, Samir, 185
Amin from Kasserine, 24
Amira, a non-veiled woman, 182
Al Aml al-Tunusi journal, 95
Ammar from Sousse, 135
Ammari, Mohamed, 73
Amnesty International, 33, 44
Anna Hazare movement (India),
    87
Anonymous, 3, 50-2, 75, 89; denial
    of service attacks, 51
Ansar al-Shari'a (AST), 98-9
anti-Islamism, 43-7
anti-terrorism legislation, 43-4
April 6 Youth Movement, 194
Arab League, 17
Arab Spring, 1, 71, 81
Arabic, colloquial Tunisian, use
    of, 77
Araissia, Latifa, 186, 190

Arfaoui from Bizerte, 110
Al-Aridha Chaabia party, 97, 144
armed struggle, 46
Arrhma : Association des Femmes
    Nahdaouis, 172–3, 186
Arwa, a student, 136
Asma from Gabès, 137
Asma from Menzel Bourguiba, 189
Association des Femmes
    Tunisiennes pour le Recherche
    et le Développement
    (AFTURD), 171
Association for the Preservation
    of the *Quran*, 39
Association of African Women for
    Research and Development,
    171
Association of Experts of
    Democratic Transition, 151
Association of Tunisian Women
    Lawyers, 172
Association Tunisienne des
    Femmes Démocrates (ATFD),
    69, 171, 187
Atef from Sidi Bouzid, 126
Atika from Ariana, 184
autonomy, reclaiming of, 82
AVDN Flavius organisation, 118
awra, 182
Ayari, Chedly, 150
Ayedi, Slim, 158
Ayman from Kasserine, 113, 139,
    193, 204
Ayoub from Bizerte, 35, 160
Aziz, a JID member, 116

Bahloul, Nizar, 141
Bahrain, protest movement in, 5
Balqaziz, Abdallah, 81
Banque Centrale de Tunisie
    (BCT), 149–50, 154
Banque Tunisienne de Solidarité,
    27

Bar Association *see* Tunisian Bar
    Association
Bassem from Kasserine, 181
Bayaoui, Nejib, 153
Bayat, Asef, 83, 85–6
Beau, Nicolas and Catherine
    Graciet, *La Régente de
    Carthage*, 29
Béji, Hélé, *Islam Pride*, 185–6
Bel Hadj, Sofiane, 52, 53–4, 105;
    detention of, 76
Belaid, Chokri: assassination of,
    203; funeral of, 204
Belhadj, Ahlem, 188
Ben Achour, Yadh, 103, 150
Ben Ahmed, Bashir, 36
Ben Ali, Zine El Abidine, 2, 17,
    23, 24, 29, 43, 50, 55, 67, 69, 76,
    95, 98, 109, 110, 111, 112, 113–14,
    140, 150, 165, 170, 171, 177, 179,
    200, 204; address to nation,
    77–8; becomes president, 22;
    departure of, 4, 79, 92, 95,
    125; embezzlement by, 154;
    overthrow of, 81, 82, 120–1, 126;
    reaction to demonstrations,
    74–5; record on human rights,
    32–3; reform of Personal Status
    Code, 40–3; repression of
    Islam, 160
Ben Ali, Leila *see* Trabelsi, Leila
Ben Ammar, Wassila, 39
Ben Ammou, Nadhir, 205
Ben Farhat, Soufiane, 80
Ben Fredj, Slaheddine, 30
Ben Hammouda, Hakim, 22, 67
Ben Hussein, Mohammad, 98
Ben Jaafar, Mustapha, 96, 145,
    149, 153
Ben Jedou, Lotfi, 205
Ben Mhenni, Lina, 75, 105, 127–8;
    'A Tunisian Girl' blog, 56
Ben Mhenni, Sadok, 56

Ben Romdhane, Mahmoud, 68
Ben Salah, Ahmed, 21, 163
Ben Salem, Mohamed, 205
Ben Youssef, Salah, 15, 16
Ben-Amor, Hamada (El Général), arrest of, 76
Bessis, Sophie, 41
Bin Dhiaf, Ahmed, 35
birth control, 38
blasphemy, 36, 163
blogs and bloggers, 48, 49, 57, 194, 200; Facebook event, 127–8; arrests of bloggers, 52; blocking of sites, 50
Bouazizi, Ali, 56
Bouazizi, Hedi, 153
Bouazizi, Mohamed, self-immolation of, 1–2, 18, 21, 56, 63, 67, 69, 71, 72, 152; funeral of, 76; visited by Ben Ali, 74
Bourdieu, Pierre, 11
Bourguiba, Habib, 15–17, 21–2, 56, 67, 94, 102, 109, 114, 140, 150, 167, 170, 179, 169–70; state feminism of, 37–40; views on women, 38–9
Bouzid, Dorra, 37, 39
Brahim, Ahmed, 157
bread, rising price of, 22
Bricorama company, 29
Bullet Skan, 51, 52, 54–6; released, 78

Caïd Essebsi, Beji, 102, 104, 109, 157; interim government of, 105, 108
caliphate, calls for return of, 148
call centres, work in, 65, 198; conditions of, 60–2
cannabis, legalisation of, 107
cellular telephony see mobile phones
censorship, 87, 172; of the internet, 108, 198; of pornography see pornography, censorship of
Centre de Recherches, d'Études de Documentation et d'Information sur la Femme (CREDIF), 41
Centre for the Study of International Affairs and Diplomacy (IDEAS), After the Arab Spring, 81
'Chabeb Tounes' Facebook page, 58
Chebbi, Ahmed Nejib, 96
Cherifaq from Tunis, 141
Chile, protest movements in, 6
Christians, in population of Tunisia, 146
Citizen Bus, 128–9
citizen journalism clubs, 107
citizenship, from below, 11
civil liberties, 19, 108, 121, 123, 201; lack of, 32–5, 70, 87
civil society, 66–8; women's movements in, 19–20, 167, 172
civil society organisations, 18, 158, 192, 193
clientelism, 27
Club d'Études de la Condition des Femmes, 171
Club Tahar al-Haddad, 171
CNN news channel, 3
Code du Statut Personnel (CSP), 37–42, 169–70, 175–6; limitations of, 187; reform of, 40–3
Communist Party see Parti Communiste des Ouvriers de Tunisie (PCOT)
Confédération Générale du Travail (CGT), 16
Congrés pour la République (CPR), 8, 93, 95–6, 99, 103, 136, 144, 148, 205

Conseil National pour la Protection de la Révolution, 100
constitution: Article 27 on women's rights, 175–6, 191; 'mini-constitution', 145; rewriting of, 7, 9, 82, 103, 120, 122, 129, 136, 144–66, 175
contraception, 38
cooperatives, agricultural, 17
corruption, 2, 13, 22, 28–32, 87, 113, 131, 132, 135, 149, 151, 155, 193, 197; among police, 32
Critchley, Simon, 196
customs officers, 64 *see also* smuggling, by customs officers
cyber activism, 2, 14, 18, 48–59, 89, 105, 106, 121, 127, 172, 198, 200; repression of, 47
cyber war, against government sites, 3, 75, 89, 105

Dailymotion, censorship of, 49
deaths of Tunisians in uprising, 4
democracy, 93, 114, 159, 191, 196, 201; education about, 128; not model for Islamists, 165; process of, 10; transition to, 93–121
Democracy in Action project, 129–30
Democratic Patriots Party (Watad), 68, 95, 100, 158, 203
Destour (Constitutional) Party, 15
Dhia, a poll observer, 136
Dilou, Samir, 152, 205
Dimassi, Houcine, 99, 150
divorce, 36, 39; extra-judicial, 38
Dridi, Kamel, 114–15
Duvall, Jack, 83

education: of women, 36, 190; reform of, 13, 25–6; women's right to, 168, 186–90

Egypt, protest movement in, 5, 11, 58, 71, 89, 193–4
El Kadhi, Zouhair, 26, 28
El Materi, Mohamed Sakher, 29
elections, 82, 122–43, 192, 193; blank ballots cast, 137; boycotting of, 135, 136–7 (calls for, 128); bribery in, 134; disarray and delays in, 136; education of voters, 142; low voter registration, 123–8; low youth turnout, 8, 142; organisation of, 106; results of, 137–41; role of foreign money in, 134; violations of regulations in, 135 *see also* youthEl Hadjm, a Salafist, 181–2, 184
embezzled property, recovery of, 154
Embezzlement Commission, 99
emigration *see* migration
employment, women's right to, 186–90
Ennahdha party, 8, 9, 17, 41, 43, 45, 46, 69, 93, 97, 100, 103, 104, 123, 131, 132–3, 134, 147, 148, 149, 155, 159–65, 166, 176, 178, 184–4, 189, 202, 203, 204, 205; attacks on offices of, 152; criticism of, 161; elections results for, 138–41, 144; funding of, 139; relations with Salafism, 162–3; women in, 172–3
Ettajdid Movement, 68, 93, 96, 99, 102, 157
Ettakatol *see* Forum Démocratique pour le Travail et les Libertés
European studies of social movements, 84–6
European Union (EU), 28; as Tunisian trading partner, 153; free trade agreement with Tunisia, 22

Index

239

Extortion and Repression Commission, 99

Ezzedine from Sousse, 160

Facebook, 80, 99, 194; censorship of, 49, 54; hacked by government, 76, 200; use of, 2, 48, 54, 58, 71, 74, 80, 106, 127, 196 (estimated usage, 49)

'Facebook revolution', criticism of term, 90

Faiza magazine, 37, 39

Fakhfakh, Elyes, 205

'family, the', 29–31; control of state apparatus, 31

family, traditional, 39, 41–2

family law, 37

family planning, 38

Farhat, Safia, 37, 39

Farhat, Zeynab, 184

feminism, 167; Islamic, 174; state feminism, 37–40; Western, 173–4

'flash mobs' against Internet censorship, 50

food, rising prices of, 151

foreign direct investment, 30, 153

Forum Démocratique pour le Travail et les Libertés (Ettakatol), 8, 68, 93, 96, 99, 100, 103, 131, 148, 205

Foued of Radio Sada Chaanbi, 117–18

France 24, 3, 57, 58, 73, 79; cultural influence of, 140; invasion of Algeria, 15

Francophone speakers, 8

free speech, 147

freedom of association, 33

freedom of worship, 163

Front Islamique Tunisien (FIT), 45–6, 98

Front Populaire, 158

Gaddafi, Muammar, 5

Gafsa, 72

Gafsa Phosphate Company, 25

gender equality, 147, 169, 175–6, 187, 191; in sexuality, 183

General Union of Tunisian Students, 65

Germany, 16

Ghali, Amine, 205

Ghannouchi, Mohamed, 99–102, 105, 109

Ghannouchi, Rached, 41, 43, 97, 139, 145, 146, 155, 160

Ghonim, Wael, 194

Godec, Robert, 29

Graciet, Catherine, 29

graduates, 59–66; employment project for, 76 *see also* unemployment, of graduates

Graeber, David, 196

Greece, protest movements in, 6

Groupe d'Études et d'Action Socialiste en Tunisie (GEAST), 95

Guevara, Ernesto 'Che', 113

Habiba from Tunis, 187

Hached, Farhat, 15, 16

Hachmi, Mongi al-, 45

Haddad, Tahar, 38, 170; *Our Women in the Sharia and Society*, 35–6

hadith, 185, 186

Hafsia from Kasserine, 65, 77, 118–19, 160

Hajer, a student, 136–7

Halioui, Jazem, 119–20

Hamdi, Fayda, 1

Hamdi, Hechmi, 97, 144

Hamdi, Mohamed, 125

Hammami, Hamma, 53

Hammami, Rema, 169

haraga migrants, 63

Health Workers' Union, 67
Hegel, G. W. F., 84; *The Phenomenology of Spirit*, 53
Hella, a JID member, 116
Hibou, Béatrice, 27, 125, 126
Hichem from Tunis, 68, 102, 110, 112–13
Hidri, Chawki, 73
Higher Authority for the Realisation of the Objectives of the Revolution (ISROR), 103, 150–1
Higher Commission for Political Reforms, 99
Hizb al-Nahda *see* Ennahdha party
Hizb Jabhat al-Islah al-Islamiyya al-Tunisiyya (JI), 98, 162, 166
Hizb ut-Tahrir, 98, 162
Hlali, Houssem, 57
honour, significance of, 1
housewives, salary for, 189
Houssem from Kasserine, 124
Human Rights League, 69

Ibrahim, Mounia, 189
identity politics, 19
Ijmaa, 168
Ijtihad, 168, 170
Ikhtiar platform, 130–1, 116
Imen from Sousse, 82
Indignados movement, 6, 197
informal economy, 12
infrastructure, social, lack of, 23
inheritance laws, and women, 39, 40, 41, 187
Instance Nationale pour la Réforme de l'Information et de la Communication (INRIC), 105
Instance Supérieure Indépendante pour les Elections (ISIE), 122, 135
Institut Arabe des Chefs d'Entreprise, 30

Institut de Sondage et de Traitement de l'Information Statistique (ISTIS), 138
interim government, formation of, 93; of Caïd Essebsi, 102–4, 122
interior regions of the country, disadvantaged, 158
International Association in Support of Political Prisoners, 44
International Crisis Group (ICG), 101, 189
International Monetary Fund (IMF), 22 26, 28, 153, 201
internet, 28; censorship of, 34, 49, 50, 51, 55, 56, 58 (protest against, 50); closure of, 4; freedom of, 107; use of, 2–3, 48, 49, 55, 66, 71, 72, 80, 86, 88–9, 116, 117–18 (by Islamists, 165)
Islam, 10, 36, 39, 133, 138, 140, 146, 157, 160, 161, 164, 191; as state religion, 163; conservative, 10; family values in, 190; political, 202; women in, 172, 186
Islamic fundamentalism, 40, 41, 45
Islamic law *see* Sharia
Islamism, 8–9, 19, 70, 88, 96, 97–9, 104, 123, 125, 126, 132, 136, 139, 144, 156, 158, 167, 192, 201; assaults carried out by Islamists, 178; detention of Islamist militants, 43; opposition to, 140; relation with secularism, 175–86; repression of, 47; use of term, 161 *see also* anti-Islamism
Islamists, patronage in elections, 141
ISROR *see* Higher Authority for the Realisation of the Objectives of the Revolution

Index

Jaafar from Metline, 160
Jarandi, Othman, 205
'jasmine revolution', use of term, contested, 79–80, 90
Jebali, Hamadi, 145, 148, 149, 160, 163, 204
Jeunes Indépendants Démocratiques (JID), 115, 130–1
Jews, in population of Tunisia, 146
jihad, 98–9, 184; resurgence of, 46
job creation, 154, 202
journalists, attacks on, 34
Jribi, Maya, 96, 101, 157
Jugham, Mohamed, 95

Kacem, Rafik Haj, 77
Kaloutcha, Hamadi, pseudonym of Sofiane Bel Hadj, 54
Karoui, Nabil, 162
Karthago airline, 29
Kasbah Square protests, 100; Kasbah two, 100
Kasserine, 2, 56–7, 58, 65, 72, 76, 77, 113, 117–19, 138, 199
Kazdaghli, Habib, 178
Khadher, Habib, 147
Khaled from Kasserine, 24, 64–5
Khalifi from Regueb, 63, 76
Kheireddine Pacha, 35
Kholoud from Monastir, 179
Khoujah, Mohammad al-, 45, 98, 163
Khouloud from Sousse, 147
Kifaya movement, 194
Kilani, Mohamed, 1
kleptocracy, 21

Labidi, Meherzia, 188
Lachheb, Monia, 42, 167
Lahlali, El Mustapha, 77–8
Lampedusa, destination of migrants, 62
Larayedh, Ali, 205

L'Aristou Gass, pseudonym of Houssem Hlali, 58
Law on the Provisional Organisation of Public Powers, 145
lawyers, demonstrations of, 4, 66, 75 *see also* Tunisian Bar Association
Leila: Revue illustrée de la femme, 36
Leila Speaks to You magazine, 37
liberalisation, political, 31
Liberation Party *see* Hizb ut-Tahrir
Libya: migration to, 63; protest movement in, 5; war in, impact of, 153
Louzir, Mohamed, 157

Mâalel, Nabil, 26, 28
Mahjar-Barducci, Anna, 145–6
Mahmoud, a Salafist, 165
Mahmoud from Metline, 113
Mahmoudi, Baghdadi Al-, 149
maisons des jeunes, 13, 14, 86, 114–15
Mansouri, Mohamed Najib, 152
Marouen from Metline, 124
marriage, 36; by consent, 38; forced, 36; minimum age of, 38
Marxism, 53, 84
Marzouki, Moncef, 96, 145, 149
Mashhour, Amira, 169–70
Al Massar coalition, 157
maximalist approach to political change, 92
McDonald's company, 30
Mebazaa, Fouad, 99, 103, 104
Meddeb, Hamza, 125
Menchari, Habiba, 37
Mendès-France, Pierre, 16
Menzel Bouzaiene, 73
Messaoudi, Ayoub, 149
middle classes, 2, 3, 8, 189; women of, 173, 190

migration: international, 27–8 (to Europe, 22, 25, 62–3, 65; to France, 64; to Libya, 63)
mining industry, 24, 25; decline in, 23
mobile phones, 28, 57
mobilisation of protest, 48–70
modernisation, and women's rights, 35–43
Mohammed from Tunis, 125
Moncef, Ali, 76
Mootez from Monastir, 160
Morjane, Kamel, 95
mosques, placed under state surveillance, 43
Al-Moubadara party, 95
Mouna from Djerba, 179
Mourou, Abdelfattah, 97
Mouvement de la Tendance Islamique (MTI), 41, 97
Mouvement des Démocrates Socialistes, 95
Mozambique, 14
Mubarak, Hosni, 5
Muhammad, Prophet, 186
Muslim Brotherhood, 97

Nabli, Mustapha Kamel, 149
Nadia from Thala, 183
Naima, 179–80
Nasraoui, Radhia, 33, 53
Nasser, Gamal Abdel, 17
Nassir from Tozeur, 27, 31, 35, 111
National Constituent Assembly (NCA), 7, 19, 94, 95, 103, 120, 127, 129, 130, 135, 136, 144, 158, 175–6; election of representatives to, 82, 122–3; mandates and action plans of, 145–7; women's representation in, 188
National Council for the Protection of the Revolution, 7, 112

National Democrats Movement Party, 158
National Employment Fund, 27
National Institute for Statistics, 27
National Syndicate of Tunisian Journalists, 66, 69
nawaat.org, 76
Néji, Hassen Ben Salah, self-electrocution of, 73
Neo-Destourian Party 15–16 see also Rassemblement Constitutionel Démocratique (RCD)
neoliberalism, 23
nepotism, 28–32
Nigam, Aditya, 87–8, 195
niqab, wearing of, 177, 178, 184
Nissa magazine, 171
Nizar from La Marsa, 111, 112
North American studies of social movements, 84–6
Nouira, Asma, 105
Nourdinne from Sidi Bouzid, 63–4, 111

Occupy movement (USA), 6, 195, 196
Olfa from Tunis, 182–3
Open Government initiative, 119–20
OpenGovTN, 119–20
opposition: fragility of, 156–9; legalisation of parties, 94
Ouertani, Manoubia, 37

Palestinian intifada, 88
Parti Communiste des Ouvriers de Tunisie (PCOT), 53, 95, 96, 100, 131
Parti de la Justice et de la Liberté, 95
Parti de la Lutte Progressiste, 158
Parti de l'Indépendance pour la Liberté, 95

Parti de l'Unité Populaire, 95
Parti Démocratique Progressiste, 68, 93, 95–6, 99, 101, 102, 134, 157
Parti des Conservateurs Progressistes, 97
Parti des Verts pour le Progrès, 95
Parti du Centre Social, 131
Parti du Travail Tunisien, 157
Parti Républicain, 131, 157
Parti Social-Libéral, 95
Parti Socialiste Destourien, 94
parties, political, 68–9, 133, 142, 143, 175, 193; creation of, 109, 110, 111; disconnected from central issues, 125; lack of trust in, 138; large numbers of, 123; youth suspicious of, 112–15, 193, 195
patriarchy, 170, 171, 173, 174
penal code, women's position in, 42
Persepolis film *see* Satrapi, Marjane, *Persepolis*
pluralism, political, 94, 113, 143
Pôle Démocratique Moderniste, 96, 157
police: brutality of, 66, 71, 72, 73, 74, 106–7, 172 (against lawyers, 75); corruption among, 32; repression by, 57, 60, 87
political, the: 'new politics', 83–4; practice of, reformulation of, 18, 72; refusal of, 9, 195–6
political culture, new, 192–7
'political process' model, 84
pollution, from factory, 24
polygamy, 35, 187; prohibition of, 38, 39, 189–90
pornography, censorship of, 107
Portugal, protest movements in, 6
Postal Workers' Union, 67
poverty, 23

power, divorced from politics, 196
president, powers of, reduced, 148
Primary School Teachers' Union, 67
prime minister, powers of, 145–6 (increased, 148)
prison, 33
privatisation, 29
prostitution, Islamists invade brothels, 162
provisional nature of things in Tunisia, 147
public sector employment, 27

Qatar, 133, 139
Al-Qayrawan Media Foundation, 98
Qiyas, 169
Quotidien, Le, 134
Quran, 36, 38, 157, 168–70, 182, 183, 185, 190

Rabhi, Samir, 24
Radio Sada Chaanbi, 117–19
Raouf from Kasserine, 114
rape, 183
Rashidi, Khaouila, 177
Rassemblement Constitutionel Démocratique (RCD), 17, 25, 27, 43, 64, 68, 75, 78, 93, 95, 99, 100, 102, 106, 109, 113, 124, 127, 157; banning of, 110–11 (call for, 100, 103); dissolution of, 199; establishment of, 94
Rawya from Kairouan, 178
Redeyef, protests in, 24–5
regional development, unequal, 21–8
regional imbalances, 24
Regueb, 73, 76, 181
religion, 69, 132, 137: not an issue for youth movement, 125; place

of, in public life, 163; relation to state, 163–4, 202; role of, 166; separation from state, 140, 166, 188

religious freedoms, absence of, 44, 47

religious identity, quest for, 43–7

remittances of migrants, 64

repression, political, 32–5

'resource mobilisation' model, 84

revolution: definition of, 81; possibility of, 198

Riahi, Slim, 133

Rihem, a PhD researcher, 180

road block protests, 151

rural population, political interests of, 159

Saadawi, Nawal El, 171

Sabbagh, Rachid, 205

Sadiki, Larbi, 16

safsari, wearing of, 180

Salafism, 8, 97–8, 157, 161, 164, 165, 166, 168, 177–9, 180, 182, 184–5, 204; attacks on TV stations and cinema, 161–2; flag taken down, 177; jihadi, 46; reported involvement in riots, 165; scientific, 46; street demonstrations, 175; Tunisian, 45; use of internet, 200; use of term, 46; violence of, 203

Saleh, Abdullah, overthrow of, 5

Sall, Macky, 195

Salma from Tunis, 133, 140

Sami from Metline, 62

Samir from Sousse, 193

Samti, Farah, 153

Satrapi, Marjane, *Persepolis*, 98, 162

Saudi Arabia, 133

Sawt Chebeb Tounes organisation, 128

Sawty: Sawr Chabeb Tounes, 117, 131–2

Secretary of State for Women and Family, office of, 41

secularism, 8–9, 10, 19, 46, 104, 123, 132, 139, 140–1, 142, 158, 164, 167, 185, 192, 201, 203; relation with Islamism, 179–86, 204

self-determination, women's right to, 188, 186–90, 191

Senegal, protest movements in, 5, 194–5

sexual harassment, 183

sexuality, 182–3

Sfax, 67, 72, 162; demonstrations in, 78

Sharia, 8, 9, 39, 46, 97, 98, 161, 162–3, 165, 167–70, 187, 191, 203; and women's rights, 168–70

Sharp, Gene, 83

Sidi Bouzid, 1, 2, 12, 49, 53, 56–7, 58, 71, 72, 74, 126, 138, 151–2, 199

single mothers, attack on, 148–9

sit-ins at government offices, 151

Slimi, a demonstrator, 76

smuggling, 64; by customs officers, 63

Société Nationale de Cellulose et de Papier Alfa, 24

social movements, 83–4; research into, 84–6; theories of, 18

social networking, 200

socialism, 17

Soufien from Menzel Bourguiba, 35

Sousse, demonstrations in, 78

sovereignty, 34; outsourcing of, 196

spiritual needs, 45

state: as employer, 27; controlled by the 'family', 31; role of, repressive, 29

Stepan, Alfred, 163

street politics and protests, 24–5, 78, 86, 105, 109, 121, 142, 152, 172, 195, 199, 203, 205; by Salafists, 175

strikes, 53, 67, 78, 86, 104, 153; general strikes, 22, 151, 152, 203; of students, 60

structural adjustment policies, 23

subsidies, reduction of, 24

Sumaya from Sidi Bouzid, 160

Sunna, 168–9, 182, 185

Supplementary Finance Law (2012), 153

Syndicat National des Enseignements (SNES), 67

Syria, protest movement in, 5

Tahrir Square, Cairo, 5

Takriz network, 55, 67, 128

Taoufik from Tunis, 161

Tapscott, Chris, 85

Tarek, a cultural trainer, 130

Thompson, Lisa, 85

torture, 33, 44

Touati, Zeineb, 37, 41

Tounes, Afek, 157

Tounes, Nida, 157

Tounesa organisation, 128

Tounsyat, Nissa, 172

tourism, 153

Trabelsi, Belhassen, 29

Trabelsi, Imed, 29, 133

Trabelsi, Leila, 29–31, 134

transition to democracy *see* democracy, transition to

transitional coalition government, 99–102

transparency, 128; procedures for, 120

troika government, 144, 159–65; inefficacy of, 164; loss of support, 155; priorities of, 166; weak performance of, 148–55

Tunis, 162; curfew in, 77; demonstrations in, 78

'Tunis' Facebook page, 127

Tunisair airline, 30, 79

Tunisia, growth in, 201

Tunisian Association of Democratic Women, 66

Tunisian Bar Association, 3, 69, 86, 100; activism of, 66; call for demonstration, 75

Tunisian Human Rights League, 66

Tunisian Internet Agency, 108

Tunisian Pirate Party, 76

Tunisian revolution, 48; achievements and limitations of, 197–202; chronology of, 71–91; discourse of, 142; use of term, 80–2

'twin tolerations', 163, 202

Twitter, use of, 2, 48, 50, 58, 71, 80, 106, 127, 196

underdevelopment, seen as deliberate, 24

unemployment, 1, 2, 13, 12, 19, 21–8, 57, 70, 123, 126, 144, 151, 154, 155, 159, 166, 188, 201, 202, 203–4; marginalised as election issue, 124; of graduates, 13, 18, 25–7, 47, 69, 87, 198; of youth, 2, 3, 17, 25, 45, 73, 125, 131–2, 142, 164 (unpublished data on, 107); protest of Hassen Ben Salah Néji, 73 *see also* job creation

UNESCO, 117

Union Démocratique Unioniste, 95

Union des Tunisiens Indépendants pour la Liberté, 128

Union Générale Tunisienne de Travail (UGTT), 4, 16, 22, 66–7,

69, 74, 86, 99, 100, 150, 152, 178, 203
Union National de la Femme Tunisienne, 170
Union Patriotique Libre, 133–4
United Nations Special Rapporteur for Freedom of Expression, 34
United Nations Special Rapporteur on Human Rights, 44
United States of America (USA), attack on embassy of, 165

veiling of women, 36, 38–9, 165, 168, 174, 177–86; as expression of feminism, 185; as reaction to modernity, 186; promotion of, 41; removal of veil, 37
violence: against women, 191; of Salafism, 203

Wade, Abdoulaye, 194; overthrow of, 6
Walid from Kasserine, 77, 117–18
Walt, Vivienne, 165
'war on terror', 34, 43
Watad see Democratic Patriots Party
water, problems of supply of, 152
'We Are All Khaled Said' movement, 194
weddings, paid for by parties, 134
Westernisation, 140, 173
Wikileaks, 29, 30, 51, 80
women: civil society movements of, 167; excluded from public office, 40; in paid employment, 186, 189; involved in street protests, 172; legal reforms related to, 20; rights of, 8, 18, 35–43, 140, 148, 167–91 (in Islam, 20; to education,

168); status of, 166; suggested exclusion from paid workforce, 188 see also single mothers, attack on and veiling of women
Women and Dignity organisation, 129
Women's Day march, 176
women's movement, 9, 19–20
World Bank, 28, 201; study of Tunisia, 26
World Transplant Games, 56

Yemen, protest movement in, 5
Y'en a Marre movement (Senegal), 5–6, 194–5
youth: abstention from elections, 137; and new political culture, 192–7; and the transition, 105–10; as trailblazers of the revolution, 10, 11, 21; associations of, 142; civic engagement of, 115–20; disengagement from formal politics, 19, 112–15; dissatisfied with progress of transition, 102, 104; left out of account, 109; movement of, 5, 9; not registered for elections, 159; role of, in elections, 108, 119, 122–43; speaking for themselves, 141–5; suspicious of politicians, 93; trailblazers of social change, 11, 21; use of term, 12; voter education initiative, 128
YouTube: censorship of, 49; use of, 2, 71, 196

Zarai from Sidi Bouzid, 114
Zarrouk, Muhammad, 36
'Zarzis internauts' case, 49
Zeinab from Tunis, 61, 111, 112

Zeitouna from Le Kef, 124

Zied, a law student, 115–17

Zied from Tunis, 78, 79, 112

Zlitni, Sami, 37, 41

Zouaiti, Neji, 94

Zuckerman, Ethan, 80

www.ingramcontent.com/pod-product-compliance
Ingram Content Group UK Ltd.
Pitfield, Milton Keynes, MK11 3LW, UK
UKHW031251020325
455689UK00008B/102